I0759779
NWK91

ALSO BY JOHN DARNIELLE

Devil House

Universal Harvester

Wolf in White Van

THIS YEAR

WITH ILLUSTRATIONS BY JOHN KEOGH

MCD FARRAR, STRAUS AND GIROUX NEW YORK

THIS YEAR

365 SONGS ANNOTATED: A BOOK OF DAYS

JOHN DARNIELLE

MCD
Farrar, Straus and Giroux
120 Broadway, New York 10271

EU Representative: Macmillan Publishers Ireland Ltd, 1st Floor, The Liffey Trust Centre, 117–126 Sheriff Street Upper, Dublin 1, DO1 YC43

Printed in the United States of America
First edition, 2025

Grateful acknowledgment is made for permission to reprint the following material:
"And Even, Even If They Take Away the Stove," originally written in Polish by Miron Bialoszewski, translated into English by Czeslaw Milosz, collected in *Postwar Polish Poetry*. Copyright © 1965, 1983, by Czeslaw Milosz, used by permission of The Wylie Agency LLC.
"Musée des Beaux Arts," copyright 1939, 1940 and © renewed 1968 by W. H. Auden; from *Collected Poems* by W. H. Auden, edited by Edward Mendelson. Used by permission of Random House, an imprint and division of Penguin Random House LLC. All rights reserved.
Lines from "To stand" from *Breathturn into Timestead: The Collected Later Poetry: Bilingual Edition* by Paul Celan, translated by Pierre Joris. Translation, Introduction, and Commentary copyright © 2014 by Pierre Joris. Reprinted by permission of Farrar, Straus and Giroux. All rights reserved.

Library of Congress Cataloging-in-Publication Data
Names: Darnielle, John author | Keogh, John illustrator
Title: This year : 365 songs annotated : a book of days / John Darnielle ; with illustrations by John Keogh.
Description: First edition. | New York : MCD / Farrar, Straus and Giroux, 2025. | Includes index.
Identifiers: LCCN 2025026841 | ISBN 9780374606497 hardcover
Subjects: LCSH: Songs—Texts | LCGFT: Song texts
Classification: LCC ML54.6.D35 T45 2025 | DDC 782.42164026/8—dc23/eng/20250801
LC record available at https://lccn.loc.gov/2025026841

Signed Edition ISBN: 978-0-374-62088-2

Designed by Abby Kagan
Illustrations by John Keogh

www.mcdbooks.com • www.fsgbooks.com
Follow us on social media at @mcdbooks and @fsgbooks

10 9 8 7 6 5 4 3 2 1

ABSOLUTELY ALL OF THIS FOR LALITREE DARNIELLE,

a real one if ever there was one

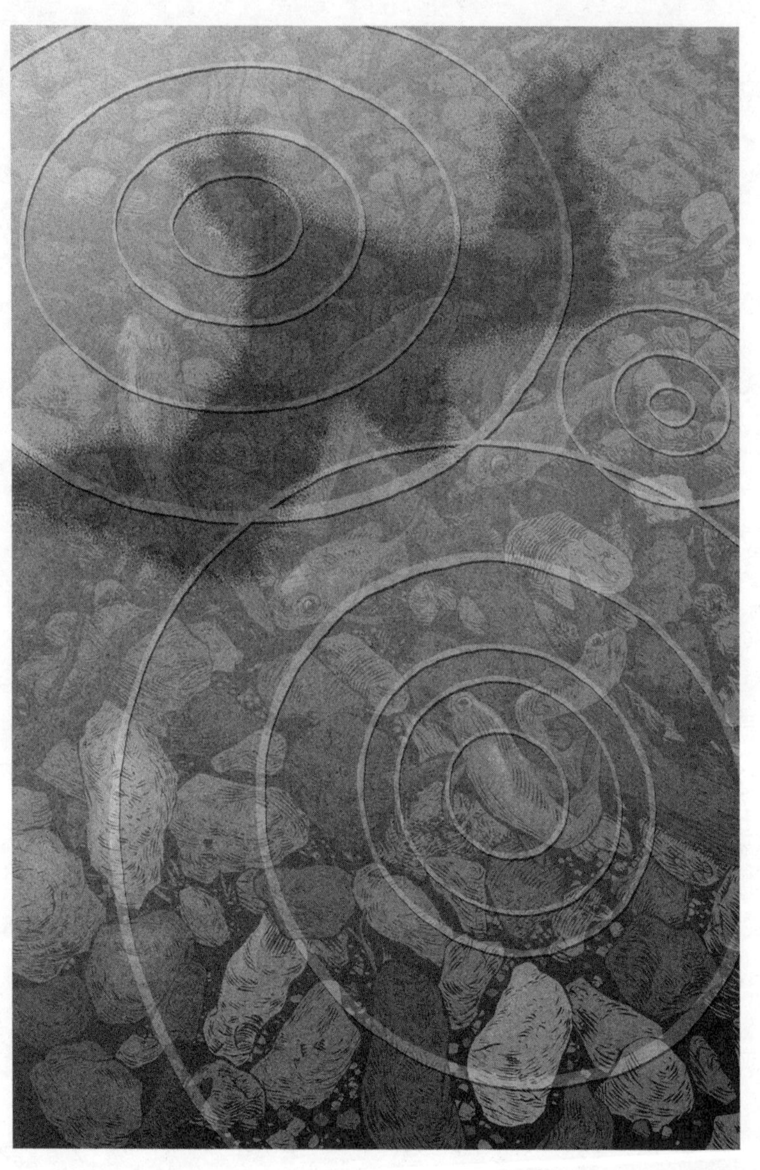

CONTENTS

PREFACE

A book can take a while to find a form. This volume began as *Compleat Lyricks*, the antiquated spelling there to mark the effort as out of step with the times: an enormous tome collecting everything, with the ones that still seemed good to me there in detail alongside their brethren, boisterous and vocal but occasionally unkempt.

I picked and pecked at *Compleat Lyricks* for several years. I wrote long pieces about the room in which I started doing this, an employee-housing apartment in Norwalk, California, to which we'll be returning frequently in the pages that follow. I dug up old songs on master tapes, ones that nobody besides me had ever heard but that felt, to me, like part of the picture. "Part of the picture"—what picture? That was the question, for me, that pushed the book past one deadline and then another: What are we trying to do here? "Trace a path across thirty-odd years of writing songs" was, I decided, the answer.

You trace a path through time methodically or it's no path at all: You use a piece of chalk and eventually it becomes a stub, or you write in a diary until it's full, or you mark a calendar from January through December.

I remembered a late Psychedelic Furs album called *Book of Days* (look it up; it's underrated), and I had my form.

There's one song for each day of the year here. Some are accompanied by detailed explications, and some by autobiographical reflections; some get elliptical glosses and some get extended question marks. Most were first released on records, or tapes, or compact discs, but some of what you'll find here has only ever been played live; a few songs in what follows have never been seen or heard by anyone but me until now. Some differ in small ways from their recorded versions: a phrase here, a line there; sometimes because that's how I found them in the notebooks where they originally resided, sometimes because that's how I sing them now. The shape they trace, together, resembles me; the songs beside which they first appeared would form a different view of the same person, but this one seems truer. That's a notion I'd have resisted fiercely back at the beginning of all this. I don't, now.

For me, the form of this book evokes that Norwalk apartment—a place where, in 1991, I hung a Warhol calendar on the wall above the radiator: This calendar became immensely useful to me as my once-chaotic life took on, or at least began to hint at, form and direction. I was only then coming around to the idea that I might live a long life, full of years. It was novel territory. Some of the ideas that emerged in that time have faded into dim memory (a one-hundred poem cycle about a man who thinks he is a pig, entitled *Theodicy*), and some have endured: specifically, the project that eventually results in this volume.

You can read *This Year* however you like; if you want to assail it in a single sitting, you can do that, but you can also take it in twenty-four-hour doses, going deep into the weeds on some days and skating across a frozen pond on others. My misconception, for the first several years of the effort, had been that I was writing a book, but in truth I was *making* a book: These are two different things. To make a book rather than write one is to assemble something whose external form masks its more flexible potential.

I did not expect, when I began writing "the Mountain Goats" on the J-cards of blank cassette tapes, that the project would encompass so many forms over time. In truth, I did not anticipate any audience at all. The existence of an audience—one that genuinely spans the globe—the privilege and honor of it, still seems, to me, like a dream, or a miracle. The distance from my station as a state hospital psych nurse grafting poems onto crude chord progressions to—well, to whatever I am now: It's a road marked by the songs that, over the years, paved it. Back in the beginning, I didn't expect that anything I was then writing would see print; indeed, I had whole theories about how lyrics weren't meant for the page. I'll still rehearse these theories aloud, if you let me get started: *Songs exist in the air! Poetry is its own discipline, which informs all the others but reserves its essence for itself!* And so on. I resisted for years; but that resistance was, really, only the search for a form, for this form. What more fortunate situation could there be, for a person, than to be glad of having been wrong? And really, come to think of it, —

JOHN DARNIELLE

DURHAM, NORTH CAROLINA, MARCH 2025

DRAMATIS PERSONAE

John Darnielle
Rachel Ware
Rosanne Lindley
Sarah Coleman
Peter Hughes
Jon Wurster
Matt Douglas

"The Mountain Goats" has, from its first usage, been a floating signifier; the only variable that never goes missing is me. The names you read above will occur and reoccur throughout this book. These are the people who helped bring these songs to such life as they attained, and none of it would exist without them. Rachel, Rosanne, and Sarah—the Bright Mountain Choir—were there at the very beginning; Peter dedicated a quarter-century to the mission of carrying our music to the world; Jon and Matt are still both over a decade in, finding new ways to make the songs breathe. In the absence of even one of these, who's to say what any of it would look like? To say so is no formality. I write lyrics, but without the Mountain Goats, those lyrics would be languishing in dusty notebooks with bent spiral spines. I am at the top of the list because I was there first. But there would be no list, nor any songs to speak about, without the list at the top of this page.

We're the Mountain Goats.

JANUARY

1 - ALPHABETIZING

The summer crawled by indetectably
and then I saw you, looking down to me
and your earrings sparkled in the noonday sun
and though it's very true that I love everyone

with every ounce of energy left in me,
I love you especially

because I saw you
coming through
the screen door
up on the second floor
up on the balcony

it was hard to even see you at all
because the air was thick with alcohol
so I kept on rubbing my eyes
for all the good it did me, for all the measurable good it did me

let the years come and take away my memory
I will not forget the shock that rang through me

when I saw you
coming through
the screen door
up on the second floor
up on the balcony

ΔΔΔ

Let's start here. It's the last song on *Chile de Árbol*, the second 7″ by the Mountain Goats and the first of several works I'd release in partnership with Chicago's Ajax Records. Ajax ran a distro whose catalog made for some of the best coffee table reading around; almost every item listed got a capsule review explaining what you could expect from the record, tape, or CD under review.

Tim Adams was the guy who ran Ajax, and he'd contacted me through Shrimper's Dennis Callaci to ask if I wanted to do a single; I did, and I had a whole lot of songs to choose from, because I almost always spent a little time every day working on songs. Some of the songs I wrote had their roots in a sequence of poems called *Songs from Alpha Privative* that I'd been working on before I got the bright idea to set some of them to music—poetry is its own discipline, one into which I'd poured countless days and nights, and the characters in the poems were like real people to me. Sometimes I'd use the word "alpha" in the titles of songs that sprung from this series: a note to myself about the song's origin, a breadcrumb for imagined listeners who might come along later to try to piece things together.

My time as an aspiring poet seems as distant to me now as our collective cellular origins beneath the ocean bed, but in this song I can still find what seemed important to me then: a central image (Richard Hugo's thoughts on anchor figures in writing and the imagination inspired me here), characters who reveal details of their past in the way they react to the present, a working cocktail of image and humor and wistfulness. A tendency to make that wistfulness the foundation upon which the other stuff is built.

Because writers are also always telling their own stories even when they're trying not to, there are also real people in this song, who I can still see, if I squint.

2 · RUNNING AWAY WITH WHAT FREUD SAID

Big city, wide corner
new flowers, cold comfort
56° Fahrenheit, early in the morning
buses passing by, black smoke in their wake
big surprises, a lot of big surprises
bones ringing
running away with what Freud said

Same morning, world breathing
far, far from home
big ringing in the bones
whose bones are these? God, please.
feel the pumping, feel the fresh blood pump inside
city's living, the city's truly living
what's the difference?
running away with what Freud said

ΔΔΔ

We weren't the Mountain Goats yet. It was just me working as a Psychiatric Technician at Norwalk's Metropolitan State Hospital, living in a studio apartment on the grounds of the hospital, cheap rent deducted from my paycheck. The building itself was very old and has almost certainly been destroyed by now; there was a tile floor in its bathroom, very Deco-aspirant in appearance, and a shower but no bathtub, and a heavy old porcelain sink. The bed was hospital standard-issue, the same as the ones the patients I cared for slept in.

I had a small black-and-white television my girlfriend had bought me, because she thought it was kind of grim that I was just up there all the time in my room with some books and a portable dual-cassette boombox. I didn't actually mind not having a TV, but once the TV was in the room, the opportunity to be weird about it kind of presented itself. I worked the three-to-eleven shift; I didn't have cable; late night broadcast TV hadn't yet been given over entirely to hucksters. You could let the televangelists on the UHF channels rave on all day and all night if you wanted, and there was a psychiatrist named Dr. David Viscott who did a call-in show on the local NBC affiliate very late on Saturday night.

I was sober by court order (random drug testing for the duration of a three-year suspended sentence; never tested dirty once, not that it was any of their business), and young, and up late pretty much every night, and one night Dr. Viscott told a guest that we shouldn't start running away with what Freud said, and somehow in that moment I remembered a day in my life just a few years earlier, when, emerging from an extended blackout, I'd walked out into the early spring in Portland, Oregon, and seen flowers in a planter on the corner. I'd thought to myself then: *You don't seem to have died yet; fancy that*; and now, back in the present day, I had a good job, and a room to myself, and also a little guitar I'd bought at a music store in a strip mall.

I wrote this song as a poem, adhering to some principles then very important to me—compress everything as tightly as possible; if there must be images, let them speak for themselves; show don't tell, sure, but suggest more than you show—and then I set it to simple music using that guitar, probably with the TV still on, which was very much part of the process most of the time in those early days.

3 - WILD PALM CITY

I see five fingers on each hand
I see only as far as my arms can stretch
After that it all gets kind of blurry

I see the air compressed and bent where it rises
Up from the hot ground, but I'm not afraid
I see what's coming through—
It's you, only it's bigger and better and brighter

I got the sofa set up right here
I got a room, a room full of sand
Open up your mouth and, buddy, you'll wish that you hadn't

I feel the new day coming on strong
I see Cindy and she's talking up a storm
I remember her, and I see who she's bringing
It's you, only it's bigger and thinner and whiter

I touch the leaves of the plant next to me
They're thicker than they were the last time I touched them
One of them curls quickly around my hand
There are stars up there even when you can't see them
I'll tell you something: that really bothers me
How are we supposed to get anything done,
With those stars casting shadows that look just like spiders?
Yeah, it's you,
but this time you're coiled up much tighter

ΔΔΔ

Day One for the Mountain Goats is hard to locate because I didn't keep, and still don't keep, records of anything at all; I'd been in other bands, and I'd written and recorded a song or two with other musicians helping me out; when I started writing "the Mountain Goats" on the spines of cassettes, sometimes I'd harvest lyrics from those other bands and projects. But "Wild Palm City," I'm pretty sure, is near the fault line—it has hallmarks of having wanted to be a poem, and of the poetic style I'd been trying to develop (conversational but formal; familiar to a point of obscurity, e.g., naming people to whom the reader could not conceivably feel any present connection; within obvious variations for a reader's mileage, at least a little funny), but it's also audibly a lyric. It has a refrain that varies with each repetition, which is something poets like better than songwriters—if you want to write a hit song, make the chorus short, to the point, memorable, and say it exactly the same every time it comes around. Say it extra times at the end. That's the formula. I think it was clear to all 150 or so people who heard "Wild Palm City" in its first appearance that its author had maybe heard about the formula, but hadn't pursued the question any further, because he wanted to tell weird stories that were one part biblical pastiche to two parts Weldon Kees.

I could not, at this time, sing and play the song while keeping the rhythm on the guitar consistent, a fact to which the recording bears extremely difficult, glorious witness.

4 - ONE WINTER AT POINT ALPHA PRIVATIVE

What the hell kind of deal is it here anyway?
How much does it cost and how long can you stay?
Should we dance? should we sing? should we curse? should we
pray?
Do I have to hang on every single word that you say?
Every hour, every minute, every second of the day
Hey, hey, hey, hey, hey, hey, hey.

What the hell's going on at the edges of your face?
Is there something eating you? Will it leave a single trace?
Will it take your pretty features and lay them all to waste?
Could we sit down over there? could we sit down any place?
Can you feel the spirit moving? can you feel God's grace?
Hey, hey, hey, hey, hey, hey, hey.

Ever since I've married you I've wondered what it means.
That every single shirt I owned has burst out at the seams
Every single piece of clothing, every last pair of jeans,
All the reds, all the whites, all the yellows, all the greens,

and I'm sure that there's a reason all of this is happening.
Hey, hey, hey, hey, hey, hey, hey.

ΔΔΔ

John Berryman was an idol to me; I wanted to do something as dogged and persistent as *The Dream Songs*, something I could just keep returning to. I'd always thought of kids from California as being more divorced than kids from elsewhere, which I think was demographically true; my own parents' divorce when I was five had given me a window into how long the legacy of a catastrophe is, how its oil keeps leaching into the present no matter how far it recedes into the past. So I decided to write a long cycle of poems, titled *Songs from Alpha Privative*: And I did write such a cycle of poems, though I don't think I ever put a final nail in it, and the only originals that survive are the ones that became songs. It still was an ongoing concern when I started singing some of the poems out loud.

The couple in the songs has become known as "the Alpha couple," and by now they've really earned the long history I'd originally hoped to drown them in; we'll be hearing more about them here later on, but this was the first time they drew a breath that exhaled into melody.

5 · GOING TO ALASKA

The jacaranda are wet with color,
and the heat is a great paintbrush, lending color to our lives,
and to the air, and to our faces; but I'm going to Alaska
where there's snow to suck the sound out from the air.

Up, yes, in the branches,
the purple blossoms go pale at the edges;
there is meaning in the shifting of the sap, and I see in them
traces

of last year, but then they hadn't grown so strong,
and their limbs were more like wires. Now they are cables,
thick and alive with alien electricity, and I am going to Alaska,
where you can go blind just by looking at the ground,
where fat is eaten by itself
just to keep the body warm.

Because from where we are now, it seems, really,
that everything is growing in a thousand different ways;
that the soil is soaked through with old blood and with relatives
who were buried here, or close to here, and they are giving rise
to what is happening. Or can you tell me otherwise?
I am going to Alaska, where the animals can kill you,
but they do so in silence, as though if no one hears them,
then it really won't matter. I am going to Alaska.
They tell me that it's perfect for my purposes.

ΔΔΔ

This one was also a poem before it was a song, but there was this store in a strip mall run by two guys, brothers, neither of whom could have been a day under sixty-eight; both wore dark glasses indoors, and I think one of them was completely blind. The store, walkable from my employee-housing apartment, was also quite old, palpably part of a time that was on its way out—small weird stores in single-story block-long stucco expanses abutting the highway.

I bought a cheap parlor-size acoustic guitar and a Mel Bay chord chart, both of which I still have, from these two; they were always the only people in the store, which was often unlit. This sounds like a story I myself would call bullshit on if Tom Waits was telling it on a talk show, but it's honestly how things were. For several weeks after getting the small guitar, I eyeballed another one hanging on the wall, labeled "Hawaiian guitar." It is an understatement to say that I'm inspired by place names. It was fifty bucks.

Eventually I bought it, and, from a jar on the counter, a glass slide with which to play it. Tuning a guitar to an open chord and running a glass bottle slide along its strings is one of the greater thrills to be had in this world when it's your first time, and when I got the guitar home, I did exactly that, then grabbed a poem from the stack near the typewriter and sang its lyrics over some I–IV–V* changes.

It was a very exciting day for me in Norwalk in 1990.

6 - THE COW SONG

Bang, pow! Look at me now
Don't let the cows stray off too far
Come down, take a good look around
See how the cows start to shine like light bulbs

I love the cows
I love the cows
I love the cows
I love the cows

Rain comes, strikes you dumb
Reseed the meadow so the cows don't starve
Mud puddle, it's a fine place to cuddle
If you're a mosquito, or a mosquito's baby

I love the cows
I love the cows

* I remain an acolyte of the I–IV–V: I is the base note of whatever scale you're playing in, IV is two and a half steps up, and V is one more. This is the basis of the blues and therefore of rock and roll, and, if you're lucky enough to be alone in a room when you notice that the IV from the I sounds like the birth of creation, it can change your life. I knew a little theory from having studied piano as a kid, but sliding the glass up to the IV lit a fire inside me, as anybody who's listened to the next, oh, ten or eleven releases will already have noted.

I love the cows
I love the cows

They're smiling in your face
All the time they wanna take your place
Yeah you know who I mean
Talking about those cow machines

I love the cows
I love the cows
I love the cows
I love the cows

ΔΔΔ

About a third of early Mountain Goats songs are idle gestures made mainly to amuse myself, or, more accurately, to preserve a record of having on some specific day amused myself. For this reason, among the early songs, it's the ones with punch lines, the funny ones, the absurdist weird ones, that are the genuinely autobiographical ones. If you hear an animal pop up in an early Mountain Goats song, or, indeed, in the band name itself, it's probably because I saw the animal in question somewhere that day and thought: Say, that animal is fantastic, someone should sing about that lovely animal.

There was a taco joint in another strip mall in Norwalk, near a dollar theater, and they had the best aguas frescas in the area, and it was a rainy day, and on the way home from lunch I drove past a field of cows milling about in the rain; and when I got back to my place, I turned on a Casio keyboard I'd bought at a Circuit City and fiddled around until I found a preset rhythm I liked; and then I wrote this song, the one for which I will be remembered if I am remembered at all. Its success—#1 in the United States for nine weeks; in England, for fourteen weeks; in Switzerland, three weeks at #1, then two at #2, and then another at #1 before beginning its slow, summer-long descent; there's not really space here to list all its global chart placements—came as a big surprise, needless to say, but the pre-SoundScan charts were a different world.

7 - PURE MILK

moon's full, and the
sky's bright, and so
you and me are gonna get
drunk tonight, we're gonna
steal some tractors,
head on into town, find the
main strip, and start
mowing them down

don't come to the window until you're sure it's me
don't ignore the obvious, take a deep breath
put your hand on the God damned radio
put your hand on the God damned radio

the fields are full of spirits,
but no one cares at all
and the light above you flickers when you
hear me call
and I'm shaking when I see you there,
'cause I don't know what it means
but the ground is looking dry tonight,
bursting near the seams

so don't come to the window until you're sure it's me
don't ignore the obvious, take a deep breath

put your hand on the God damned radio
put your hand on the God damned radio
yeah

ΔΔΔ

One of my absolute favorites among the earlier songs—because it has a narrative voice whose roots are hard to locate, and because, if I sing it today, I still find myself interested in the story. Who is this narrator? What's going on in his life? The immediate situation in the song: What is it? Who's he talking to? Is it more than one person, is the "you" collective? Are we arriving at the beginning of the action, or in the middle, or toward the end? What assumptions does our selectively disclosing narrator have about the listener—the actual listener, out there in the world with a copy of a cassette for which he paid three dollars, and also the person who will steal tractors with him, what are they to each other, who's to say, we can't, we don't have enough information, we just have some scattered but not static images and a guy who, once he's laid them out before us, says "yeah."

I still aim for this kind of effect, but I'm a little less wedded to the obscurity of the effort.

8 - ICE CREAM, COBRA MAN

I have a hand disfigured by snakebite.
I have a couple of things that I really like,
and I am heading your way all the time.

I'm going to move all my vital organs
to someplace outside my body—
the wiring is something you would not believe.

I feel no pain
as I float across your ceiling, and I—

I have no shame.
I am in a thousand rooms all at the same time,
yeah, and I have a glass
filled with water and light, and I feel good tonight.
I am climbing up this mountain.
You can watch me. You can watch me.

ΔΔΔ

Seen on the page, this lyric from the *Taboo VI* tape reveals the still-submitting-poems-to-small-press-magazines guy who wrote it, almost certainly on a manual typewriter—over the years I've developed a "lyrics are written by hand, prose on a keyboard" rule, but there weren't any rules at the time of *Taboo VI*. I now think the ideal place for a song lyric is in the air, and that a transcription of one is a rough approximation of what happens when you listen; but the guy at the typewriter thought otherwise, and, although he stubbornly resisted including lyrics on his releases until 2017, believed that a lyric should be able to stand on its own on the page.

I interpret this song as a statement of purpose by a guy at the dawn of a thirty-year career in music working under the name "the Mountain Goats." This seems genuinely clear to me; I see symbols in here, most about writing and ambition. But I'm just as certain that all I meant to do at the time was sketch a small scenario that was somewhat disquieting but not lurid or explicit, and then house it within a generally celebratory musical framework, the better to enjoy the tension between these two impulses for a couple of minutes.

9 - SOLOMON REVISITED REVISITED

You say you came to see me,
because you had nothing else to do,
but I've got a radio.
You say you'd thought you'd stop on by

and let me have a look at you,
but I've got a radio.
I've got a radio.
I've got a radio.
I've got a radio.
I've got a radio.

You say you brought some photographs,
but I don't care to see them,
'cause I've got a radio.

You say this place must get dull sometimes,
but that's not the way I see it.
'cause I've got a radio.
I've got a radio.
I've got a radio.
I've got me a radio.
I've got a radio.

You say these rocks are treacherous,
but how long has it been since you've seen my feet?
You see, I've got a radio.
You warn me about all sorts of things,
but this is not the sort of warning that I need.
You see, I've got a radio.
I've got a radio.
I've got a radio.
I've got a radio.
I've got a radio.

ΔΔΔ

Somewhere in a long-lost notebook there was almost certainly a poem called "Solomon Revisited," and it was probably about a Jonah-like figure celebrating the last thing he has that connects him to the world he used to inhabit. That seems, knowing my own habit, like the most likely explanation for the reduplication in this song's proper title, which does not appear correctly on the tape sleeve, because we were all winging it at the time. The source text for characters like this, who in many subsequent songs would reappear in different situations and wearing different hats, was a poem by Miron Białoszewski I'd read in Czeslaw Milosz's *Postwar Polish Poetry*—an anthology whose tendrils can, with a little digging, be found all through my writing, down to the present day. The poem bears reproducing in full here, because a pretty sizeable chunk of the Mountain Goats poetics germinated in the moment I first read it, at the age of seventeen or so, trying to figure out how I thought about writing.

And Even, Even If They Take Away the Stove
My Inexhaustible Ode to Joy

I have a stove
similar to a triumphal arch!

They take away my stove
similar to a triumphal arch!!

Give me back my stove
similar to a triumphal arch!!!

They took it away.
What remains is
a grey
    naked
        hole.

And this is enough for me;
grey naked hole
grey naked hole.
greynakedhole.
—MIRON BIAŁOSZEWSKI

10 - SEEING DAYLIGHT

Two cans clear chicken broth;
two white onions;
one bulb garlic.

Boil, boil.
Boil, boil.

And the screams of delight from the pool outside—
the splashing sounds;
the coffee heating up on the stove,
and the sky outside the color of pure, fresh milk.

Boil, boil.
Boil, boil.

And the phone ringing, and me picking it up,
and watching myself do so
in the quiet room
in the June evening.
And your voice on the other end,
and the impossibility of your voice on the other end.

And the impossible echo inside.
Boil, boil.
Boil, boil.

ΔΔΔ

Not the first song in the catalog to find a narrator expressing vulnerability, nor the first to orbit loss and absence, both central concerns for me then and all the way down to the present day: But the story inside the song sketches a scene where the particulars are recognizable pieces of an ordinary life, and then opens a window into what those particularities might mean. The main character is the space left by an absence whose loss renders any physical object a potential oracle. It is almost certainly the case that I had just made some soup when I got the idea for this song, and that it was a little overcast. The rest is me trying out different ways to spin a web.

11 - NEW STAR SONG

I hung pictures of you from every lamppost in town
As the humidity climbed into numbers I don't care to repeat
The air was heavy and the sky was alive
And the Pacific Starlight train wasn't due in 'til 11:45

I thought about how cold you must be
I thought about things I thought that I'd soon be forgetting
I thought of you up in Canada as the lightning storms lit up
All downtown Redding

There were teenagers in mini trucks coming around every corner
You could taste the adrenaline coming out through their skin
I came to the well-lit doorway of a sheet music store
I saw my face in the glass, sat down in the doorway, and I settled in

I thought about how cold you must be
I thought about things I thought that I'd soon be forgetting

I thought of you up in Canada as the lightning storms lit up
All downtown Redding

ΔΔΔ

My friends Mark Givens and Joel Huschle—memorialized by name on the same EP that hosts "New Star Song"—had moved to northern California. We were close, and had made music together for several years; the Mountain Goats came into existence in part because of the vacuum left by their decampment to McKinleyville. Still in Norwalk, working at the hospital, living alone, and not good at making new friends nor particularly interested in doing so, I spent some paid leave on a trip to visit my friends. I took the train as far as Redding; from there you had to get on the bus. It was a very long trip. On the way home, my layover in Redding lasted eight hours; most of the physical details in this song are observations from that day I spent wandering around, too broke to really do anything but see movies in the dollar theater (I think I saw one on each of the four screens in the local multiplex). The freezing person up in Canada is an invention. This, again, is the working ethos of the early lyrics. Set a scene and put some ghosts in it, then get excited about the ghosts.

12 · SONG FOR CLEOMENES

Seventy-three years before the advent of the Christian era
as Rome was taking over any land within reach
setting up proxy governments in the conquered lands
there lived one such man, given just such a job:
Gaius Verres

A praetor held a position which operated on trust
he was to govern in the stead of the emperor himself
it was an easy, easy privilege to abuse
and Verres did so

He was the governor of Agrigentum, which we now know as
Sicily
and he stole everything that wasn't nailed down
took improper advantage of other men's wives
the list goes on, trust me
Cicero wrote it all down

At Syracuse, Verres welcomed a band of pirates
they all drank and danced and sang on the shore
and when the husband of one of Verres's paramours came
bringing a fleet of boats with him
Verres, clever if diabolical, gave him a job
and enlisted the pirates to burn the whole fleet down

The boats burned in the Sicilian harbor
the flames rose hundreds of feet into the air
we stood on the shore, watching them burn
we stood on the shore, we heard the old songs

ΔΔΔ

I was working on a double major in English and Classical Studies at Pitzer College; it was a joy, for me, to be learning about things I'd wondered about all my life, to be finally making good on the promise my earliest teachers had insisted they'd seen in me. I showed up on time to class and worked diligently, and practically everything I learned I'd shoehorn into the songs I was writing at a breakneck pace—two or three a day, sometimes; they were still mainly sketches that insisted on the inherent dignity of the sketch; they were caprices, I didn't really care if they had blemishes by the dozen, the blemishes were half the point. Hence this, written while learning *In Verrem* from Jones and Sidwell's *Reading Latin* and railing constantly—really just constantly—against that book's diabolical need to turn all citizens of Rome into British citizens wearing Roman costumes. For me, the history felt alive—I saw and heard and smelled and sensed real people as I read Cicero insisting to an imaginary jury (the case was never actually delivered; Verres fled) that the crimes of Verres were so heinous as to cause animals—even stones, gentlemen, even unfeeling stones!—to weep, were they to hear of them. I'd seldom succeeded in connecting with history when younger. Surprise! The trick is so simple a child could do it, so simple it's exactly what we were told as children all along: Imagine it's you; a trick I get to at the end of this song, a thing that happened by accident as I was singing and improvising and which was, on that day, a valuable lesson. To satisfactorily correct all the errata in this song would take up the rest of this book; I sing "common era" on the rare occasions when I still do this song.

13 - THE LAST DAY OF JIMI HENDRIX'S LIFE

On the last day of his life, Jimi Hendrix woke up,
and made his way down the hall;
and he adjusted the knobs in the shower 'til the water came out just the way he
liked it.

It was hot, but not too hot;
It was hot, but not too hot.

On the last afternoon of his life, Jimi Hendrix went to the kitchen
and he got himself a glass of water.
And he put four ice cubes into the glass;
there is nothing like cold water,
there is nothing.

ΔΔΔ

When I was a child, my father read me Auden's "Museé des Beaux Arts," more than once, I think; I imagine that it was one of the poems he taught in his Intro to English Lit courses at California Polytechnic State University, San Luis Obispo. Here's that poem, if you don't know it:

> About suffering they were never wrong,
> The old Masters: how well they understood
> Its human position; how it takes place
> While someone else is eating or opening a window or just
>   walking dully along
>
> How, when the aged are reverently, passionately waiting
> For the miraculous birth, there always must be
> Children who did not specially want it to happen, skating
> On a pond at the edge of the wood:
> They never forgot
> That even the dreadful martyrdom must run its course
> Anyhow in a corner, some untidy spot
> Where the dogs go on with their doggy life and the torturer's
>   horse
> Scratches its innocent behind on a tree.
>
> In Breughel's *Icarus*, for instance: how everything turns away
> Quite leisurely from the disaster; the ploughman may
> Have heard the splash, the forsaken cry,
> But for him it was not an important failure; the sun shone
> As it had to on the white legs disappearing into the green
> Water; and the expensive delicate ship that must have seen
> Something amazing, a boy falling out of the sky,
> Had somewhere to get to and sailed calmly on.

"The Last Day of Jimi Hendrix's Life" is a version of Auden's poem, in some ways, or a response to it, though in neither case a direct one: I didn't sit down and say "What then, W.H., what say'st thou to this?" Rather, my father's explanation of this poem to me—we had a framed copy of the painting in question on the wall of our house when I was small—made an impression on me, and formed no small part of what I hesitate to call "my poetics," because honestly, who talks like that, but I don't know how else to put it. The details of everything around something big are, for me, the places wherein the poignancy of a given scene can be most deeply sensed. Not the cars crashing but the person a block away who hears the crash. Not the fire but the way the room looked before the fire. Not the moment of the overdose, but the dozen things the man who overdoses, beloved by so many and with so much more to do in the world, will do, without thinking much about them, for the last time on that day.

14 · GOING TO NORWALK

At one thirty on a Thursday night,
I saw a pair of raccoons, heading to the gutter—
they stopped at the storm drain;
their tails hung down and out of sight.
They looked up at me;
their eyes were shining;
I thought of you,

and I can't stand
the way the moon expands and fills out the corners of the
  California sky,
I can't stand it.

The old buildings stood tall against the sky;
the windows had old sheets hanging over them, doubling as
  curtains,

and the silhouettes moving in the bright lights behind the
curtains
looked like you—
I stopped moving momentarily;

the world will
stand still on nights like these without any kind of warning,
and I can't stand it.

ΔΔΔ

The verses in this song are a simple description of something I saw—two raccoons making for a storm drain on the grounds of Metropolitan State Hospital, late at night—and the choruses are an invention: of a character, not me, but somebody who, seeing the same things, calls a person to mind whose memory is, evidently, hard to carry. This is among my very favorites among the early songs, because its narrator withholds more than he shares, and the effect, for me, is one of great tension. I think that for most people who liked my early stuff, the chaos and the energy and the humor and the sheer drive of it are the things that drew them in. For me, in a moment like "Going to Norwalk," I saw a place where I wanted to spend more time: a weaving together of real places and the imagined ghosts who live there.

15 · SONG FOR MARK AND JOEL

I opened up the window and the cold air came in
And I saw a bird on a branch outside
That I had never seen before
It looked like a robin, but it had an upside-down V-shaped
Red mark on its chest
And I had a special feeling in my mind
I had a special feeling in my mind

I had a certain glint in my eye
On the morning the trouble came by

There was a map of the American Midwest on one wall
And there was a map of the American West on another wall
And there was a map of Rome on the third wall
And there were maps in all directions
I was looking at them, pondering connections
When trouble came by

Then I stuck my head out the window
I had to stick my head out the window
It was much colder than I'd imagined it would be
It was much, much colder than I'd imagined it would be
It was much, much colder
It was much, much colder and trouble came by

ΔΔΔ

Joel and Mark, who you met back in "New Star Song," were, and are, dear friends who had, and have, a band called Wckr Spgt. Probably none of what you're reading in this book would exist at all without Wckr Spgt, the first band among my friends to do something really weird and insist on its inherent—dignity? value? worth? It's hard to say how Wckr Spgt conceived of itself in terms you'd apply to other bands, which is a big part of what made and makes them great. Their second 7″ was called *Fortune Came Today*, and to play its title track you fingered an A inversion at the seventh fret and then moved it around the neck; both E strings and the B rang constantly as you did this, which caused a drone effect. It was badass; Mark showed me how it was done. When I applied this A-inversion-up-the-neck strategy to a song of my own, I made the chorus "trouble came by," which echoes "fortune came today," and then I gave the song the title it bears so as to increase the tribute to Wckr Spgt by a factor of one. Joel asked me, several years later, for an explanation, and I told him what I'm telling you now, but he sounded suspicious; but abiding suspicion of simple explanations is itself part of the Spgt protocol.

16 - FRESH CHERRIES IN TRINIDAD

When I woke up on Saturday and you came in
And you brought the sunlight in
I felt sleep slipping away from me
I feel things occasionally like this:
Fresh cherries
Hanging from your fingers

When the water on the window let the sunlight through
And I got a good look at you
Standing above me bright and tall
There are no words for it
There are no words at all
I saw
Fresh cherries
Hanging from your fingers

ΔΔΔ

Water, windows, fruit: the inviolate early Mountain Goats troika! The second person, in medias res, and a specific point in time (Saturday): the troika of secondary necessity! But it's the note of longing in a song like this that, for me, made the song a keeper instead of one among many other songs featuring water, windows, and fruit that never got released. The details are there only to get to the longing: to frame it in a way that makes it feel real. And it is real; I wrote this song after Joel, now mentioned for at least the fourth time, either wrote or called to tell me his partner, Kim, had brought him fresh cherries. They lived in Trinidad at the time. Trinidad,

California. It's up near Humboldt, but I was under no obligation to tell you that.

17 - BILLY THE KID'S DREAM OF THE MAGIC SHOES

They're going to hang me out to dry
They're going to hang me out to dry
I don't really care
I don't really care
I got special shoes
I got special shoes

They're gonna fill me full of holes
They're gonna fill me full of holes
I don't give a rat's ass
I don't give a rat's ass, you rat bastards
I got special shoes on
I got special shoes on

ΔΔΔ

The grasping hands of theory! They beckon from this tune, they reach out through a thick fog of twenty-plus years passed and seize me by the neck! Their fingers press into my larynx and bid me speak! Speak, servant, you who once would no sooner have printed lyrics on an album sleeve than suffer a photograph of yourself on the front cover! Speak of the union you sought, between the high-minded poetry of the academy and the physical force of the poem as one receives it, alive in the air, extant only for the moment in which it's heard, livable only in that moment, incommunicable outside of it! The space of song, that original form, the place within which all is possible and outside of which none of it's possible at all, that self-contained gesture that seeks to make something where nothing was, the impossible arrogance of it! Only gods and mothers can do that, fool! But nevertheless: here. A song whose text is meaningless without its title, a song that concludes with the singer saying "yeah," essential to the song but unwritten on the page and not reproduced here, because the theory still exerts its force, the printed lyric is an echo and not a simulation, even the recording is only the physical evidence that something happened, something spectral and momentary, something maybe worth remembering but impossible to remember with total accuracy, and yet.

It's a lot, I know. But this was the sort of sea-spray inside my brain making this stuff, these loose ideas about poetry and its place in folk music, in rock music, the intersection. The interstice, if you wanna dredge up a then popular term among academics, and why wouldn't you.

18 - GOING TO JAPAN

There's a north wind coming in
and there's a west wind coming in
and there's an east wind coming in
and there's a strong wind blowing in from the south
and there's a sweet metallic taste in my mouth
there's a dead feeling lingering over the land
and there's a one-way ticket in my hot little hand
and I'm kissing your eyelids and I'm going to Japan

There's life and liberty on my tongue
and there's a dead silence where the wind chimes hung
and on some mountain somewhere in the world it's snowing
but here in the fields there's not a thing growing
maybe next year, you know, but there is no way of knowing
there's wind coming in from all directions
there's a coat on my shoulders, midnight connections
and I'm kissing you and leaving you behind in the sand
I'm holding you awhile then I'm going to Japan

ΔΔΔ

There are songs that appear to me as flashpoints, growth spurts, songs within which I'm audibly getting better at the thing I'm trying to do: songs where I'm both gathering up the skills I've learned so far and locating, within them, my own voice—as a writer, as a songwriter. This is one of those for me. It's kind of a song about form: image, image, image, image, image, mood, image, physical fact in time and space, physical fact in time and space. That's the structure of the first verse. The second verse retains the formal characteristics of the first for two lines, and then begins to wander—a "but" instead of an "and," a "maybe" after that; there's an instability taking hold that echoes both the chord progression's wild neck wanderings and the melodic modulation that happens in the second half of the verse, deeply uncharacteristic of the Mountain Goats in that time and for the next twenty years or so until *Goths* breaks the seal. The structure of the lyric is rigid for half the song, and fragments across the space of the second half. Finally, you can't miss that there's a story inside it—a person, he's leaving, something seismic has happened, the world is too much with him, he appears to be in the desert but it's time to go, somebody else has to stay behind, it's a time of excitement and sorrow and fear and uncertainty, something has happened and can't un-happen and we're not sure what.

That's the soil I sought out in those days, and occasionally, with some luck, I found it.

19 - THANKS FOR THE DRESS

the young sun
the old story forming
it hasn't been the same
since dad came by this morning

did you see the way mom's looking at us?
mark it well

your eyes meet mine
when we hear her call
and strange birds in the yard
are perched above the symbols that she painted on the garden
  wall
did you see the way mom's looking at us?
did you see the way mom's looking at us?
don't say anything

ΔΔΔ

This book is about the lyrics; over time, I've grown to be as interested or more so in the music that serves as a place for words to do their thing. But this song is one of the strangest things in the catalog. Counting time to it is very difficult if it's even possible, but the guy playing it—me, that was me, I did this—has an internal clock that's pretty consistent: The main guitar figure that introduces the first lines of the song happens twenty-two times in total, and begins in the middle of the bar—on the three, and runs for two bars; in the middle of those two, the vocal comes in. The guitar is not tuned to concert E; it's very hard to figure out what the chords are until, in the chorus, we go to the five chord, which is what usually happens in any early Mountain Goats song. From there, things get even hairier; the chorus is a modulation, maybe a double modulation; it's deeply unstable but the vocal line is rock solid, utterly consistent—I appear to know what I want. I sound like I hear a structure that's almost impossible for the listener to locate in space. Reconstructing this song to play it live, which I've now been trying to do for the last thirty minutes, here at my dining room table thirty-one years later, is possible, but extremely challenging. I could no more write a song like this today than slip into the skin of the guy who wrote it.

The text is from when Medea sends her children offstage before murdering them in the Euripides play that bears her name, and, since Greek plays orbit questions of order and disorder a lot, I give Medea full credit for this vortex of uneasy waters. The dress in question is the one she gives to her husband, Jason's new wife, Creusa, a magical dress that will kill the person who wears it. There should be more songs about this.

20 - QUETZALCOATL COMES THROUGH

He came spitting fire
on a day like no other
tried to hold you near to me
I heard him passing over
he made a banquet for the stray dogs of the air
he put our love in clear perspective

Blue red and green plumage
trailing behind him now
swaddling the sky in its aftermath
the last day coming down
he made a banquet for the stray dogs of the air
he put our love in clear perspective
rising, rising, rising, rising

ΔΔΔ

I had a book called *Aztec Thought and Culture* by Miguel León-Portilla, translated into English by Jack Emory Davis. I don't remember where or when I got it, but it was a very important volume in my small, growing library. I wanted to know about polytheistic religions, specifically their pantheons; the many faces of God is a theme that holds me still, and felt transgressive to me in 1994, when I was still a fifty-two-Sundays-a-year practicing Catholic. A little perceived transgression is a reliable source of inspiration if you know where to look.

Aztec Thought and Culture's impact on the early Mountain Goats catalog can hardly be overstated; finding sources of information for the images and stories that attracted me was difficult. León-Portilla's volume was like a codex for me, and I wasn't yet a scholar of any stripe; I was an undergrad at Pitzer by this time, learning how to do things with words. This song—from *Yam, the King of Crops*, possibly the best of the cassette releases—is actually just a breakup song. The whole tape was recorded in the wake of parting ways with a woman I'd loved for five years. It was our second breakup; she initiated the first one, and the second one was all me. I didn't want to write breakup songs. They're generally boring. But I also couldn't just write as though things weren't going on in my life, so I submerged details in myth, in image, in grand themes.

This pattern would continue for about eleven years.

21 · CHINESE RIFLE SONG

I lay out on the patio, dreaming
I lay out on the patio, dreaming
And the Chinese rifles sounded in the evening air
I heard them popping off everywhere

I lay out on the patio, on the chaise lounge
I lay out on the patio, and I let my hand
        rest against the hot redwood frame
And the Chinese rifles sounded again
I could not stomach their acumen

ΔΔΔ

Yam, the King of Crops is, for me, a big moment. Partly this is because my friend Tom, whom I'd known since high school but was only occasionally in touch with, told me it was my best work; I'd learned a lot from Tom when we were young, and I held his opinion in high esteem. Partly it's because, as an artifact, it's a snapshot of a time that won't come again—a time of small tape labels around the world whose quarter-page ads you might happen across in zines, or whose tapes you might see reviewed in *Factsheet Five*, and to whom you might, out of a clear blue sky, send your latest eight songs, because you liked the one weird noise tape you'd gotten from them. That's what happened here: most of Oska's other releases were very noisy affairs, and the scene, so hard to connect with at any but the most localized and random of levels, felt like a secret society. I had eight new songs and they felt fresh and of-the-moment to me; I was getting somewhere. I sent them to Jod, who ran Oska, with the cover art complete. He sent me back eight copies, and I sold seven of them, and now one of them is in a drawer in the next room.

This is a song about Chinese rifles.

22 - LOVE CUTS THE STRINGS

First thing that happened was the river overflowed
The water running through the streets was sweet and cold
I knelt by the water like a doe by a stream
Punch-drunk, snow-blind, as though the whole thing were a bad dream

And then love called out the heavy artillery
And Kypris took the horses by the bit for the morning ride
I count my blessings but you can only be expected to count so high
When love cuts the strings

I smeared myself with pennyroyal to keep the hounds at bay
And you poked your head out from an alley half a block away
And I recognized you though I'm not sure how
And the air turned red around you
As a dull chill came down over me

And then love summoned up the infantry
And the green-eyed goddess got ready for all-out war
I count my blessings
But I don't even know what the word "blessing" means
When love cuts the strings

ΔΔΔ

Speaking of small English indie labels, there was and is a guy named Russell Hill from Brighton, which is a city in the county of Sussex, both places so exotic to the twenty-something-year-old mind of a young songwriter in California that an invitation from such a place to send a song for a compilation felt like something from a dream. I don't remember whether I'd been on one or two Theme Park compilations—that was Russell's label, which he ran from his home, in the manner of most indie labels of the time—and I don't remember whether the idea of doing a 7″ was mine or Russell's, but I was writing pretty much constantly by this point, and everything I was learning in college felt deeply inspirational to me, especially the Greek and Latin stuff. The 7″ was called *Philyra*, which is a word attested to only rarely in the Latin lexicography; Horace used it, Ovid used it, I understood it to mean "lime tree" at the time and it's probably better not to get me started on how I feel about trees, what is better than trees, "nothing" is your answer, that's your answer right there, nothing is better than trees and it's wonderful that trees have names.

Of the four songs on *Philyra*, "Love Cuts the Strings" was the fastest and the best. Within a year, the fastest songs would no longer reliably be the best ones, but in 1994 it was still often the case that if my right hand was moving faster, the song was going to be better. The lyric itself is essentially an attempt at writing a Greek ode to love. One tries.

23 - NOCTIFER BIRMINGHAM

I had to stop and catch my breath
When the telephone rang out as loud as death
It was three in the morning
There was a low drone of katydids behind your voice
And then I came down from Harrisburg, Pennsylvania
And I saw you by the highway

You asked me if the north was all right
And I said it got kind of cold at night
I could feel your bones shivering way down there in Birmingham
And then I came down from Harrisburg, Pennsylvania
And I saw you by the highway

You reminded me of all the things you'd given up forever
And you asked about the children
And you asked about the weather
And then I came down from Harrisburg, Pennsylvania
And I saw you by the highway

ΔΔΔ

Rachel and I were invited to tour Europe; it was my senior year in college, I was pursuing a double major with a thesis in each, it was sheer madness to contemplate ten days away from school to play music abroad; but I thought, *This chance may never come again*; I begged my thesis advisors, and they gave their hesitant blessings; the festival footing the bill for the tour was releasing a compilation album featuring all the artists who would play at the festival, so we went into the studio to record my newest song, which felt like a big step up for me rhythmically and melodically; as I've probably mentioned, I took pride, in those days, in giving some of my best work to compilation tapes and EPs and albums—let the others give the castoffs to the compilations, let the Mountain Goats always stand out as the best song on the compilation, this was my position; I declined to reuse these songs on albums; I was no longer strictly boom box but a purist can always find some new outlet for his ascetic urges. We recorded the song in December, I think—I remember it was a little cold in San Dimas though within a year I'd be learning that California cold and Chicago cold were two very different things; and, indeed, in the song itself, a story about a phone call from someone the speaker is trying not to lose, a person from a warmer place remarks that it gets kind of cold at night in the new place. Songs can see into the future, if you let them.

24 - GOING TO KIRBY SIGSTON

We boarded up the windows
And we sealed the door shut
And we let the special chicken
Build a nest right by the window
Your face was glowing
The heat was strong
We ate cold black eggs all day long
In the winter when the wind kicked up

I saw your body moving
Through the incandescent light
You were dancing by yourself there
Your sweater hugged your shoulders and it was all right
We plucked sugar crystals from the cold English air
I had a present for you hidden somewhere
In the winter when the wind kicked up

ΔΔΔ

In West Yorkshire there was a fellow named Rik Albatross—heir to the Albatross fortune; they made their money in ironworks and their forge dated back to the age of Saxon kings—who took a liking to the

Mountain Goats. He'd send me postcards and, later, songs on cassette, documenting his wanderings, his interests and obsessions, his view of things. He loved fish and he loved old, weird England. I loved getting postcards and letters from Rik; sometimes he'd draw a comic strip depicting his workday, or a weekend exploring the countryside. One such postcard arrived one day in, probably, 1994, and bore the handwritten emblem "GOING TO KIRBY SIGSTON."

The song itself is one of the last few John-and-Rachel recordings and is honestly one of our best tunes; the story is one of those self-contained little snow globe scenes I had learned to specialize in, the sort of view that, when you tilt the globe just right, catches some light that makes it feel like a whole bunch of things are happening all at once.

25 · GOING TO HUNGARY

We touched down in Budapest
Headed straight for the motel room and got undressed
We had not slept for three or four days
We slipped underneath the covers
It felt okay

About twelve hours later
The sun came out to play
I felt it on my eyelids
I pushed your hair away

You put on your old gloves
You put on your new skirt
I put on my cowboy boots
I slipped on my yellow shirt

We headed out, sweat drying on our bodies
And I got all sentimental

We were heading straight to hell
In a Lincoln Continental

ΔΔΔ

The best cassette releases of the 1990s were albums by Furniture Huschle, albums that will probably never see rerelease, in part because at one point in the mid-aughts Joel sent me digitized versions of them on compact disc so I could write liner notes for them, and I got distracted and the CDs went missing and then it turned out they were the masters. Sorry about that, Joel. "Going to Hungary" represents the sole occasion to date of Furniture Huschle and the Mountain Goats appearing on a single slab of wax, a 7″ out of Oklahoma. The sleeve of the 7″ omitted the first *n* in the word "Mountain" in the band name and I was very out of sorts about it, and probably vented my frustration ungently at the young dude named Brad who was releasing the record. Sorry, Brad! The song itself is in that weird half-song-half-dream mode that I really like from the early days, and is hell-bent on rhyming "sentimental," so it does. Joel said, at the time: "I don't like the Lincoln Continental." Joel was right! But the options are all fairly rough—"dental," "rental," you could maybe get some mileage out of if you worked at it, "gentle" is what I'd almost certainly go with today. "We headed out, sweat drying on our bodies / And I got all sentimental / We were heading straight to hell / The road rolled on, the turns were gentle." Nice crescendo on the last two syllables to drive home that the only gentle thing in the picture is the road. Something like that.

26 - SONG FOR TURA SATANA

Doll Squad's at the drive-in,
It's 1973,
and the fruit is full and fat this year on the orange trees,
which grow in clusters;

the city's sixty miles away
as the sunset tries desperately to break through the grey;
and the stardust came down, royal blue,
as the San Bernardino sky
showered over you.

Coming home early is always a mistake,
but when you see that woman on the sofa something in you breaks.
You've got a celluloid tendency to flare out and blaze,
and the report sounds once like a failed hymn of praise:
and the stardust came down, royal blue,
as the San Bernardino sky
showered over you.

ΔΔΔ

"I nearly died after The Doll Squad when I got shot, I was shot in the stomach by my ex-boyfriend. I told him to go but he didn't want to. I caught him fooling around, so I told him to go. He felt he should have his cake and eat it too, so he shot me. So I spent some time in the hospital for that."
—TURA SATANA, interviewed in *Psychotronic Video* 12

I was on the couch devouring this issue of *Psychotronic* and the story seemed like something I wanted to preserve—for myself, to remember it, to be able to call it to memory when I liked. The point of the story is not that Tura Satana gets shot. The point is that she lives to tell to tale. For years—decades—I misremembered the story, and believed that it was Satana who'd done the shooting, and I still prefer to remember it that way. Satana died in 2011; may some rendition of the afterlife find her shooting her ex-boyfriend on an endless loop in glorious Technicolor.

27 - GOING TO CLEVELAND

We both know you're leaving
You just don't want to say it yet
'Cause you don't want to hurt my feelings
So you gnaw your little holes in the net

And you torture me with those big eyes
And you punish me with pity
But I'm going to Cleveland

You say you wanted to strike first
Because one of us was leaving
That's what you say
But I've always been real fond of you
So I never would've treated you this way

And you torture me with those big eyes
And you punish me with pity
But I'm going to Cleveland

I hear the Cuyahoga calling, now I know
What I was born for
And you say: "Hey John, where are you going?"
But that's not my name any more

And you torture me with those big eyes
And you punish me with pity
But I'm going to Cleveland

ΔΔΔ

So at some point I met this guy named Peter Hughes, who played guitar and sang in a band called Diskothi-Q. He was from Chino. I'd done some home health care gigs in Chino and was quietly obsessed with the whole vast terrain east of Claremont, where I'd grown up.

Peter ran a tape label called Sonic Enemy and I was writing pretty much all the time. I got this idea to record ten songs in ten days, and then just to release the tape as is, a document of ten days' work. When I'd finished the tape, I gave it to Peter, sort of conscripting him in my plan. Peter would be conscripted into several future plans down the line, hopefully all to his pleasure on balance.

The tape was released quickly with Sonic Enemy's signature home paste-up sleeves. "Going to Cleveland" mainly interests me for its chord progression; thematically it covers terrain that was irresistible to me then and less so now. Still, some of these internal alliterations are slick, and saying my own name mid-song? That was a transgression and felt like it, and the kick I got from doing it laid a little track for greater self-transgressions down the line.

28 - EARLY SPRING

The pictures that you paint aren't as pretty as they once seemed
to me
And the coffee's bitter 'cause it's been boiling too long
And the jokes you tell aren't as funny as they once seemed to me
And the songs you sing are just plain hackneyed
But the stars shine down on all God's children
And the sun sets on the good and on the evil
And I know you
And I know you

The throbbing flowers outside: I get it
And the paint peeling from the bathroom wall
And the smile on your face: It's a lie
And the smile on your face is real pretty

And the sun shines down on all God's children
And the stars burn for the good and the evil
And I know you
And I know you

ΔΔΔ

"The incantatory mode" is a phrase I use to describe this thing I did a fair bit back then, probably rooted in the rosary but also in poetry: phrases that all begin with the same conjunction in a great big block, phrases heralding images one right after another with a view toward flooding the conceptual plain, phrases that indicate or gesture toward a scene they decline to fully outline, phrases that suggest details withheld. Of the early lyrics in the incantatory mode this is one of the best—little asides like "I get it" situate the narrator within his resentment but don't dwell on it, because what we're meant to see is that the narrator has a pretty vivid view of everything in his environment except himself. He should invest in a mirror! But maybe the world needs a few narrators who live in rooms without mirrors. Rooms with mirrors sort of dominate the real estate landscape in song. We have to have a room or two where the surrounding details get to have their say.

29 · GOING TO MONACO

The sea gobbles up the full sun,
And I look at you and I know you're the one:
The one I used to know something about,
And I try to say what it was, but the words won't come out,
And you ask me to hold you: that's the devil's work.

You show your palms and I see they're empty,
And I'd check them twice, if you'd let me—
But you wouldn't do that, now, would you?

I didn't think so.
And you ask me to hold you: that's the devil's work.

We stand on the sand and we watch the world turn
And we stand on the sand and we watch the water burn
And we stand on the sand six inches from one another
And the sands burn and blow, but neither one of us runs for cover,
And you ask me to hold you: that's the devil's work
And you ask me to hold you: but that's the devil's work.

ΔΔΔ

The definitive version of this was on a radio session, at either KUCI or KSPC, in which members of the Bright Mountain Choir sang "oooh, oooh / devil's work!" over the chorus. That version is lost to time, but the pleasure of trying to nail down the narrator remains fresh for me. One possibility is that he's just one of two people in a relationship having reached its nadir, and he's being dramatic. Not an unheard-of situation! But several details—the scene with the empty upturned palms, the cinematic staging on the sands—suggest a more fleshed-out backstory. "The one I used to know something about": And you don't, now? Why not? Were you wrong about what you thought you knew? Or have you forgotten? Did you forget over the course of time, as happens in life, or was this forgetting more of a renunciation? Nobody seeks cover when the desert is on fire: They just remain in close proximity, either fearless or foolish, or both? As for the devil and his work, whether the narrator means what he says is the song's most pressing question, but the other song that might have shed light on this—"Radical Evil Song," played at least twice, but only once since people started keeping track—remains unreleased.

30 - ORANGE BALL OF PEACE

They wanted me to be a lawyer
They wanted me to work in a machine shop
They wanted me to be a designer
But I came out on top
I'm a fireman
I'm a fireman

Stand and watch the smoke
See the flames rise to the sky
I stand and watch the flames climb higher
I feel the smoke get in my eyes
I'm a fireman
I'm a fireman

ΔΔΔ

It's the attraction of the difficult equation, you know—wanting to write something that's really simple but that's also hard to solve; wanting to write things that have a solid enough surface for even a child to be able to take in at one glance, but that craze when the light hits them. Wanting to write stories that work just fine as themselves but that hide at least one more story inside of them. Given the choice between giving away too much or not giving away enough, I will, in my personal life, always overdisclose, and, in my professional life, always hold something back. My professional self and my personal self are barely even on speaking terms, and who can blame them? They don't really understand each other. This song is obviously about a guy who has realized his lifelong ambition of becoming a fireman. That's why it's such a happy song, in D major with a happy little riff between lines. It's also about how he didn't actually pass the exam you have to take to work for the Fire Department, but that's okay. There are a lot of ways to be a fireman.

31 - GOING TO WISCONSIN

There was the sound of a lake boiling over
On that day
And everyone said just to sit still
But the thickening air got in my way

So the hook's been baited now
The cheese is on the water
The water's been cleansed of all impurities
But now it really doesn't matter

Wisconsin bound
Wisconsin bound
Wisconsin bound
Wisconsin bound

The bottom of the boat was a hotplate come alive
But the boat wasn't real, and this is how I feel:
        You don't know where you're going until you arrive
And the frogs sang out from the distant banks,
And you say you need me in California, but no thanks

Wisconsin bound
Wisconsin bound
Wisconsin bound
Wisconsin bound

ΔΔΔ

It seems like a lot of nonsense, but I would defend it in court—"the boat wasn't real, and this is how I feel: / You don't know where you're going until you arrive" is practically a precis for my method for the next, what, thirty years? Some of these early songs get me into a dreamy state where I imagine nothing, nothing of my work surviving except this. This one weird song where a guy is going to Wisconsin and wants to tell you why, but has a strange idea about how to tell you. I have to tell you that I am pretty attached to this idea.

FEBRUARY

1 - ALPHA GELIDA

Popcorn was snapping in the hot oil on the kitchen stove
And the sky through the kitchen window was cold and poised
and threatening
I heard your voice come lilting through the wall
I heard your voice come sailing from the other room

Let the young lions come out
Let me break their jaws
Let the young lions come out
Let me break their jaws with my bare fingers

Coffee was dripping through the paper filter cone
The heady scent of it nearly knocked me out
I heard your voice come lilting through the back of the
refrigerator
I heard your voice come breaking through the wall

Let the young lions come
Let me talk them out of it
Let the young lions come out
Let me break their jaws with my bare fingers

ΔΔΔ

The eternally divorcing Alpha Couple would be hard to locate in this song if the title weren't there to indicate their presence; what's going on? An angry person in a haunted house, a half memory of Psalm 56 by way of Diamanda Galás, a chord progression that indicates I'm getting nimble enough to do more fun things. "Alpha Gelida" ("Cold Alpha"; perhaps by the end of the calendar year we'll have a clear understanding of how the titles work in this series, though I wouldn't go betting the ranch on it) feels on the page like it belongs more to the setting-poems-to-music moment of just a year or two earlier, but for me it's a moment worth marking: It's a song, not a poem. It is an expression that has found the right skin within which to live and breathe. It's also not a love song, which sets it apart from many of its bedmates in this series early on. We see more of the internal life of the house here. It's jagged.

2 - GOING TO JAMAICA

We saw the last of the brightly colored birds
Check out and make for the other world
And you asked me how much longer we were going to have to
  stay here
But I'm not at liberty to say

And what flowers there were around Kingston were blue
I ripped them up from the dry soil
Draped them over you

We saw the last of the bright birds coming home
I saw you address them through your megaphone
And you asked me when we were leaving
Well, it's any day now

And what flowers there were around Trenchtown were red
I stole them from the hands of children
Braided them around your head

ΔΔΔ

The timeline's vague but that first stanza sounds to me like I've been rereading Didion's *Democracy*, whose elliptical approach to narrative is something of a lodestar to me. It's not clear whether the birds in the opening stanza are just flying away or if they've died, though they do come back in the next verse, in who knows what state of being.

3 · PURE HEAT

The wind from the north fattens the yellow corn
You come in through the house with your dress torn
I can see you now, as though through a screen
Smile on your face, fingers dripping kerosene

And your hair hangs down over me
Your hair casts a shadow to cover me
I can see you now, as though through a screen
Smile on your face, fingers dripping kerosene

And the wind from the north cools me
The wind from the north doesn't fool me
I can see you now, as though through a screen
Smile on your face, fingers dripping kerosene

ΔΔΔ

At some point around '93–'94 I get considerably better at vocal melodies, and for me this song is an example of that—the lyric is a little thin on the page, but set it over I–V–IIm–IV and keep the main line consistent and something magic happens: Spare phrases take on a little weight, like flesh and clothes spontaneously forming around a skeleton.

4 · GOING TO TENNESSEE

Baseball season will be starting soon
But we have no baseball team here

I got a house right by the river
I can see Arkansas from where I am
And the dogs are gathering
And the birds are chattering
And the sun is setting on Memphis
And the sun is setting on Memphis

Medicine bottle collection on the window ledge
Shakes when the cars go past on Interstate 55
You are standing above me
You've washed your face with that apricot scrub again
I am glad I am alive
And your skin is warming up
And my skin is warming up
And the sun is setting on Memphis
And the sun is setting on Memphis

ΔΔΔ

Not sure if a generality like "most of the early Mountain Goats songs are really about sex" is especially useful, but still, one notes that the imagery seems most vivid, and the tone most urgent, when there's two people whose senses seem keenly attuned to the physical particularities of their surroundings, but whose focus narrows, as the song progresses toward its climax, to one another—together, away from the world and together in the ebbing glow of sunset, which, unless somebody turns a light on, and why would they do that, probably leads to a warm and dark room, possibly with the window open, but possibly not.

5 - THE RECOGNITION SCENE

We broke the doorknob off of the door,
and the door swung open easily

We sauntered into the poorly lit store
and looked around lazily
We stole every bit of candy they had inside
and gobbled it all up greedily on our three-month ride,
and I'm going to miss you when you're gone
I'm going to miss you when you're gone

We made our way to the getaway car,
and hit the open road
I saw something written in tall, clear letters on your face
but I could not break the code
You had hot caramel sticking to your teeth
and the only love I've ever known burning underneath
and I'm going to miss you when you're gone
I'm going to miss you when you're gone

ΔΔΔ

The scene in a Greek tragedy where the hero understands that he's too deep in the machinery—the specific machinery of tragedy—to escape it alive: That's the recognition scene. The scene in your life where you remember that there are only two types of stories ever, comedies and tragedies, and the one you've found yourself in probably isn't a comedy: That's this song.

6 - THIRD SNOW SONG

In January, I took the short walk
down the Broadway Bridge—two and a half blocks
when you scrape the ice away,
you can read the bridge dedication

I could feel the cold air coming in through my teeth
I saw the bridge, I saw the water underneath

that's a whole lot of water
that's a whole lot of water

I took out the key that I'd forgotten the function of
Twisted it from the keyring as the bridge loomed above
I hammered it against the ice
I hammered it against the ice

ΔΔΔ

More early autobiography, embellished for effect—I really did live right up the street from Portland's Broadway Bridge, and I'd moved there constitutionally unprepared for colder, rainier, sometimes icier weather. Having lived, since then, in the Midwest, I know that younger me was really a little dramatic about the cold in Portland. Imagine that, younger me being a little dramatic, I mean who could really picture it.

7 - SNOW CRUSH KILLING SONG

When I ask you to look at me, you look away
When I ask you to say something nice once,
you come at me with all your hot lights on display
I know you're changing
Damn you
I know you're changing
God damn you

When the wild snow stacked up outside
You looked around
I could see you from the window
I could see the snow coming down
I know you're changing
Damn you

I know you're changing
God damn you for that

ΔΔΔ

Rachel, a keen reader of English texts, laughed when she first heard "hot lights" here, and she was right, but I have affection for the off phrase that interrupts a line, that just sits there demanding to be regarded as sensible, serious even. *Sweden* was my first attempt at an album where recurring characters tell a story without worrying much about beginnings and endings; I had various big theories about narrative strategies at the time. I still have theories about narrative strategy but they are smaller theories, and denser, more nutritious.

8 - SEPT 19 TRIPLE X LOVE! LOVE!

I cut down that withered peach tree
just like you asked me to
and I hacked it into pieces
set it on fire with your face in plain view
at the near window where you stood
watching me split the wood
I will do as I am told
I will keep away the cold

The fire pit in the snow
Gave off a rich, ripe, orange-red glow
and a familiar scent rose up into the air
and I remembered something special from a long time ago
you opened up the door
you stepped away from the killing floor
your footprint on the snow was fresh and new
when you touched me I felt fire come through
I will do as I am told

I will keep away the cold
I will do as I am told
I will keep away the cold

ΔΔΔ

I know few if any people are here for analysis of lyrics as sentences, but I'm a little mystical about sentences—people don't think of the mighty sentence as really being a player in the field of song, but this one gets its power precisely from the way the sentence keeps tightening the knots: "set it on fire," okay, "with your face in plain view," okay, "at the near window," okay okay, "where you stood / watching me split the wood"—this is repetition, right, beloved repetition, which is actually impossible, cf. the river in "Rain in Soho" (September 20) several chapters hence, but there's a desire in the first stanza to linger, to repeat while we can, because it's going to get so active in the second one that the just-gone time of sought-after repetition will seem like a lost era of safety and known outcomes. I think it's that movement that accounts for the developing urgency of the second verse, although it would also be fair to say that "the developing urgency of the second verse" is one of the most reached-for tools in my kit.

9 - SOME SWEDISH TREES

While you were standing by the door
And while I wondered what we were waiting for
I saw the wild strawberries on the vine
Out of control

While I was trying to think of something clever
You were saying nothing whatsoever
I saw the berries throw their hooks into the soil
Felt the blood between us burning thick as motor oil

We'd come from California
the air around you was familiar to me now
and you were gazing westward
I was looking at you again

ΔΔΔ

It's cryptic! But it comes across like it doesn't really think of itself as cryptic at all, like it's just talking the way people talk, doing the whole "communication" thing, right? Here I am, still quite happily tethered to the poem as ideal, infatuated with the notion of bringing together a number of poems that, considered individually, feel like incomplete broadcasts, partial views of something private, but which, in one another's company, do more than suggest or outline the whole story but less than tell it outright like a gossip.

10 - WHOLE WIDE WORLD

When the last of the repercussions
died off real slow
and the sky was still,
and the cold sun sank down beneath the snow
I hung by my hands
from the tree outside
and I looked on the whole wide world

When the voices came quietly
I shut them down
When a tricky young southerly wind
Came at me with its high whistling sound
I turned around to face it
Real arrogance burning inside
And I drank in the whole wide world

ΔΔΔ

In contrast to "Some Swedish Trees," this feels more song than poem to me—even if its refrain line isn't properly a chorus, it has a home to return to, a structural reliability that might have been used in the service of something less hermetic, had I been interested in less hermetic things at the time. Popular music seeks to be understood. The Mountain Goats in 1995 cannot fairly be called "popular."

11 - WRONG!

You know
You know
You see
What's going on with me
But you don't do anything
You don't do anything
You don't do anything

You feel
You feel
And you hear
That the time is near
But you don't do anything
You don't do anything
You don't do anything
You don't do anything
. . . two, three, four

ΔΔΔ

"Wrong!" is from *Taking the Dative*, a six-song cassette single released on Joel Huschle's Car in Car label operating out of McKinleyville, California. *Taking the Dative* is a weird release, and the weird releases are my favorites. Weird is something you can't really do on purpose, people will clock you doing it; weird has to come naturally. I was in a weird place at the time, and *Taking the Dative* happened as organically for me as sleeping or eating. Just make six songs, send them to Joel. That's what we're doing now, right? On the page, "Wrong!" reads like something you might have found scrawled in the gigantic Yellow Pages hanging from a coiled cable at a phone booth, something someone once took the time to write there, at who knows what time of night or early morning. There's a whole story hiding in that scrawl. This is part of it.

12 - PURE GOLD

Hey, don't touch the door,
because the door will surely kill you.
I hear you saying that you don't see what I mean;
well, you'd better look again.

Stop looking at the floor,
because the whole building's turning, and turning, and turning.
And don't touch the door.
Can't you see the door's burning?

And all at once the street is filled with light,
and all at once the street is filled with sound.
When I hold you, I know our number's being called somewhere.
Let them come on down.

ΔΔΔ

"Don't touch the door!" is a warning issued by the *Twilight Zone* pinball machine, designed by Pat Lawlor and released by Midway under the Bally label in 1993. There are fourteen panels in the door on the playfield; each panel refers to a task, and once the player completes that task, the corresponding panel in the door becomes lit. When all fourteen panels are lit, the player can become "Lost in the Zone" by completing one of three tasks. When Lost in the Zone is activated, the machine sends six balls into play and lights all features for forty-five seconds. EVERYTHING IS LIT, reads the display. It's a whole scene. The machine keeps track of who has the highest Lost in the Zone score; at the time of this song's composition, the initials for "Lost in the Zone Champion" at the co-op at the Pomona College student union read "MTN." Who, one wonders, was this mysterious pinball player MTN, who also held the high score on Bad Cats, and, just up the road, on the *Doctor Who* machine at CMC? Who, indeed?

13 - SONG FOR JOHN DAVIS

The day we set sail from England,
the wind behind us was fair.
The day we set sail from England,
there were smiling faces everywhere.
And the snow came down on New Hampshire today.
And the snow came down on New Hampshire today.

The day we put the grain into the ground,
there were smiling faces all around
and underneath the trees we'd planted when we landed.
And when I was a child,
I spoke with the language of a child,
but when I became a man, I put away childish things;
And the snow came down on New Hampshire today.
And the snow came down on New Hampshire today.

ΔΔΔ

John Davis was a fellow Shrimper stablemate whose work inspired in me, then as now, real envy: hermetic, self-contained, solitary. I don't remember why I dedicated this song to him, except that it takes place in New England, and John lived in Massachusetts. The obvious source for the sort of story it's telling is Robert Lowell, specifically his first two volumes, *Lord Weary's Castle* and *The Mills of the Kavanaughs*, books with which I'd spent more than a little time in the years immediately preceding the whole Mountain Goats project. I didn't go in for the later Lowell of *Life Studies*, but now, thirty-odd years later, I keep thinking of giving it another try.

14 - GOING TO PORT WASHINGTON

The trees were all decked out in their best fall colors;
there was a snap in the air
when you eased down the window
and the New York sun brought out the highlights in your hair
and gently, gently
the constellations aligned
and as we crossed over the Throg's Neck Bridge
I had something on my mind

When we rolled down the street
in the cool of the morning
I could feel the new day dawn
and somebody'd gone and turned the waterworks on
and slowly, surely
I saw the whole story unwind
I had never loved anyone like I loved you
and I had something on my mind

ΔΔΔ

A love song written to mark the occasion of the wedding of two friends who had long supported the band. "Long" in this context means "for a year or two," which was a long time, in 1994, for a band that had only existed since 1991.

15 - HATHA HILL

As the sun went away,
you were sending out signals.
You had sugar on your stomach.
You had sugar on your hair.
You had sugar underneath your eyes;
You had sugar on your mouth.
I know that trick, too,
and I know what it means, coming from you.

ΔΔΔ

Some of the early songs are postcards to my future self about a moment in time; at the time, they were snapshots whose context was knowable mainly, and often only, by me; so I'll say here only that this song marks an occasion, and that now, decades later, I'm very glad to have so marked that occasion, which would otherwise be lost entirely. When I sent the track to Alastair Galbraith for violins, he knew the text only on its merits, but I felt like he understood it, and that his contribution underscored that. That's all I have to say about any of that; this isn't a memoir, unless it is.

16 - NOCHE DEL GUAJOLOTE

The glowing world, the bench backed up against the house.
The chicken coops, the darkness surrounding everything.
It was late, and the night was moving slowly.
We lay down on the ground because the world was lonely.

If you keep quiet, it will stay like this forever.
If you'll just keep quiet, it'll stay like this forever,
I feel certain of it now.
And all the birds were sleeping in their perches.
A little wind, swaying birches—

and the North American wild turkey that your father brought
home
woke up and came towards us.

And the moonlight, and the turkey waking up.
And the night air, and the moonlight on your skin.
And the moonlight, and the turkey waking up.
And the quiet yard, and the turkey, and the moon:
Unimaginable, unimaginable, unimaginable
Unimaginable.

ΔΔΔ

I should say that while birches do actually grow in California, the birch is really only there for the rhyme. All this takes place in the backyard of my girlfriend, but the scene itself never actually occurred. Her father kept chickens, and he did bring a turkey home at one point, and turkeys are really quite incredible creatures, beautiful in a way no other animal is beautiful; social but only according to their own terms; melodious, magnificent animals. Sometimes I think poetry is what happens when a person imposes a vision he's had onto a time and place, when the imagination steps in to improve the conditions within which the author exists. This is more poem than song.

17 - SONG FOR DANA PLATO

The three-month ride sticks in your mind as though the insides of your head were a big screen; and, coming in on the evening wind, it's the unmistakable scent of brilliantine. What kind of memory serves? What kind of world is it that comes headlong at you and then swerves at the last possible second? It's this one; yeah, it's this one. And it's easy to slow down. And it's easy to slow down. And it's easy just to lie out by the blue pools in the squinting sun and slow down. And it's easy to slow down, and in situations like these, it's sometimes useful to think of life as one long, continuous evening that never turns into night. Hey, hey.

ΔΔΔ

I've rendered this one as a prose poem rather than a lyric because that's how it feels to me; the original draft is long gone, and there may not have even been an original draft—something about it feels improvised to me. Nodding at Joni Mitchell without saying her name. I know that, at the time, I was in possession of a Karl Shapiro volume that had a whole block of prose poems, and that they impressed me. I also know that Dana Plato was still alive, but not for much longer. I don't know what informs the feeling I have for people who got famous too young and who struggled to define themselves in the wake of the catastrophe of fame, but I do know that this is probably the first time I connected with that feeling. It would not be the last.

18 - THE ONLY THING I KNOW

When you came back from Trenton,
all the sparkle was gone
and you stood in the shadow
and the curtains were drawn

And I know you're lying
you know you're lying, too
that is just about
the only thing I know about you

When you pocketed your eye shadow
and you picked up the phone
I stepped out on the balcony
and I drank in the drone

And I know you're leaving
you know you're leaving, too
that is just about
the only thing I know about you

When you stopped on the sidewalk
and you looked up above you
the warm, wet air came down to shelter me
how much do I love you?

Well, you know you're dying
and I know you're dying, too
that is just about the only thing I know about you

ΔΔΔ

There is more narrative movement in this song than in many of its stablemates from the '93–'95 era; I'd call that the single most important arc to follow in that time—from obsessive focus on self-constructed dioramas to scenes with moving parts, people who have backstories and futures, or backstories and no futures, or futures and no reliable backstory.

19 - DUKE ELLINGTON

Light hit the rings
glimmering on his fingers
the light came down
and his hands hit the keys
it utterly wasted me in Sweden.

Horns punched the air;
the aftermath fell around everywhere.
I saw the spotlight land on his rings

and I'd had just about enough of losing things in Sweden,
in 1962: quite some distance from you.

ΔΔΔ

In contrast to "The Only Thing I Know," here I'm still burrowing into a scene in which very little happens, teasing out the story that necessarily hides underneath even the stillest of surfaces. A man in 1962 watches Duke Ellington play with his orchestra and remembers someone. Louis Armstrong played Sweden in 1962 and so did Count Basie, but I don't find Duke Ellington there until he plays Lund in '63. If I have the choice between rhyming "you" or "me," though, I mean that's not really even a choice, the second person is the preferred person where possible.

20 - AGAINST AGAMEMNON

Red, red—
red everywhere.
Bright red all along the thin canvas walls.
I stepped outside
to get a little air.
I stepped outside
to get away from it all.
I looked around;
I saw the purple sky
making jokes about my condition.

I am going for a walk.
I'll be back in half an hour.
Watch over the children.
I'll be back in half an hour.

ΔΔΔ

The source text for this is *Ajax* by Sophocles. Ajax, in the frenzied madness of Aphrodite, has bound and flayed livestock, believing them to be his enemies, Agamemnon and Achilles. But they're just sheep. His imagined triumph over his enemies has been a dream. He does not return from his walk; he is overcome by shame, and takes his own life. *Ajax* is not mentioned in the same company as the Oedipus cycle or *The Oresteia* of Aeschylus, but its pain feels personal to me: a man led to ruin by something he's imagined, a man for whom mockery is worse than death. I'm not that man, but I'm older than Ajax was when his moment came.

21 - FULL FLOWER

I saw the ceiling spin
and I saw the room shift
and I watched the television flicker
and I let my mind drift
and I would give anything in the world up for you,
but I will not stop

I saw the blossom form
and I saw the screen glow black
and I let my arm fall to my side
and I took one step back
I would give anything in the world up for you,
but I will not stop

ΔΔΔ

This is a song about heroin addiction and usage, and it's considerably more blunt and less coy about its theme than many of the early songs, which probably accounts for why I sent it to Graeme Jefferies to slather it in gorgeous, painterly, very loud layers of electric guitar, which moved the spotlight off of the lyric some, a dynamic you almost never find at work on early Mountain Goats records. I don't do advice, as a general rule, but I will say that if you're looking to move the focus a little away from whatever it is you feel you need to sing about, I recommend loud electric guitars.

22 - ORANGE BALL OF PAIN

When I saw it on the bakery carousel,
I knew I had to have it for my own.
I eased it out,
And I brought it home.
Why don't you try some?
I already had some myself.

Is that the most delicious thing
You ever tasted in your life?
Is that the most delicious thing
You ever tasted in your life?

And then cold sorrow gripped me by the throat.
And then I felt the colder sadness taking hold.
I knew I had to have it for my own.
Why don't you try some?
Why don't you try some?

Is that the most delicious thing
You ever tasted in your life?
Is that the most delicious thing
You ever tasted in your life?

And I saw the snow against the window.
And I saw the snow hit the window.

And I saw the snow brush against the window.
And then I saw the snow again.

ΔΔΔ

The self-hypnotic effect of the coda here was a hallmark of that time: Say something, then say it again, say it in a lower register, drag out the syllable a little longer, see where you end up. This is really a Nick Drake pastiche—still a fairly obscure figure then, but I had a copy of *Pink Moon* that a friend had copied for me on cassette. The other side had Leonard Cohen's *Live Songs*, the one with "Please Don't Pass Me By (A Disgrace)." I would listen to this tape on the same machine I used to record this song; it was a quasi-alchemical practice.

23 · BLOOD ROYAL

I remembered you
I remembered where you'd come from
I remembered you
I remembered where you'd gone
and in the shifting neon air
I saw the colors of the revolution everywhere
blood royal

I remembered you
I remembered all the little things you'd said
I remembered the shape of your face
I let the thought go to my head
and in the iron-blue dawn
I felt power coming on
blood royal

ΔΔΔ

There are times, as in the entry of the previous day, where I would revise phrases, lines, stanzas—fix what I now perceive as shortcomings. And then there are times like these, where I remember the act of writing the song but not what was going through my head as I did so—sitting on the floor by the boom box, playing a little riff in D, seeing a scene in my head and saying some lines out loud that came from within that scene, the story assembling itself through improvised details and evocative phrases—and remember listening back and feeling something magical. "Getting somewhere" is what I say to myself when I write a song that feels like it's taking me a little further along the road toward some desired place. Here I'm still moving toward it. But I can feel the movement. Getting somewhere.

24 - GOING TO SCOTLAND

There was a barn owl trapped in the rafters
the ground underneath us was wet and cold
we heard the owl thrashing about
trying desperately to get out
we stood outside and watched the night unfold

We watched the sun go down on Scotland
and I watched the moon come up over you
when a pack of dogs went silently past us
we knew we'd been given fair warning
but that was the only thing we knew

And you threw all your luggage out onto the water
and I tore the shirt away from my back
the cold came on with a newfound intensity
and you pressed your warm body against me
and I loved you so much, it was making me sick

We watched the sun go down on Scotland
we were glad that we'd left Oklahoma behind
I took your hips in my hands and I drew you down
to the newfound deep brown rich wet ground
had a vision of you burning in my mind

We watched the sun go down on Scotland
and I watched the moon come up over you
when a pack of dogs went silently past us
we knew we'd been given fair warning
but that was the only thing we knew

ΔΔΔ

A lot going on and not many words wasted: I'm aiming for maximum density, for some movement inside a scene—something from which an entire novel, or play, or film might proceed, then drawing the curtain forever on that scene. An entire life can occur within the confines of a song, and be pretty vividly sketched by just a few details from a single morning within that life—or within two lives, maybe. It's fair to say that at the time of "Going to Scotland" I am somewhat obsessively interested in this possibility.

25 - GOING TO REYKJAVIK

I've been drinking that coffee you sent me from Thailand
I've been watching the lamps burn
I've been listening to the wind chime
I've been waiting my turn

And I'm coming to you
I am coming to you
I am coming to you

And I heated the milk 'til it boiled, and I drank it down
And I stepped outside and I checked my reflection in the rain
And there were voices on the wind
Winter coming on in
And I made myself up again: brand new,

And I am broken, and I am tired,
and I'm coming to you
with my mouth
dripping.

ΔΔΔ

I avoid speaking in generalities about writing, but: Growth, for me, is a dialectical process—my style develops in reaction to its present state, and as commentary on whatever state it was in before that. "All writing is correction," I would like to proclaim in some marvelously opaque essay on style, or maybe on voice, or perspective. The pyrotechnics of "Going to Scotland" coexist in a state of happy tension with the static scene here, where a person is thinking about going somewhere instead of having already arrived there to scenes of great drama. Neither impulse can win: They can only conspire to push the style forward. The marvelously opaque essay will be called "Going to Reykjavik" and the editor of the journal who publishes it will have my gratitude for letting me keep the title.

26 - HEIGHTS

When the seashells crumbled in your hand,
You looked up at me;
And the sands shifting underneath your feet
Softened for you, and, incredibly,
The sun withdrew from the sky,
And I was certain I was going to cry—

But then you reached up, and you reached out.
We'd been staring at the water all day.
And then you touched me—you were golden.
You were giving the game away.

When the sand crabs ran across your face,
You didn't even twitch;
And the salt scent came across the water—
Impossibly rich, impossibly cold.
We were just nineteen years old,

And then you reached up, and you reached out.
We'd been staring at the water all day.
And then you touched me—you were golden.
You were giving the game away.

ΔΔΔ

I would like to know more about this narrator—why does the sun sinking into the water at the end of the day make him want to cry? How old is he now, if he was "just nineteen" at the time when this scene burned itself into his memory? What is, or was, the game, given away once and for good in this moment, since you can't take up the game again once it's been seen, revealed, confessed, recorded. I would like to know more about him, I say, and that's not a conceit: I know about him only what the listener knows; my insight is limited to the images I gave him to remember, the phrases I put in his mouth. For me, that mystery is one of the great pleasures of writing lyrics, and the tending of it is a cherished errand.

27 - MILLION

When I came back from Finland,
and the taxi took me down the street

I saw the red flowers growing like they used to
by the roadside in the smothering summer heat.

You were standing out in front of the house
with your floral print dress on
and you had questions only a masochist would ask
written all over your big, brown eyes,

and the moon is high over Iowa tonight,
and the moon is high over Iowa tonight—
and I brought you a blanket—handwoven, hand-dyed,
and the moon is high over Iowa tonight.

ΔΔΔ

Within a year of writing this song I would be living in Iowa, where I would remain for the next seven years or so. Had I noticed this connection prior to today, I'd have begun an earlier start on my new song "John Darnielle Unifies the Heavyweight Title at the Age of Fifty-Seven Despite Never Having Boxed." Still, as my father used to say, there's no time like the present: I repeat this for those who, like myself, need to hear something several times before it sinks in. There's no time like the present. I'm not just riffing here, I mean it, and this song means it, too. There is no time like the present.

28 - COLD MILK BOTTLE

Rainbows shone on the glass
Dewdrops gathered on the grass
And the yellow sun came into view:
another God damned message from you;

Well, despite your best efforts, I feel all right.
Against my better judgment, I feel all right.

Despite your random acts of violence, I feel all right.
Despite the force of your fury, I feel all right.

You're mean to me. Why must you be mean to me?
You shouldn't forget, you see,
What you mean to me.

ΔΔΔ

Trying to track down the origin of the phrase "random acts of violence" yields plenty of information about the phrase coined as a response to it ("random acts of kindness," Anne Herbert, *CoEvolution Quarterly*, 1982; these acts and this notion are certainly better for the world than random acts of violence, although I'll posit that the power of random chance will, reliably, be more keenly felt when its effects harm rather than help; why is this? Because kindness and violence are not two sides of the same coin; violence can be accidental, truly random, but kindness cannot; to be kind is to act with intention; kindness cultivates the self, while violence fragments as many selves as it touches; indeed, kindness is its own intention, it is a stranger to chance, whose wiles have been the subject of much invective since at least the age of the Romans, and probably the Greeks). I know I heard it somewhere as a kid and found it hilarious: the *National Lampoon* feels like the best candidate to me, but it might also have been Monty Python, or the Firesign Theatre. It is, at any rate, a wholly borrowed phrase, one of two loaners in this song, the second being the coda, taken wholesale from "Mean to Me," Fred E. Ahlert and Roy Turk, 1929, and sung by so many of the greats: Billie Holiday, Sarah Vaughan, Judy Garland, Frank Sinatra, Rosemary Clooney, Ella Fitzgerald. Murderer's row. This is the last song on *Sweden* because it's one my favorite songs on *Sweden*. I retain this aesthetic preference even in the streaming age. It's worth retaining.

29 · SONG FOR ROGER MARIS

When the power of God shows up in your swing,
and the people start to notice, and you can't do anything about it,
and they all come out to see you, and they start to crowd around—
let me tell you, brother, you can feel it coming down,

And I've got an angel watching over me
A monkey on my back
The devil at my heels
Reporters breathing down my neck

My father always told me to finish what you start
And my wife's about to leave me, and it's going to break my heart
And I no longer have my youth, and I no longer have my looks
I got a God damned one-way ticket to the God damned history books

And I've got an angel watching over me
A monkey on my back
The devil at my heels
Reporters breathing down my neck

ΔΔΔ

Speaking of cribbings, "I no longer have my youth, and I no longer have my looks" is a version of "I have my youth; I used to have a lot more" (Robert Forster, "Rock 'n' Roll Friend"—1988, maybe?)—but the thing that interests me here is "the people start to notice, and you can't do anything about it." Roger Maris held the record for most home runs in a season from 1961 until 1998, when both Mark McGwire and Sammy Sosa gave him chase; Claremont's own McGwire got there first. This song is about the pressure of increasing success in the public eye, something its author could, at the time of its writing, only really guess at, but what is an author if not a person who makes a good guess every now and again? And, certainly, when the power of God shows up in your swing, and the people start to notice, you could always stop swinging, or at least swing worse: That'll get them off your back, won't it? But you won't do that, now, will you. If you were that sort the power wouldn't have shown up in the first place.

MARCH

1 - CUBS IN FIVE

They're going to find intelligent life up there on the moon,
and *The Canterbury Tales* will shoot up to the top of the bestseller list,
and stay there for twenty-seven weeks;
and the Chicago Cubs will beat every team in the league,
and the Tampa Bay Bucs will make it all the way through January,
and I will love you again—
I will love you, like I used to.
I will love you again.
I will love you, like I used to.

The stars are going to spell out all the answers to tomorrow's corporation
and the Philips Corporation will admit that they've made an awful mistake
and Bill Gates will singlehandedly spearhead the Heaven 17 revival;
and the Chicago Cubs will beat every team in the league,
and the Tampa Bay Bucs will take it all the way to the top,
and I will love you again—
I will love you, like I used to.
I will love you again.
I will love you, like I used to.

ΔΔΔ

I had the idea for the song, and then I wrote the song, and I called Peter Hughes, the singer from Diskothi-Q and bassist for Nothing Painted Blue, and, as important to me at the time, a fellow baseball fan; and I said, Peter, I got a live one, come over and sing harmonies on it. We did it into the boom box, facing each other from chairs at my mom's dining room table. Many years later, Peter and I, along with Jon Wurster and Matt Douglas, played "Word on a Wing" at Carnegie Hall in tribute to the late David Bowie. Checking out of the hotel the morning after that remarkable evening, I made conversation with the guy who'd sung "The Width of a Circle" with Tony Visconti and the house band at the same show. He was the nicest dude, sharply dressed, positive and energetic, the icing on the cake of our trip to New York. His name was Glenn Gregory, and in a bygone age he'd been the singer for Heaven 17.

I didn't say anything.

2 - PURE MONEY

Waves crashed all around and near your body;
The waves came all over you.
And I saw the sky reflected on the ocean, deadly blue.
Yeah, and I used to know you.
I used to know you.
I used to know you.
I used to know you.

ΔΔΔ

There is something about the songs I did on the Casio instead of the guitar. There is just something about them, for me. Had I committed to the Casio, this book would not exist; perhaps I would be a Registered Nurse; perhaps nursing in Hawaii, a state that was offering considerable signing bonuses for new nurses around the time when this song was written and recorded within the space of no more than half an hour. Perhaps I would be teaching English somewhere, having sent out more graduate school applications than I did in 1995 (four), with more of these schools having accepted me than did back then (zero).

Perhaps I would reflect on the short period of time during which I made a few albums using only a Casio SA-7, albums whose songs were spare, cryptic, spectral, odd, and entirely commercially unviable. Then might I say, from my office, or from behind my med cart: You know, I'm glad things turned out for me the way they did, but still, there is something about those old Casio songs. Maybe I would listen to a few of them when I got home from work, or maybe I would just go over them in memory, to see how much of them I could remember. I think I would remember this one.

3 · NINE BLACK POPPIES

When I got home I meant to bring you some
sweet chrysanthemum
but the wind chimes were ringing all wrong
and you were standing in the doorway, singing along,
and I tried to remember how nice it had been
a long, long time ago,
and then I couldn't remember; I honestly could not remember.

And a package came for you today from Hunan Province,
the postmark burning jet-black in the summer sun
Someone was changing, someone was changing from the inside out;
and I turned around to face you.

Sweet peas in the garden—
all in full bloom,
and I swore I heard the traces of an old song
murmuring in the room
like a half-remembered conversation,
but I let it fall away, and then I couldn't remember.
I honestly could not remember.

And a package came for you today from Hunan Province
the postmark burning jet-black in the summer sun
Someone was changing, someone was changing from the inside
out;
and I turned around to face you.

ΔΔΔ

Norman Dubie, from whose poem "Nine Black Poppies for Chac" I cribbed the title of this one, was a poet whose star seemed ascendant to me in the early nineties; I became aware of him when he made the cover of the *American Poetry Review*, which I bought at Chancery Lane Bookstore on Second Street in Claremont. I had two of his books—*Groom Falconer* and *Radio Sky*—and I spent some good time with them, reading and rereading, trying to get inside Dubie's vision, as you do with poets. "Nine Black Poppies for Chac" is a vivid and intense poem rife with allusions to political violence and death; my song, all physical signposts and the memories they trigger, might take place in that poem's distant future.

4 - THAT HIPPOLYTINE FEELING

We sat together on the porch
as the sunset bled,
and you playfully leveled your semiautomatic handgun
right at my head
and then God,
in another stroke of His genius—
He opened up the floodgates,
and the bulls came out, the bulls came out.

We heard the heavy hooves beating on the earth
as the moment came near.
I felt the chamber of your pistol kissing my jaw,

I felt your red lips brushing my ear
and then God,
convincing if not transparent in His motives—
He opened up the floodgates,
but the rivers were dry, because it was late August,
and the bulls came out, and the bulls came out.

ΔΔΔ

Firearms Suite Song No. 1

Hippolytus meets his death in the Euripidean play that bears his name when a bull suddenly charges from the surf at Troezen, frightening his horses, who bolt, dashing his chariot with him in it against the rocks. He meets this fate for having offended Poseidon, but the original insult was his having neglected to honor Aphrodite; therefore let me ask, here, with you, assembled, as my witness—who, O goddess to whom the dove is sacred, and also the white goose, is greater than you? To whose beauty, goddess, can yours be compared? The red rose blooms for you; yea, and myrtle. From the cockle shell you have emerged in splendor, to spread word of fruit ripe upon the tree, both pomegranate and apple. As a young man writing songs I lauded your power, because I lived in its thrall; nor, goddess, do I yield to others in my service. Behold, lovers with handguns. I knew you'd like it.

5 - GOING TO GEORGIA

The most remarkable thing about coming home to you is the
feeling of being in motion again; it's the most extraordinary
thing in the world. I have two big hands, and a heart pumping
blood, and a 1967 Colt .45 with a busted safety catch. The world
shines as I cross the Macon County line going to Georgia.

The most remarkable thing about you standing in the doorway is
that it's you, and that you're standing in the doorway; and you

smile when you ease the gun from my hand, and I'm frozen with joy right where I stand. The world throws its light underneath your hair, forty miles from Atlanta. This is nowhere. Going to Georgia.

ΔΔΔ

Firearms Suite Song No. 2

Written during the winter break between semesters, possibly on Christmas morning though I don't have the documentation to prove or disprove that; recorded four or five times, one take after another, certain I was onto something but not liking any rendition enough to mark as a keeper. There was one in 2/4, I remember, with a galloping strum pattern, a last-ditch effort after a solid hour of trying to get a take I liked. That 2/4 version sounded kind of like the theme from *Rawhide*, but the version that got released was the original draft as performed live on KSPC Claremont. Its perennial status as one of the most requested songs in the Mountain Goats catalog supports my longstanding claim that the people, while not actively demanding blood, would still like the occasional assurance that blood, should they need it, is certainly on the menu, both as a starter and as a main dish.

6 - BLACK MOLLY

Black mollies in the aquarium
darted back and forth as though an earthquake were certain,
and I turned up the heater
and I ripped off my shirt
and I grabbed hold of my stereo
and I threw it out the window.
You were in town again.
You'd come around again.
You were dragging me down again with you.

Siamese fighting fish flashing like sparklers
It started to rain
and the telephone rang a couple of times
I put a bullet through its cold, dead brain
and I got out my photographs of you
and I put bullets through all of them, too:
You were in town again.
You'd come around again.
You were dragging me down again,
dragging me right down with you.

ΔΔΔ

Firearms Suite Song No. 3

Like so many of my early lyrics, this one cloaks several autobiographical details of the moment in a story otherwise unrelatable to that moment, except maybe via metaphor. I had an aquarium with some very cool tropical fish in it, because there was a way cool pet store just down the street—just a few storefronts down from the Bang Luck Market, where I bought some peanuts we'll be talking about on March 22. Black mollies were small, velvety-black fish, inexpensive and hardy. I did indeed watch them swim back and forth, and they did seem to anticipate earthquakes, sometimes even breaking the surface of the water in the tank right before a big tremor hit. I worried a lot about something breaking the glass tank. From this worry, a vision of a guy with a fish tank, a firearm, and an anxiety meter way up in the red. The tank doesn't catch a bullet in this song, but when I sing it, I still worry about the tank and its inhabitants.

7 • CHESHIRE COUNTY

When the sun came up
I got up
Because you were saying my name backwards in your sleep again

The field outside the door was fresh and green,
and the most gorgeous cow I'd ever seen
was coming right at me, right at you

Her udder was fat with fresh milk,
and her black-and-white coat was as smooth as silk
and in the waning of a long, long year
I felt the remnants of last night disappear.

Disappear.
Disappear.
Disappear.
Disappear.

ΔΔΔ

We interrupt the *Firearms Suite* with a song that, for me, really lands squarely on the "it's a song, but it's a poem" nexus I was so often trying to reach in those days. You could count the syllables in this song without much effort, but inside them there's a whole world: That is, for me, what poetry's good at—dense economies of rhythm, sound, and meaning. In those early days one thing people tended to notice was the high energy of my performances, but my intense love affair with repetition is the more important quality to my mind: Say "disappear," then say it four more times. Make it the coda. What is the song then? How does it work differently from other songs? I wanted songs that both made these questions explicit and were brave enough to leave those questions open.

8 - STARS FELL ON ALABAMA

You looked real calm
as we made our way up the walk
there were lazy kisses,

and hands brushing, and small talk
the moon was high
your smooth face was dry
and the kudzu
grew

And the stars fell on Alabama
and your eyes filled up with light
and the stars fell on Alabama

The warm earth underneath us gave way
dry grass crinkled like paper as a breeze came in across the bay
cold, clean water nearby
glimmered in your eye
and your pistol
glistened

And the stars fell on Alabama
and your eyes filled up with light
and the stars fell on Alabama,
but if you think I'll take a bullet for you, you're dreaming

ΔΔΔ

Firearms Suite Song No. 4

Oh, yes, there were other early songs with guns, but the *Firearms Suite* ends here. "Stars Fell on Alabama" shares its title with a jazz standard to which it otherwise bears no resemblance. I have a specific memory of wanting to name the bay across which that breeze comes in the second verse, but I didn't have any maps of Alabama to hand, which left me with two choices, both unacceptable: put off writing the song until I could get to the map room of a library somewhere, thereby breaking my "either the song gets finished in a single sitting or it doesn't get written" rule (which remained in place for another ten years at least), or make up a name for a bay that didn't exist. This latter idea I liked, but I couldn't come up with a bay name I liked well enough. "Half Moon Bay" was what I wanted to say, but Half Moon Bay is a city south of San Francisco. You can do a lot of things as a writer, but putting Half Moon Bay in Alabama isn't one of them.

9 - RED CHORAL DIAMOND SPRAY

As we pull into the harbor in New York today
I ask you how you're doing, you swear up and down you're okay
but I can see what's gotten into your eyes
and it's written all over your face tonight
we will never see Ireland again
we will never see Ireland again

As we hang up the map on the motel wall
count up the places that we've left behind
add the distances between them all
all the bridges someone's burned down for us
all the chances that we burned all by ourselves
makes us wonder what we were thinking then
'cause we will never see Ireland again
we will never see Ireland again
we will never see Ireland again

ΔΔΔ

This is from *Hail and Farewell, Gothenburg*, an album written and recorded on a borrowed boom box during a week in somebody's apartment in Bavaria that they loaned me as a favor to a friend, and it's rather a long story, all that, and I know that if you're here at all part of what you're here for is the long stories, but the song really is a mirror of what I prioritize in any story at all: details that will evoke, not explain; characters whose presence solidifies and becomes real as they speak; resonance. I didn't release the album but it got leaked to the internet eleven years down the line; I was very mad about that at the time, but now? Now I don't have to book a session with somebody who's got a DAT player to recover the lyrics. On balance, victory!

10 - FOUR NEW TREES

The first new tree is tall and good
it gives hard, dark, brown burning wood
when winter comes it stands right outside
with its blossom-laden arms spread wide

the second new tree gives out sweet sticky fruit
and it took a long time to take root
sometimes we thought it had given up the spirit
but now it makes me happy when I'm just standing near it

the third new tree stands just west of the barn
its best branch is no thicker than my arm
I will water him every day
and I will chase all the termites away

but the fourth new tree
is my enemy
the fourth new tree shouldn't be here
the fourth new tree
sends its tendrils through the water mains and tries to poison me
its leaves are thick, and always falling, and pure

ΔΔΔ

"Four New Trees" seems to situate the narrator of *Hail and Farewell, Gothenburg* as unreliable (it is a single narrator throughout). It's the only song of the bunch where he sounds fixated, paranoid—somehow off. The other songs have various degrees of distress, but for me they read as "normal" distress—reactions to undesired outcomes, honest responses. I mark this song's presence in the cycle as indicative of some tension I was feeling back then about always pathologizing my narrators. As with some of the songs on *Sweden*, I'd bicker with my choices now—I wonder how else this song might resolve, where else it might go. But then I note that by forcing the narrator a little too far around the bend, I've ended up with "the fourth new tree / is my enemy," and an interior "sends its tendrils" rhyme just a couple of beats later, all in a song with the title "Four New Trees," a title certainly given to no song before this one, and I think: Sometimes it's fine to just be a little weird, to dawdle in the weirdness.

11 - GHOSTS

I went down Yale today, just in the old way
and a black dog hobbled past me
its tags jangled on its collar
it made me wish I was dead
it made me wish I was dead

And the familiar sun on me
just like it would always be
rocky soil, dry land
I knew it all like the back of my hand
it made me wish I was dead
it made me wish I was dead

Terrific view from here
sky's clear
sun's high
I let things lie,

and I know what is and isn't mine
and it was good to get back to the sunshine
but five years is a long time,
and I spent five years in Sweden dying for you;
I spent five years in Sweden dying for you.

ΔΔΔ

Sometimes I think of a song as "justifying" the album it comes from—not just in my work but elsewhere, too. It's a way of reading: of thinking of one point as exerting gravity on all around it, of regarding the other points as supporting structures, not without their own virtues but ultimately there to help. "Ghosts" is why *Hail and Farewell, Gothenburg* exists; it's the step forward here. It's very focused, and economical, and moves briskly toward a dramatic and romantic climax. To speak plainly, I'm working out some personal stuff in this song, something I didn't do all that often then and that I'm still careful about now; it's not autobiographical insofar as I didn't wish I was dead, and I wasn't in Claremont, where Yale Avenue is, and I hadn't seen the black dog in question for at least a year. Maybe two. But this song is a close examination of that "maybe two," which is to say, it's a song about calculating distances.

12 - RAID ON ENTEBBE

On the shores of a lake named after a late queen of England
I heard new rumors of war
the sun was a red ball up in the summer sky
I heard my sister standing in the doorway

She had that look on her face that reminded me of you
The reports were coming hourly and the sky was blue
They were shifting the power again
They always do this when I come home

I tucked my shirt in though I don't know why
Shielded my eyes from the light up in the sky
'cause it was shining shifting like a highway flare
In the incredibly, impossibly dry air

I heard my mother call my sister to the kitchen again
And knew that everything was headed straight down the drain
They'd positioned themselves in strategic locations
I was beginning to lose my patience

If you'll just put your hand in mine,
we're going to leave all our troubles behind

ΔΔΔ

We all have things we like best about ourselves. Sometimes these line up with the things others like best in us, and sometimes not. "Stories that take place against a backdrop of hazily defined political tension and that seem to be careening toward an unhappy resolution for all involved" is probably not high on anybody's list of most desired qualities in a Mountain Goats song, but on my list it's very high indeed. I imagine a shadow career in which this was all I did, in which emotions were bottled up in the urgency of the action and had to be inferred from their context, song after song and album after album. Deeply obscure song after deeply obscure song and unreleased album after unreleased album, most likely, but still.

13 - AN INSCRIPTION AT SALONAE

There was a guy up on the hill
with a trumpet to his lips
I mean to tell you he knew how to blow that thing

There were women dressed in purple
banging on their tambourines
and hammering on cymbals

It was not that long ago
When we gathered in the valley below
I loved you more than I loved my own life;
I was falling to pieces

There was a young man on the altar
you saw me poised above him
I saw you watching me

There were singers, there were dancers
there was glittering gold
spring breaking out gradually

It was not that long ago
But the memory's kind of dying out, you know
Like a flower caught in the overgrowth
Falling, falling to pieces

ΔΔΔ

The *Jack and Faye* EP is a moment in time, and it's hard for me to separate the songs, which I don't really remember writing at all, from that moment, which I do. We were in the studio; I was booked to leave California for good. Whatever the Mountain Goats were going to become in the future would look different from what they would be for the last time on the day when that EP's two studio songs were recorded. We didn't mark the occasion, because we didn't know there was any occasion to mark. We just went in and did a couple of songs. We were getting better at it.

"An Inscription" shares some formal qualities with "Raid on Entebbe" that I like, especially my growing tendency to sublimate the love story aspect of the song; to trust that a spare allusion here or there will suffice. It is also, to the best of my knowledge, the only Mountain Goats song in which the thing one character has as a whole card to play against the other is actual human sacrifice. None of this metaphorical sacrifice for our friends at the festival. Only the real thing will do.

14 - NEW BRITAIN

You've had it up to here with my west country talk.
You can hardly understand a word I say.
The shortest tree around here is a hundred feet tall.
It's going to rain today.

I try to tell you secrets 'til my face turns blue.
I am not getting through to you.
And all the way across the ocean, they're gathering their strength again.
Lining up along the country's length again

This morning I know who you are.
This morning I know who you are.

On the river, the sun is bright gold,
and the things you try to say to me make my blood run cold.
But I hold you anyway,
and we stare into the sun all day.

And you're about to leave again: I've learned to read your movements,
and I'm learning how to read your mind.

The sun climbs the sky for us above the Mississippi,
and I can feel you in my arms, but you're hardly even with me.

This morning I know who you are.
This morning I know who you are.

ΔΔΔ

Full Force Galesburg is the first Mountain Goats album where none of the songs were written in California, where I grew up. It takes its title from a town I passed on a train heading from Chicago to Ottumwa, but it's an Iowa album through and through: rivers, trees, big skies. I like this narrator who steps into the frame and immediately makes four declarations of which he seems absolutely convinced: supposition, accusation, declaration, prediction. I like him not because he's going places, but because he has decided that going places is for the birds. He's going to stay put until he gets a clearer picture. If only his creator would grant him that mercy, but alas.

15 · MASHER

Most of the brine has got to boil away.
Most of the air has got to choke you.
Most of June I spent in jail again;
I don't mean jail, exactly.

Up in a pine tree,
red squirrel looking down at me
and I am losing control of the language again.
I am losing control of the language again.

Most of the things I used to hold on to,
most of the things I used to say to you.

All of the ways I knew around the local roads
are disappearing daily.

High in a cottonwood,
you were looking down at me and you sure looked good.
Hair hanging down in the leaves.
Your neck tilted back to make a rainbow.

I was losing control of the language again.
I am losing control of the language again.

ΔΔΔ

Beautiful lofty things; the Parkisons, from Dublin, by post: Would you like to come and play for us?; an exhausted man with a guitar in a new airport; a club on Capel Street, and a soundman who'd roadied for Thin Lizzy; no more than forty people present, a generous estimate, with me premiering, at mid-set, this song, which felt like a step in a new direction; and John Parkinson seeing to it that I knew he'd marked that step, and the cobblestone clacking a little under it; each step its own un-retraceable step; a thing never known again.

16 · CUTTER

I've been living hand to mouth for a year or better
When the mailman comes and brings me your letter
And I recognize the handwriting even now
But I go ahead and open it anyhow
No one's been buying from my roadside stand
And I hold your letter like a Cross in my hand
I'm going to wrap up my troubles
I'm going to wrap up my troubles
I'm going to wrap up my troubles
in you

I went out into the kitchen, where the light
Comes through the four-paneled window clear and bright
And it's taken me this long to realize
How much I like the way that you dot your *i*'s
I was born in Indiana thirty years ago
I've got a mean, mean hunger down below
I'm going to wrap up my troubles
I'm going to wrap up my troubles
I'm going to wrap up my troubles
in you

ΔΔΔ

"Cutter" is what they called working-class Indiana guys who worked at the stone quarry; I learned this from the movie *Hoosiers* when I was a kid. Because I was born in Bloomington but moved with my then intact family to California while still an infant, and because that family would no longer be intact four years after the move, Indiana occupied a corner of the pre-divorce Eden I held in my head for much of childhood. Its name still resonates for me as it did in those early years—the place I come from, the place I first saw light on the sixteenth of March, 1967. The court of King Arthur and his Knights of the Round Table. Xanadu, whereat Kubla Khan a stately pleasure dome did decree. The lost city of Atlantis. Indiana.

17 · CALCUTTA

Wild donkeys kicking, braying in the meadow
Made you wanna kick and bray yourself, at least you said so
You were wild-eyed, your lips were flecked with foam
'Til warm Calcutta called you home

Twin rivers flowing brought a flush into your cheek
At the spot where the trickling streams and rivers meet

The wind from off the snowcapped mountain cooled you down
'Til warm Calcutta brought you back around

I could hear the prophets yelling in the street
How your eyes were pure poison, but your skin was sweet

ΔΔΔ

The internet tells me that this song was only played once—at NYU in March 1997. I remember that it was a festival date of some kind, and that I also gave a reading of an essay, which I believe was called "What We Do Is Secret" and which may have later been published in a magazine called *Jaboni Youth*, or possibly elsewhere, or possibly not at all and probably for the best. The extant recording reveals a song that I like a lot, in fact as well as many of its contemporaries that made the cut for *Full Force Galesburg*. Maybe I wrote this after I'd already sequenced the album to DAT and sent it to Craig at Emperor Jones? Maybe I didn't have a recorded version I liked well enough to release? Maybe I was unhappy with a line I didn't want to take the trouble to fix? Fine, yes, I know that last bit is true, and I even know which line, but I feel gentler toward this song now—it gets a lot done in ten lines of verse, it tells a story that draws me in, and it has a coda but no chorus; in short, it's the sort of song that people then urging me to really go for that brass ring of success would have urged me to revise until it had a chorus that repeated at least twice, and maybe no coda. But I wasn't interested in any of that then. What we do: It was secret.

18 - ORIGINAL AIR-BLUE GOWN

rain all burned away
horseflies are an iridescent green
plums boiled down to pulp
drying on a screen

bright red air inside the house here
I can barely draw breath
dark blue shapes pop behind my eyelids
I am not afraid of death,

and on the television
black-and-white footage of the young Cassius Clay:
my God, my God, my God,
he was something—

fists flashing as he comes toward the screen
sailing headlong into nothing
and disappearing, reappearing
out there in the clearing
floating down the slight breeze
that plays along the edges of the leaves:
it's you, it's you, it's you.

ΔΔΔ

This song has no chorus, a characteristic it shares with ten of its comrades on *Full Force Galesburg*, the sixteen-song album on which it appears. That's 63 percent songs with no proper chorus—and of the ones that do have a chorus, several are really only half choruses, because the words change here or there when they come back around. Most folk songs have choruses that people can remember and sing; indeed, most popular music prizes the hook, the singable and memorable earworm that keeps people coming back for more. And yet, when I sent a copy of this album to an A&R guy at Reprise with whom I had a correspondence going because Tanita Tikaram was on Reprise and I sought news of new music from her, he did not offer me a record contract. "Thanks for the CD," he said, but that was all. Still can't figure it out.

19 - SONG FOR THE JULIAN CALENDAR

Sun twinkling on the river this evening
the taste of chocolate on my tongue
darkness climbing down the ladders to the sky
rung by agonizing rung

I heard firecrackers popping next door
wondered what it was I'd bargained for
when I lay quiet on the floor and You were knocking

Let me be Your witness
let me walk out on the edge
the sun refused to shine on my backyard today
darkness climbing up the house, coming through the window
ledge

I saw the firecrackers bursting on the sidewalk
heard you talking that baby talk
saw the bright lights again and I felt the shock
when You were knocking

ΔΔΔ

We find our idiosyncrasies either charming or embarrassing, depending on a number of factors—our moods, the level at which these idiosyncrasies do or don't help with our desired ends, whether they charm or offend others. I'll venture that this is almost universally true: We all have our tics. Sometimes we feel affectionate toward them, even protective of them. That this song addresses two different people as "you" when one of them requires a capital *Y*, but that the person who released it was adamant that his albums didn't have lyric sheets: I don't have this tic any more, but when I remember it, I still like it. There is something hilarious—no, something *fun* to me—about working in a communicative medium while expressing, in that medium, a palpable ambivalence toward the whole project of communication.

20 - NARAKALOKA

The cabbages that I will grow
One by one and row on row
Will fatten in the spring sun,
And breathe in the evening air

And you may hear them breathing
If you go by at night;
And you may not hear them after all,
But that's all right:

I've set the tables for two
I've cleaned the windows for you
I've got cinnamon from Jakarta
For making French toast
The doctors say that I've got
Thirty days left at most

The cabbages that I will grow
The love songs on the radio
Will fatten in the spring sun
And be brighter than the stars.

ΔΔΔ

A personal favorite; a song about a person anticipating death, although only one line toward the end makes it explicit. Also pointedly not a love song; the addressee could be a living friend, or a dead one, or God. For the first five years or so of the Mountain Goats I would have made the case to anyone within earshot that the love song was a sufficient form for an entire life's work; I think it's good to have strong convictions like this, and that it's also very good to practice the transgression of going against your aesthetic convictions and eventually overruling them entirely. "Narakaloka"'s first line probably came after rereading "To His Coy Mistress" for the *n*th time, but I was, at this point, looking to Marvell more for form than content.

21 - TREETOP SONG

All along the interstate
The palm trees were calling out to me
And the line of them stretched down the highway forever
As far as I could see
And I waited 'til the sun was coming up
Light morning traffic and a cool spring breeze
And I heard the old voices calling out to me
From the tops of the trees

And when I got up to the top,
My head got light
And for a minute,
Everything in the world was all right
I saw the next tree just ten feet away—
Give or take a few feet, I guess—

And then I pushed off into the air with all my might
And headed off into the center of the morning light,
And I knew that I was going to make it
The new tree hardly shook to acknowledge my arrival
And I knew that I would be all right

ΔΔΔ

What's interesting to me about "Treetop Song" is that it divides its time between two schools of thought about song lyrics—and on the page this is clear, but in the recording it's not. One school is the "lyrics are poems set to music" school; the other is the "lyrics have no independent existence outside of their musical context" school, which school I attended and where I used to have an endowed chair, now retired. For the first two-thirds of this song: That's a poem! I'd know one anywhere! For the climax: Only the turnaround of the progression can bring it to life; it's left poetry behind; it's a song now, and it can't go back to its old ways. Was I thinking about this while writing it? No, I was just writing. But on the page it's a fascinating, for me, tug of war between two impulses.

22 - GOLDEN BOY

You must try to lead a good life
You must do unto others as you would have them do
So that, when you die, you'll find Golden Boy peanuts
waiting in the afterlife for you

There are no pan-Asian supermarkets down in Hell,
So you can't buy Golden Boy peanuts
There are no pan-Asian supermarkets down in Hell,
So you can't buy Golden Boy peanuts

If thine enemy oppresseth thee,
You must let him oppress you some more
So that when you go shopping in paradise
You'll find those magnificent peanuts from Singapore

With the drawing of the young Chinese farmer
With the eastern sun behind him, smiling at you from the shelves

If we're going to spend eternity in paradise,
We're going to have to watch ourselves

You must give to the March of Dimes
You must be on guard against wickedness at all times
And you will find that your efforts have brought you great joy
When your spirit is munching on that Golden Boy

There are no pan-Asian supermarkets down in Hell,
So you can't buy Golden Boy peanuts there
But the streets of Heaven are lined with shells,
And there's billboards of the Golden Boy everywhere

There are no pan-Asian supermarkets down in Hell,
So you can't buy Golden Boy peanuts
There are no pan-Asian supermarkets down in Hell,
So you can't buy Golden Boy peanuts

ΔΔΔ

Ladies and gentlemen, birds of the air, beasts of the field, children of all ages: the longest lyric in the book so far. The peanuts in question seem still to exist in two forms that differ from the bagged peanuts I bought at the Bang Luck market in Pomona in the mid-nineties. The existence of same-but-different Golden Boy peanuts in the here and now either complicates my general theory of cosmology or affirms that we all died at an unspecified date and are now in Hell, roasting away, oblivious. Neither option leaves us with much hope, but at least we have a song to sing.

23 - COBSCOOK BAY

We're alone most of the time these days
Jill used to come by, but she went away, and

Gail used to come around and trash the joint, but
She moved off to Dana Point, and
You went along, just for the ride, and
You both committed suicide,

And day is breaking over Cobscook Bay,
and I've never seen anything like it in my life.

The cow gave birth and her calves are snow white
They huddle up close together at night, and the
Mama cow leans down and cleans her young
Licking their faces with her tongue, yes and
Unmarked airplanes buzz the air,
And you're falling off that cliff somewhere in California,

Which I've never seen.
I put the pieces all together, but I don't know what they mean.
And day is breaking over Cobscook Bay,
and I've never seen anything like it in my life.

ΔΔΔ

One longstanding aesthetic goal of mine is to be writing in poetic language that comes out sounding like speech—there are a lot of ways to think about poetry, and about how it relates to speech, and still more ways to think about how song does or doesn't differ from poetry in how it does or doesn't resemble speech. My own ethos, my aim, anyway, is for a lyric to allow the listener to indulge in the fantasy that the singer, or speaker, is making the whole thing up from scratch—pulling the words from the air—while retaining and exhibiting form so apparently that this could not be (and obviously is not) true. I think this song comes as close to that goal as I've ever gotten, so I've rendered the line stops here as they occur sonically—little end-of-breath "and"s that sound like I'm just relating the details of my life. I hold that good theory makes for good practice. For me "Cobscook Bay" makes a pretty good case for this claim.

24 - DUTCH ORCHESTRA BLUES

Somewhere in secret, the Dutch Orchestra's playing.
Somewhere in secret, the Dutch Orchestra's playing
real nice; real nice.

And they play so quiet, you can hear the passing traffic.
They play so quiet, you can hear the passing traffic,
And the cars buzz by, and the wind blows.

And I may walk past, and I may not.
And someone may notice, or it may all glide right by.
And you may love me, or you may not love me at all any more,
but the sun will shine on Holland in the spring;

And God will watch over the members of the orchestra for me
with all His available energies.

ΔΔΔ

What's happening in my personal life when I write this song is that I'm thinking about God a lot—about how it is in God's nature to locate the cheering note in the sad thing, the grace in the gut punch, the prayer within the litany of complaints. I'm thinking about this in this moment of my life because my faith is in a weird space, I'm no longer going to Church but I keep noticing the small-c church I seem to carry around inside me, and I like it, I'm finding God in a lot of places. I'm finding God in His absence, I'm finding the shapes God leaves on surfaces once He's touched them with His presence, which is, of course, on every surface, even the hard, hurting surfaces. This is, for me, a process of growth, but I'm trying, in this moment, to be at least a little subtle about it, and a little funny about it, because I feel like that's what I'm supposed to do.

That is what is happening in this song.

25 - THE LAST LIMIT OF BHAKTI

Let me serve You with my mind
Let me serve You with my mind
Let me leave this grieving sand and sky far behind

Let me serve You with my tongue
Let me serve You with my tongue
Let me say Your Name all day 'til my mouth goes numb

And when the sun comes up
Open up the blinds
Let me feel the machine's great gears squeal and grind

Let me serve You 'til it's all over
Let me serve You 'til it's all over
When the world is giving Your secrets all away,
Let me give You cover

Let me serve You with my body
Let me serve You with my body
Let me find, now, and 'til the end of time,
The last limit

ΔΔΔ

Few songs better illustrate my longstanding but apparently now resolved ambivalence toward printing out my lyrics (no Mountain Goats album had a lyric printout until 2017) than this one. To me, that capitalized *Y* throughout (cf. "Song for the Julian Calendar") is self-evident both from the song's title and from its text, but until I render it on the page, you're free to think of it however you like—the speaker might just be a very devoted lover, or he might be talking to a ghost, or he might be Henry David Thoreau talking to Walden Pond. But when I put it on the page, your options as a reader narrow. Songs exist in the air; the moment you take them out of the air they are changed. There's something *You* might do about that, if *You* saw fit, but there is really nothing you can do about it at all. This song is in my personal top five and so aside from this formal observation I leave it to speak for itself.

26 - CROWS

Well, I went way out
North Carolina way
to that old graveyard
where my great-grandmother lay
and the day was bright
and I hadn't slept all night
and they'd sold the place
to some guys
who were building graduate student housing.

No one had raised any objections;
they were knocking the headstones down
and the sun was high
when I rolled into town
stood by a nameless hole in the ground
the air was sweet and hot
maybe it was the right grave
maybe not

but the crows, crows, crows
rose, rose, rose

from the grave
yeah the crows, crows, crows
rose, rose, rose
from the grave

ΔΔΔ

I live in North Carolina now and I have to say, people who say "I saw this coming" are a dime a dozen and tiresome besides, but this song was genuinely a dispatch from my own distant future, except it's not graduate student housing (the new construction of which in Ames was probably the immediate inspiration), it's mixed-use residential, and if you get me going on the subject, we will be here all day.

27 · GENESIS 19:1–2

The girl who'd been haunting your dreams all your life;
The butcher from Brooklyn; the butcher's wife;
The girl who kissed you in the second grade;
her and all the others, lined up behind the gate.
The two angels came to Sodom in the evening
when the sun up in the sky was bleeding all, all over you.

And you had your camera,
and you had your felt-tip,
and you had some money,
and you had everything you needed.
The two angels came to Sodom in the evening
they saw you coming up the boulevard
The two angels came to Sodom in the evening
when the sun up in the sky was bleeding all, all over you.

ΔΔΔ

This one really pushes the limits of "assumes facts not in evidence," which is, I think, one of the first imperatives of song—to assume facts not in evidence, whole bunches of them, as many as the song can stand without collapsing. What remains then is for the songwriter to locate a headspace where those facts not in evidence palpably feel like the most pressing details, i.e., the Actually Important Parts, the ones most in need of a little air to breathe in—at which point, we need only get into position and breathe.

28 - COMMANDANTE

I'm going to drink more whiskey than Brendan Behan
I'm going to send my belongings all to Tripoli
And I'm going to ride home to California
With a banjo on my knee

I'm never going to turn off the television
No, I'm just going to let it run all night
I'm going to plant root vegetables out in the backyard
And come summer, I am going to treat you right

So put on your Chairman Mao coat
And let me clear my throat
Let's turn this whole town upside down
And shake it 'til the coins come tumbling out of its pockets
Put on your Che Guevara pin
And call the troops on in
We're going to sail through the night sky like a bottle rocket

I've got a great big secret written down somewhere
I've got a rosary to protect us both from harm
I've got a storage locker full of cow figurines
And a laundry list of grievances longer than my arm

And I am never going back to Cincinnati
All those bridges have been burned down to the ground
I've got the jet pack strapped to my back
And I'm waiting for you to come around

put on your Chairman Mao coat
And let me clear my throat
Let's turn this whole town upside down
And shake it 'til the coins come tumbling out of its pockets
Put on your Che Guevara pin
And call the troops on in
We're going to sail through the night sky like a bottle rocket

ΔΔΔ

There is a tradition, from the earliest folk musics, of songs in which the speaker boasts of his talents, or his successes, or his sexual prowess. There is a tradition in Mountain Goats songs of boasting about having, e.g., "a storage locker full of cow figurines." This song is as firmly inside that tradition as you can get.

29 - SHOWER

Blackest wind I ever saw
Was coming in from Omaha
And the latest news from Tokyo
Was a lot of ugly numbers
I was checking pay phones for forgotten coins
As the clouds came over West Des Moines
Got into the house, got the curtains drawn
Got into the shower with all my clothes on

Hey, hey! Let the water run down
Hey, hey! Let the water run down

By noon it was clear that winter'd come
So I just let the water run
I got soap suds in my eyes and they stung like iodine
Phone started ringing like a fire alarm
And the voice on the machine was brutally calm
New numbers coming down the wire
Got out of the shower with my eyes on fire

Hey, hey! Let it fall on me
Let it all come down relentlessly
And you swore that you would stick around
When days like this started coming down—well,

Get out the crystal
Get out the good champagne
We're going down
In flames

ΔΔΔ

If I follow my heart and start talking here about the Swedish death metal band In Flames, whose early work is some of the best heavy metal to be found anywhere, the copy editor won't mind, but the editor will; so instead I'll tell you this—"Shower" was supposed to be on *The Coroner's Gambit*, but there was no recorded version of it that I liked, and so that was that. Financial ruin is an almost irresistible theme for me; as soon as I feel tempted to drain a character's bank account, I do it, whether owing to bank error or poor money management skills on their part, it does me no force, I must have their money, the better to flush it down the toilet for them. To my dreamworld alternate versions of the Mountain Goats you may add the one that wrote only and exclusively songs of this sort, album after album, for years on end. In this dreamworld you might meet somebody at a bar or a party who would tell you about the band whose songs were all vivid imaginings of people facing total financial devastation. The band who seemed to have an infinite library of sound samples from the long-defunct Financial News Network. The band whose work, over time, began to seem quite obsessive indeed about this sort of thing. The Mountain Goats.

30 - SURE DO LOVE YOU, BABY, BUT I CAN'T DO 60 NO MORE

Well, Dale moved down here, and you came down, too
Where the surf's always wild and the skies are blue
Got my blood pressure measured down in Pahokee:
One sixty-five over one twenty-three
And the lights are low over Pompano Beach tonight
And one light is flickering out for the last time

Coconuts growing in the coconut tree
Surf and turf and sand and sea
Down here in the wreckage, just us three
Him and you, you and me
And the lights are low over Pompano Beach tonight
And one light is flickering out
For the last time

ΔΔΔ

Like "Shower," this song is unreleased, and that's fine—it's slight; but I'm fond of it, because it covers a lot of ground in a short space, which always pleases me, and because formally I think the quadruple rhyme is one of the most fun things there is to do in song. It's necessarily relentless: The ear is ready for a new beginning when the third rhyme comes, and then is made to understand that it's under assault when the fourth one lands. Happens. Hits. I don't usually recycle a song I'm not happy with but just throw the whole thing away, so the second verse of this never got much daylight, but I like it. The light that's flickering out for the last time is the problem for me—there's sufficient drama in the high blood pressure and the twists of the triangle; "the lights are low, and it's time to go" would have been a better resolve line for this chorus. Well, sometimes we revise in time to salvage a song, and sometimes we don't: the luck of the draw!

31 - HORSERADISH ROAD

The way that everybody's voice
comes out muffled when they speak
The way we take our diminishing inventories
Month to month, and week to week
And the Maria Callas records
On the stereo all the time
You're gonna get yours
And I'm gonna get mine

Because in this car, in this car
Somebody's bound to get burned
I know, I know
Because I've been watching the road turn

The *Enigma Variations*
On the stereo
The things that I could guess at
The things that I already know
And the twelve thousand dollars
That just somehow turned up in your purse
You've done something awful
I've done something worse

Because in this car, in this car
Somebody's bound to get burned

I know, I know
Because I've been watching the road turn

ΔΔΔ

The Coroner's Gambit took a long time to write by my standards—"Shower" I wrote in Grinnell before we moved to Colo, so probably in 1997 or possibly in December '96; "We Were Patriots" (April 7) was probably summer of '97 in Grinnell, too. I was writing a lot during this time—the three EPs for Yo Yo, appearances on compilations; I'd started writing some long-form essays about records I liked. "Horse-radish Road" interests me because it's trying to be a financial ruin song or a song of bitter separation, but if I approach it as a reader rather than as its author, I say it's neither of those. It's a song whose speaker is telling the addressee that they are both smaller, in the world, than they think, and that they are even now receding from the world, which is a hard feeling; and *The Coroner's Gambit* would be the first album where the hard feelings took center stage.

APRIL

1 - JAIPUR

I was having visions of sugared pastry
cooked up in clarified butter
I tried to turn my visions into prayer
but I built my castles way high up in the air,

and I came to the gates of the fabled pink city
hungry and tired and cold
swing low, sweet chariot
chrome tailpipe shining bright as spun gold

my brothers picked me up out of the rushes
traded me into the company of evil men,
but I have inched my way down the Eastern Seaboard
I am coming to Atlanta again

yes, I came to the gates of the fabled pink city
hungry and tired, mad as all Hell
swing low, sweet jewel-encrusted chariot
make me young again, make me well

I am the killer dressed in pilgrim's clothing
I am the hard to get stations on the AM band
I am the white sky high over Tripoli
I am the landmine hidden in the sand,

and I came to the gates of the fabled pink city
hungry and tired and alone
swing low, sweet chariot
coming for to carry me home

ΔΔΔ

"This isn't a memoir, unless it is," the text of the February 15 entry in this book states; I resist the terrain of memoir where I can. In a book like this, it's hard to retain such a resistance, but I cling to the spirit of it: My lyrics are more than me; there are more interesting things going on in them than the circumstances of their creation; what's most interesting about them, both to me and, I'd argue, empirically, is their freedom from me, their independence as songs. One reason I began performing under a collective name was to put distance between what I was doing and the confessional mode of songwriting. I prefer that my stories speak for themselves. They seem stronger to me when they do.

But "Jaipur"—the recording that appears as the first song on side one of *The Coroner's Gambit*, released on October 17, 2000, on the Absolutely Kosher label, then operating out of San Francisco; not "Jaipur" the lyric, but "Jaipur" the event in time represented by that recording—is, itself, a kind of cloaked memoir. It's a snippet of autobiography disguised as a fragmented story, a codex of the time that preceded it, personally, "professionally," generally. It doesn't, and can't, sound to others as it does to me, because only I can place it accurately in time and space: but in the pages that follow I will make that time as alive as I can, because I think "Jaipur" is the moment when I begin to make peace with the idea that storytelling is self-expression no matter what stories you tell.

✦✦✦

We lived in Colo, which is a town in northeast Story County, Iowa. By "we" I mean my girlfriend and I; I proposed marriage to her in the kitchen of our Colo house one day after she came home from her job in Nevada, the town adjacent, whose name rhymes with cicada. We are still married, twenty-five years later.

At the time, she was the breadwinner and I was . . . the bread baker: I'd spent my first two years after college earning poorly—bringing home only the tour receipts of a little-known musician, mixed in with some royalties on the early albums and singles. Royalties like these were more plentiful for a prolific writer working in the pre-Napster age; some months they might make half the rent, if your rent was low. Ours was. Beyond these, one town farther over in Ames, I had an on-call job as a Mental Health Worker—in college, I'd let my nursing license expire, and at any rate my specific licensure (licensed Psychiatric Technician) wasn't a recognized classification in Iowa. I felt sheepish being the underearning partner; I taught myself to bake and to cook, so that the person contributing more to the household's finances wouldn't have to also be the person contributing more labor.

I also taught myself to bake and cook because I was fairly—albeit very faultily: I hadn't even quit smoking yet—immersed in Gaudiya Vaiṣṇavism at the time. Vaiṣṇavism is worship of Vishnu, but Gaudiya Vaiṣṇavism, so-called because it originated in 1920 at the Gaudiya Math in Calcutta, holds that the saint Chaitanya Mahaprabhu (1486–1534) was the incarnation of the god Krishna for this age, and that all gods in the Hindu cosmology are avatars of Him. I'd been given a copy of a book called *The Science of Self-Realization* by a devotee at Los Angeles International Airport in the spring of 1995; my Catholicism was in ebb tide, and I was curious. I didn't read it right away, and I didn't read it when somehow I brought it with me to Chicago the same year, but it traveled with me through five different changes of residence. In Colo, my curiosity about it increased—in Vaiṣṇava terms, I began to nurture my devotional creeper. I sought out primary texts and commentaries; I got myself some japa beads and chanted Hare Krsna on them. Nightly, I cooked, and offered the first taste of my cooking to two bronze Gaura-Nitai deities housed in a small cabinet in the kitchen. This offering is analogous to Holy Communion: transubstantiation takes place when you offer your food before eating it, and afterward, when you eat, you are taking God Himself into your body, burning off karma while divining His presence in the spiritually transformed food. Vaiṣṇava cooking fills the whole house with the caramel scent of ghee—clarified butter—used as both a cooking medium and an ingredient. Our house in Colo was, I think it is safe to say, like few if any houses in Colo before it.

I wasn't, as I say, diligent. There are four regulations to be followed, and like a good American I tailored my own program—"No meat, fish, or eggs" became "no meat or fish" in our house; "no intoxicants"—well, I didn't use drugs, anyway; "chant sixteen rounds of the maha-mantra each day"—sixteen rounds? That's several hours, I did what I could. You were also not supposed to have sex outside of marriage. We did get married, anyway. You do what you can.

The house itself, which no longer exists, because, when we left it, the city of Colo immediately bought it from its landlord owner and demolished it entirely, stood at the corner of West and Main, at a railroad crossing.

✦✦✦

Around May or June of what must have been 1999 a sign went up, handwritten, on the bulletin board at Brannen's, the lone grocery store in Colo: "Harvest Help needed," it said. "Farmer's Cooperative Exchange." This was the co-op down the street—the grain elevator. A grain elevator consists of one or more structures that store grain—that elevate it from the ground and regulate its temperature until it's shipped back out to whoever's bought it. I applied for this job, and I got it; trucks loaded with corn or soybeans would roll in from morning to afternoon, stop over a grate, and I'd empty their cargo by opening up the bay with a socket wrench, sweeping all the excess into a grating in the concrete. In lulls between trucks I'd clean the elevator office, or sit idly scribbling in a pocket notebook. Most of the songs I scribbled ideas for in this notebook didn't amount to much, but "The Alphonse Mambo" was entirely written at the grain elevator.

The summer got hotter and I wasn't very good at the job, which was occasionally physically punishing—soybeans, down at the other end of the complex, were stored not in an elevator but in a big Morton building. They formed huge hills whose peaks needed to be knocked down with a shovel; I'd climb the hills, thigh-deep in beans, and shovel from that position. My supervisor was in his early sixties and had been doing this sort of work most of his life; when he had to climb a hill himself he'd come down red-faced, sweating. I feared for his health.

I took a week off at some point and rode a Greyhound out to Omaha to record some of the songs for *The Coroner's Gambit* with Simon Joyner and some musicians he'd wrangled to help out. I caught a cold on the bus, and by the second day of the session I was barely able to sing above a whisper. We did what we could and then I got back on the bus.

The Coroner's Gambit is the last Mountain Goats album from the brief period during which the band could fairly be described as me and whoever else I felt like playing with. (*Full Force Galesburg*, which featured guest appearances from several people, is the other.) After this, I made one more album at home, and then that's it for the Panasonic until late winter of 2020. It was the last album until *Get Lonely* to be written without an organizing principle to guide me: There were countless other songs written "for" the record, before the record was a record or even had a title (competing titles survive in my notebooks: *Jab-Jab*, *Blanchot*). *Nothing for Juice* had been the end of the early going, but *The Coroner's Gambit* crowns a fertile and strange sequence during which I was thematically very restless, sonically curious, and as busy as ever. For years, I've had a title for an unnamed work on one of the pages where I collect titles—for books, for songs, for albums: *The Last of Something*. That's exactly what *The Coroner's Gambit* is, more than any other album in the discography, and for that reason it's special to me. "Jaipur," right there at the top, neatly if violently summarizes what makes it stand out.

✦✦✦

I had two methods of recording at my disposal: The first was my trusty Panasonic RX-FT500, which I had by this point been using for eight years. The grind of its wheels was becoming more pronounced and harder to ignore. The other deck I'd ordered from Broadcast Supply Worldwide when we lived in Grinnell; it was a Marantz professional cassette recorder, intended mainly for journalists in the field—for city sounds, and interviews. Home recordings on *The Coroner's Gambit* and *All Hail West Texas* where you can't hear wheels grinding are the Marantz. Marantz, as producer for the Mountain Goats, was usually the reserved counterpoint to Panasonic's unmistakable thumbprint, but on the day I recorded "Jaipur," I discovered that I could turn the expensive machine into a decent simulation of the cheaper one if I just turned the input dial until it wouldn't go any further.

The Marantz was made for transparency, but the man singing into it on this day is interested in the blur you get on the other side of clarity. As a student of the Panasonic school, he seeks to understand the machine as a collaborator with full agency, someone whose input he can't mitigate or tame. That man is me, and we are playing together on this track, the Marantz and me. We invoke the spirit of the Panasonic, who was almost certainly looking on, not jealously but approvingly. Its lessons persist. We are a team, we three.

Gaudiya Vaiṣṇavism wasn't, of course, my entry point into spirituality. I was baptized Catholic and attended parochial school until my parents divorced; I feared God until, on entering adolescence, I decided He didn't exist, whereupon I became a very tiresome atheist for several years. I began to reapproach the Church in Portland, in 1985, attending Dominican Mass a few blocks from my apartment several times, but I felt ashamed to be bringing a wreck such as I was to the Church; I know now that the Church is for the wrecks and that it's the wrecks who make the Church, but I didn't then. But I kept trying; back home in California in 1987, working the night shift in an acute care facility for children, I listened to the all-night gospel station, hearing Shirley Caesar, and the Williams Brothers, and Rev. Clay Evans, whose "I'm Blessed" I revisit routinely to this day. I would venture, some Sundays, into small local churches—storefront places with names like Holy Ghost Temple, churches affiliated with the C.O.G.I.C., the Church of God in Christ. These were Black churches that welcomed me, and music was central to the worship experience; at the Holy Ghost Temple in Pomona, the preacher was also the drummer.

I returned to the Catholic Church a few years later. Any current or former Catholic—there are no former Catholics; I should know, I am one—knows the songs that now reached my searching heart and made it ache: "Here I Am, Lord," "On Eagles' Wings," "Lord of the Dance" (which is "Simple Gifts" reconfigured, either stripped or relieved of its simplicity). I had, and have, the post–"Dover Beach" ailment that afflicts us all; I struggled, and struggle, to believe. But having come through childhood and adolescence alive, a proposition on which I wouldn't have bet you a dollar when I was eighteen because I needed that dollar for speed, I felt gratitude, and wonder. I wasn't going to die young, or not so young, anyway.

I went to Church and I stayed there; I read the Bible in various translations, and I learned a little Hebrew and some Latin and Greek, and I tried to square my politics, which are radical, with the Church's, which are a mixed bag; and I came up short, and so stopped going to Mass after about five years of weekly attendance. But the damage was done, or the gift obtained, depending on how you look at it. Five years is long enough to gather a lot of material if you're a writer. I didn't consider myself a writer yet. I was getting there.

✦✦✦

Which brings us to "Jaipur," which is a city in India about which I would have learned from some Vaiṣṇava text—"the Pink City" because of how the buildings in its old quarter are colored, "fabled" for many reasons but within Vaiṣṇavism for a strong connection dating back no later than 1570 and a rich history of worship within the tradition. "Sugared pastry cooked up in clarified butter"—these would be jalebi, "visions" because while I was learning to cook I didn't consider my skills sufficient to attempt sweets (my one attempt at burfi in the Colo kitchen hadn't gone well), "visions into prayer" because I was at this point twenty-nine years old and trying, like my father had done throughout his life, to understand my position in the realm of spiritual things.

The images and phrases in this song are a hodgepodge of daily concerns, obsessions, interests, and yearnings; the action described within it—a narrator who returns to Atlanta after a bitter exodus in the world, who understands his homecoming as a pilgrim's voyage home—a parsable metaphor for my life as I then saw it. "Killer"? Well, no, but the songs are rather violent. "Hard to get stations on the AM band"? Bon Iver wouldn't win a Grammy for over a decade; if you wanted to hear the kind of music I was making you had to seek it out. "The white sky high over Tripoli"? This is my favorite kind of internal reference—one that can't be traced: my 1993 no-real-instruments noise project Pneumatic Ezra, which exists on tapes in a drawer but has been heard by no one, had a song about Libya in which the narrator yearns for a bygone time there that can't be regained.

A song is a place that can contain as many things as you like. I like mine to rhyme, and to head for the wings before wearing out their welcome, but beyond that, they are allowed to condense as much or as little of myself as I choose. The ones that resonate most for me are the ones where I accidentally snap a self-portrait.

"Jaipur," however obscure its narrative, offers me as clear a picture of myself as I could get in or around the winter of 1999, and a clearer picture than any of the photographs that survive from that time. Our rent was $275 a month; we had a single used car, paid off; I had a college loan on which I was paying the monthly minimum but no further debts; I spent half my day in the kitchen unless I'd been called in to work at the hospital. Our furniture was all secondhand, stuff bought at an auction house down the street, which was a source of monthly entertainment and socialization. The way I wrote songs was changing; I had become less interested in stories about people who've been hurt in love, and more interested in ones that let the images speak for themselves. In this sense I had sort of returned to the aesthetic dicta of *Taboo VI*, but having had the experience of an audience, and having learned that obscurity comes in several different colors, some quite flashy and bright. This was the lesson I learned on the morning, or afternoon, or evening, who knows, when I wrote "Jaipur," and, setting the tape deck on an organ bench we'd bought at auction—it came with the organ, we got the whole package for a dollar—leaned in toward the condenser mic and played.

"Jaipur" is what came out. It was the first song on *The Coroner's Gambit* because it felt like both a summary of my progress up to then and an opening onto whatever might be coming next. It taught me that anything I'm doing will contain what came before it, to trust my hand as it moved across the page. More on that later, probably.

I now return you to our book of days.

2 · COOL HUNDRED

Tuscaloosa, Alabama. Way out in the back trace. Me with that chrome taste in the back of my throat. You with that stupid look on your face. Taking the lock off the barn. Swinging the door open wide. Letting the yellow light fall on the prize inside. We had an amazing machine. It was going to change everything. It was money in the bank. We were written on the water.

Diamonds in the engine. Canaries in the mine. Slight songs echoing through the darkness. Everything was going to work out fine. Watching it gleam in the musty air. Hearing it purring in the straw. Teetering dumbly over the long night's open jaw. We had an amazing machine. It was going to change everything. It was money in the bank. We were written on the water.

ΔΔΔ

This song doesn't exist—it's in an undated red Mead notebook with a price tag still stuck to the front: "GROCERY $.99." The first song in the notebook is "Family Happiness" (April 6), and it's also in this format: paragraphs instead of lines in the style of some Karl Shapiro prose poems I'd seen a few years earlier. The notebooks of this era are full of things like this: cast-offs and latter-round draft picks who never made the team. I have a great fondness for these stray fish. Their flaws are clear to me—here, mainly the chorus, which has no rhyme line but is too vague about the action to get over on energy—but they swim in their own stream, which runs through hills almost nobody's ever seen.

3 - ISLAND GARDEN SONG

I will sail to the far shore
and I will chop a hole in the hull too big to repair
and I will till the soil with my hands
and I will make my home there

My garden will grow so high that I will be completely hidden.

I will go where I will go,
and I will jettison all dead weight
and I will use these words for kindling
and I will sleep by the garden gate

My garden will grow so high that I will be completely hidden.

ΔΔΔ

I mean all writing is about writing—that's a way of reading things, right? All writing is about writing. To write about writing is to disclose the intimacy of the process, to go naked before the world. When I wrote this I was just telling a story about a guy on an island, I don't set metaphorical terms and then go about satisfying them: I just write. But it seems pretty clear, here.

4 · ELIJAH

Streak the windows—smear the walls with coconut oil
Fill a cast-iron kettle with water and magnolia blossom
Let it boil, let the water roll
Let the fire take its toll
I'm coming home

Dust off the idols, give them something to eat
I think they're hungry; I know I'm starving half to death
I know you're waiting. I know you've been waiting
for a long, long time, and I'm
coming home
I'm coming home

Set the table those three extra places:
one for me; one for your doubts; one for God

Let the incense burn in every room
See the fullness of time in the empty tomb
Feel the future kicking in your womb
I'm coming home
I'm coming home

ΔΔΔ

Consult the "Jaipur" codex and then parse this one, another study in cryptic self-portraiture. You can argue, and indeed I might, that that's all any songs ever are, but I can speak with authority only about the ones I wrote. Here, the idols are real, the incense is real, the mood of ritual is pervasive and actual. Magnolia blossom? Womb? I would not move to the South for another five years, nor become a parent for another thirteen. In order to really hide you need some fairly vivid details.

5 - ONIONS

The last white slabs of snow
melted off seven weeks ago
and the geese are headed north again
through the tightening sky, and I
can feel my heart in my throat again
new onions growing in the ground

The cows come gingerly out of the barn
and when they see that the ground is warm
They pick up a little speed, and it makes me feel so good
And then I feel it rushing down my throat: fresh blood

I head out onto the earth: its cold heart is melting
I don't know if I can stand it
springtime's coming—that means you'll be coming back around
new onions growing underground

ΔΔΔ

Like others in the red Mead notebook this one exists there as a single paragraph. Vanity demands that I render it here in verse, so that the internal rhyme at the end of the fourth line won't go missing amidst the prose. Sometimes we must do what vanity demands.

6 - FAMILY HAPPINESS

As we cruised across the Canadian border,
You reached into your handbag
    and pulled out a micro-cassette recorder
You started quoting Tolstoy into the machine,
I had no idea what you meant.
I guess I'm supposed to figure these things out,
Or maybe it's supposed to be self-evident,
but I've gone feral, and I don't speak the language any more.
We're headed deep into the forest.
I've got the pedal to the floor.
The engine shudders like a dying man
When you reach out to grab my hand;
You can bring out all your weapons.
You can't make me go to war.

Long winding Canadian highways;
Innumerable evergreens.
Weather forecast on the AM radio
Says we'll be expecting highs in the low teens.
When I mouth my silent curses at you,
I can see my breath.
I hope the stars don't even bother to come out tonight.
I hope we both freeze to death.
Look at the person I've turned into:
Tell me how do you like him now.
No standards of any kind to break. No creeds to disavow.
I am right here where you want me.
Do what you brought me out here for.

You can arm me to the teeth.
You can't make me go to war.

ΔΔΔ

The sonics of the Colo house could occasionally conspire with my machines to make songs come out extra-brutal, which pleased me to no end. Expatriate Californian on the floor of a glorified shack wailing loud enough not just to wake the dead but to make them dance for their supper. The "I hope" lines look down the line toward "No Children" (May 10), but *Tallahassee* pointedly insists that dying isn't an option. It's absolutely an option here.

7 - WE WERE PATRIOTS

Clear sky over Calcutta
warm wind
Dvořák on the shortwave
clear signal coming in

Long vowels spill like liquid from your mouth
I hang on every word you say
an army of transistor radios on the bookshelf
left on all day

Let them play
let them all play on, and on, and on
let them all play longer and louder
after you're gone

Clear sky sheltering our fragile little house
listening to the radio all the time
your hand on my shoulder as though to check for fever
big plans in mind

ΔΔΔ

This song has a chorus—"la la / la la la la la / la la"—and indeed I am a big believer in the "la la" and its antediluvian power. But I think most "la la" is worthless on the page. There are those who disagree, to whom the printed "la la" seems just and good—I have no quarrel with them, may they "la" where they will! As for me and this song, however, I here withhold the "la la" in favor of a sparer presentation from which, given more days on this earth than I'll likely get, I would construct an entire novel, or maybe a Broadway musical: the combination of the title and the small details here (the location, the music and how we're hearing it, the fear of fever) suggest to me a big story full of hard choices and intrigue, and set design featuring a bunch of really cool old radios.

8 - THERE WILL BE NO DIVORCE

The rain fell all night
and it kept me awake
it was still falling by morning
it was hard to take,

And you were sleeping on the floor,
breathing free and even
if I ever want to drive myself insane
all I have to do is watch you breathing

And at 5 a.m., I turned the radio on
and an old man's voice sang a short, sweet song

And then the static roared again
it was hungry for blood

I heard the rain falling from the rainspout
down, down into the sweet, wet mud

And you punched out all the windows,
and the wind began to wail
and you gathered your hair behind your head
like God was going to catch you by the ponytail

And then the old voice crackled through the static,
and I felt young and alive
and the hair stood up on the back of my neck
we were rising from the grave again

ΔΔΔ

It's fair to say that at this time I was near obsessed with writing songs that were catchy and memorable but that didn't have a chorus. Going no-chorus is like riding a bicycle blindfolded: if you don't crash, something magic might happen. This is a love song for my wife, who did not actually punch out any windows, but who would have looked pretty bitchin' punching out windows, her ponytail springing out from behind her Cubs ballcap.

9 - BLUEJAYS AND CARDINALS

Bluejays and cardinals all come out to play
and highway traffic gets out of your way
skies clear up if they're overcast
pit bulls are gentle when you come past
stars come out of hiding for you—
and I would, too,

But this world couldn't hold you,
and you slipped free.

This world couldn't hold you,
and you slipped free,
without me.

There's a new sheen all over everything
when you open up your mouth to sing
Baseballs travel further when you watch them fly
and apples fatten on the trees when you walk by
You bring something unreplaceable to each and every day
or you used to, anyway,

But this world couldn't hold you,
and you slipped free
This world couldn't hold you,
and you slipped free,
without me.

ΔΔΔ

It's one of several songs on *The Coroner's Gambit* where I'm trying to put together my thoughts about the death of a friend—someone I hadn't seen or spoken with since 1987, possibly 1986, his arc one that crossed mine at a brief and chaotic juncture. Addressing him by name in the album's original liner notes was a way of marking distances: The version of me who'd briefly been friends with Rozz hadn't existed, at this point, since 1988 at the latest. Eulogies aren't mirrors, but they have shards of mirror affixed to them. It comes with the bargain and is nonnegotiable.

10 - SHADOW SONG

If you get there before me, would you save me a seat?
If you get there before me, would you save me a seat?

And if I never get there at all,
Would you leave the seat empty?

If you get there before me, would you light us a fire?
If you get there before me, would you light us a fire?
And if I never show,
You can watch the embers glow, you can keep the fire burning.

This is a song for you in case I never make it through
to where you are.
This is a song for you in case I never make it through
to where you are.

ΔΔΔ

This one was also for Rozz. As I say, I had only known Rozz for a short span of time—in the summer of 1985, we got drunk or high or both every night for the better part of a month, and then I saw him a few times after that a year later. He hanged himself in 1998. When someone I know dies, they take a part of me with them. The part Rozz took with him was a broken and flawed part, and I had mixed feelings about knowing that it was gone. Because it's not gone any more than the people who leave are ever gone, and it's also that gone, that unrecoverable.

11 - THE CORONER'S GAMBIT

When death came calling today
I heard the gentle grace of his cadences
I couldn't say no
I couldn't say no.

When he showed me his new silk scarves
Laid out on a shiny black plastic tray

I couldn't say no
I couldn't say no.

And I'm sorry I couldn't—
you know how badly I wanted to—
didn't want, didn't want, didn't want, didn't want
to lose you.

But his smile was dazzling,
and his eyes were shining
like moonlight
on the water at midnight.
I couldn't say no.
I couldn't say no.

ΔΔΔ

Rozz's death gave shape to *The Coroner's Gambit*. One of us would be growing older and the other would not. This is an Aeschylean paradox: the ongoing life that continues only within the people who carry the memory of the departed. Here, I am trying to understand not just Rozz's suicide but my own attraction to the act, an attraction that, mercifully, had become a memory on the day I recorded this song—but not a distant one. The desire to kill myself had been a pronounced urge from around the time I was fourteen, and for seven or eight years after that. I came to understand this feeling not as part of me but as a response to external realities, and I worked hard to change myself so that that response would no longer find harbor in me. I have written several songs about this feeling. Most of them I did not record. This one I did.

12 - THE BEST EVER DEATH METAL BAND IN DENTON

The best ever death metal band out of Denton
Was a couple of guys who'd been friends since grade school

One was named Cyrus, the other was Jeff
And they'd practice twice a week in Jeff's bedroom

The best ever death metal band out of Denton
Never settled on a name,
But the top three contenders, after weeks of debate,
Were Satan's Fingers, and the Killers, and the Hospital Bombers

Jeff and Cyrus believed in their hearts that they were headed
for stage lights and Learjets, and fortune and fame
So in script that made prominent use of a pentagram
They stenciled their drumheads and guitars with their names

And this was how Cyrus got sent to the school
Where they told him he'd never be famous
And this was why Jeff, in the letters he'd write to his friend,
Helped develop a plan to get even

When you punish a person for dreaming his dream
Don't expect him to thank or forgive you
The best ever death metal band out of Denton
Will in time both outpace and outlive you

Hail, Satan! Hail, Satan, tonight!
Hail, Satan! Hail, hail!

ΔΔΔ

I was in a frenzy: I had a new job, and I'd started writing lyrics in the margins of the handouts they made us read in the week-long orientation. I'd been doing this at job orientations for years—in health care jobs, they're required by law to go over a lot of stuff that you probably already know if you've already worked a health care job or two. My wife was out of town, so I'd come home and start working on whatever ideas I'd sketched on the handouts.

I was working with young people again. People talk all kinds of trash about young people—grown-ups who should know better will talk about the children in their care behind their backs as if they were lost causes. Columbine happened and a bunch of people on TV tried to tie in the atrocity to music or video games. They always do this. It made me angry; this is an angry song. The "hail, Satan!" was an adlib. I don't actually worship Satan, but at the same time it's fair to say that it came from the heart.

13 · FALL OF THE STAR HIGH SCHOOL RUNNING BACK

Sophomore year—
You rushed for an average of eight-and-a-third yards per carry.
All eyes were on you!
Junior year—
you blew your knee out at an out-of-town game.
Nowhere to go to but down, down, down.
Nothing but the ground left for you to fall to.

By July,
you'd made a whole bunch of brand-new friends—
people you used to look down on,
and you'd figured out
a way to make real money—
"Givin' ends to your friends, and it felt stupendous."
Chrome spokes on your Japanese bike;
but selling acid was a bad idea,
and selling it to a cop was a worse one.
And the new laws said that seventeen-year-olds
could do federal time. You were the first one,

so I sing this song for you,
William Staniforth Donahue.
Your grandfather rode the boat over from Ireland,
but you made a bad decision or two. Yeah.

ΔΔΔ

"And early though the laurel grows / It withers quicker than the rose," right? But William doesn't die, he goes to prison, because the laws passed in the nineties let prosecutors charge LSD possession by weight—including the weight of the paper the drug saturated. Those laws fed the increasingly hungry prison-industrial complex; they are a stain. This is an explicitly political song. *All Hail West Texas* is probably my most political album; its politics favor the people who don't have the means to escape the grinding gears of the system. Those are still my politics, which I was learning to articulate as things got, I think it's fair to say, worse.

14 - BALANCE

Two tall glasses of sweet iced tea
Underneath the sweet gum tree
And the love we once nurtured, you and me
Disintegrating violently

Stick your tongue out
Catch the pieces as they drift down the air
We are too slow to catch them all
Not too far gone to care

Two slow summer hours spent picking at the bones
Figuring the interest on delinquent loans
Speaking in sad and mournful tones
Trying to squeeze tears out of mute stones

Wet your finger
Feel disaster in the air
We are too slow to outrun it now
Not too far gone to care

ΔΔΔ

"Balance" because the chord progression, I–VI–IV–VII with one string left open on each chord, seemed internally well-balanced, and the lyric reflected that: A-A-A-A rhymes in the verses, mirrored gestures and phrases in the nonidentical choruses. I know: This feels like a dry sort of description for a song in which people are suffering, preparing to bury something that was precious to them both, but formal properties can carry, for me, their own emotional weight. The one feeds the other. The mute stones are from Cicero—the orator, not the town in Illinois. He can't help these people, either.

15 · STRAIGHT SIX

Dull powder blue paint job, Earl Scheib special
Dashboard full of talismans to try and push fate
Rabbit skull hanging from the rearview mirror
Six kicking cylinders lined up straight,
And I ride,
And I glide down the streets of this city
All night, uptight
Jenny's on the cellular, high as a kite

There's a crack in the windshield eighteen inches long
Evaporating snow forming crystals on the chrome
Brand-new battery I shoplifted from the Pep Boys
Cold cranking power to bring me on home
And I ride,
And I glide down the streets of this city

All night, uptight
Jenny's on the cellular, high as a kite—

Sometimes, the moon shines like a beacon to the weary and the sick in spirit, and sometimes, sometimes
it's dark

ΔΔΔ

World, meet Jenny, a recurring character in a body of work that will shortly move on from recurring characters. This is her first appearance, or maybe her second; I don't date my notebook pages and I tend to start writing anywhere I see blank space. For the first twenty-plus years of her existence, Jenny is best known by her absence—what else is going on here? She's calling somebody who either doesn't have enough money to replace the battery in his car, or just has a compulsion to steal stuff, and does. He's driving a car that got work recently but still needs more. She is high, and the recipient of her car might be, too: It's not clear but seems probable. When Jenny arrives, there are, as far as we can see, only two people visible in the world, and really only to each other.

16 · FAULT LINES

Down here where the heat's so fine
I'll drink to your health and you drink to mine
as we try to make the money we scored out in Vegas
hold out for a while
we drink vodka from Russia
we get our chocolates from Belgium
we have our strawberries flown in from England

But none of the money we spend
seems to do us much good in the end

I got a cracked engine block, both of us do
yeah the house, and the jewels,
the Italian race car
they don't make us feel better about who we are
I got termites in the framework
so do you

Down here where the watermelon grows so sweet
where I worship the ground underneath of your feet
we are experts in the art of frivolous spending
and it's gone on like this for three years I guess
and we're drunk all the time, and our lives are a mess
and the deathless love we swore to protect with our bodies
is stumbling across its bleak ending

But none of the rage in our eyes
seems to finish it off where it lies
I got sugar in the fuel lines, both of us do
Yeah the fights, and the lies that we both love to tell
fail to send our love to its reward down in hell
I got pudding for a backbone
so do you

ΔΔΔ

I did not yet know, when I wrote this, that I would, a year later, be revisiting the drunken divorcing couple who'd occupied my imagination for several years in the early days of the Mountain Goats—and while this canonically "isn't" "them," it also has to be: It's maybe a little too clear-eyed about the situation to fit into the series, but water from the same well, an inadvertent study for what will become my new project about a year from here.

17 · RICHES AND WONDERS

We live high, our love gorges
on the alcohol we feed it
and it grows all fat and friendly
we have surplus if we need it
we hold on as hard as we can
our knuckles are white

we write letters to each other
invent secrets to confess to
I learn foreign and exotic
terms of endearment by which to address you
we feed fresh fruit to one another
we stay up all night

and I am healthy, I am whole
but I have poor impulse control
and I want to go home, but I am home.

We are strong, we are faithful
we are guardians of a rare thing
we pay close, careful attention
to the news the evening air brings
we show great loyalty
to the hard times we've been through

we are filled with riches and wonders
our love keeps the things it finds
and we dance like drunken sailors
lost at sea, out of our minds
you find shelter somewhere in me
I find great comfort in you

and I keep you safe from harm
and you hold me in your arms, and I want to go home
but I am home.

ΔΔΔ

I'll be saying this again later, at least once: People ask me to come play this at their weddings, and I always decline. If a person yearns to go home but is already home, then that person is saying that they do not feel at home in their home. A hard state of affairs! It's a love song, yes. The love is real and palpable. But I hear it darker than others do, I think. I don't trust the speaker to keep his priorities straight. He's having a good moment here, but I'm the guy who built him from whole clay, and I have reason to suspect that out there in the imaginary world beyond the song's text, the good times won't last.

18 - TRANSJORDANIAN BLUES

This church is rotten from the top down
This church is rotten from the top down
But I, I am going to clean house tonight

These walls can't keep the world at bay
These walls can't keep the world at bay
Our time, our time
Is limited and precious
But this place, this place
Is limitless and pernicious

Would you all just follow me
Out into the open?
Leave your coats and handbags, damn it all
Can't you see the floors are smoking?

This church is not long for this world
This church is not long for this world
And if you're wondering Who to blame,
I want to praise His Name with songs and feasting
Follow me into the open field
Where the truth will be revealed, if you're really listening.

Hosanna! Hosanna! I am saved by the blood of the Lamb!
One day when I was lost, He died upon that Cross.
I am saved by the blood of the Lamb!

ΔΔΔ

This one, on the other hand, I will absolutely play at your wedding, whether you ask me to or not.

19 - JENNY

You roared into the driveway
of our southwestern ranch-style house
on a new Kawasaki, all yellow and black
fresh out of the showroom.
Our house faced west,
so the new orange sun
positioned at your back

lit up your magnificent silhouette.
How much better, how much better
can my life get?
Nine hundred cubic centimeters of raw, whining power,
no outstanding warrants for my arrest.
Whoa, whoa! Whoa, Whoa! The pirate's life for me!

I hopped on back of the bike,
slipped my arms around you
and I let my face sink
down into your hair.
Inhaled as deeply
as I possibly could.
You were sweet and delicious
as the warm desert air

and you pointed your headlamp toward the horizon.
We were the one thing in the galaxy God didn't have His eyes on.
900cc of raw, whining power,
no outstanding warrants for my arrest.
Hi-diddle-dee-dee! God damn! The pirate's life for me!

ΔΔΔ

Happier days here for the people we met in "Straight Six"—maybe their happiest day. Even the least careful reader will have noted that I don't generally do happy endings, but this is one if there ever was one. Whether it ever actually happens or not, or is just a dream inside the head of a guy who misses the woman who changed his heart for the better, well, that's not for me to say.

20 - HOTEL ROAD

Thirty-story hotel overlooking the sea
Friends on either arm supporting me
It's hard to walk now
But I will go down somehow

I'm going down the old road.
I'm going down the old road.

Children kick a soccer ball around in the street
Kalpadruma trees are melting in the heat
It's hard to walk here
Where the waves shine so clear

I'm going down the old road.
I'm going down, down the old road.

Above the swollen ocean, the burning yellow sun
Hits the hotel's mylar windows, catching every one
It's hard to say why
I should come here to die

I'm going down the old road
I'm going down the old road

ΔΔΔ

This, like "Transjordanian Blues," was released on *On Juhu Beach*, a 3″ CD housed in a hand-sewn sleeve on the Japanese label Nursecall. Its five songs constitute a song cycle about a sanyasi—a Vaiṣṇava renunciant—dying in India. One hundred copies of *On Juhu Beach* were made, and for many years, it existed in near-total obscurity. It's one of my favorite things I've ever made; it's self-contained and complete in itself. To elucidate is one errand of the writer, and to obscure is another. When I can do both at once, I'm happy.

21 - BURNED MY TONGUE

Woke up this morning about a quarter to five
Said the prayer You'd taught me to keep myself alive
It burned my tongue
It burned my tongue

Fried some grains in butter, said a simple grace
Sat down at the table, fed my greedy face
It burned my tongue
It burned my tongue

Looked out at the ocean, I could see it so clear
Said the only Name I can ever stand to hear
It burned my tongue
It burned my tongue

When I ask you to sing with me, I wish you'd sing along
Thirty years in this world, thirty years too long
It burns my tongue
It burns my tongue

You took away my friends, You took my will to live
I gave you all I got, what more've I got to give
It burns my tongue
It burns my tongue
It burns my tongue
It burns my tongue

ΔΔΔ

Another of *On Juhu Beach*'s five hermetic byways, "Burned My Tongue" tells a lot of story without clarifying much of it at all. The "simple grace," anyway, is:

নমো মহাবদান্যায় কৃষ্ণপ্রেমপ্রদায় তে ।
কৃষ্ণায় কৃষ্ণচৈতন্যনাম্নে গৌরত্বিষে নমঃ ॥ ৫৩ ॥
namo mahā-vadānyāya
kṛṣṇa-prema-pradāya te
kṛṣṇāya kṛṣṇa-caitanya-
nāmne gaura-tviṣe namaḥ

Which means: "O most munificent incarnation! You are Kṛṣṇa Himself appearing as Śrī Kṛṣṇa Caitanya Mahāprabhu. You have assumed the golden color of Śrīmatī Rādhārāṇī, and you are widely distributing pure love of Kṛṣṇa. We offer our respectful obeisances unto you."

22 - WORLD CYLINDER

I don't like going to the doctor
I don't like looking in the mirror
I like looking out the window
Watching the waves break

Do I have to hit you over the head with it?
Do I have to hit you over the head with it?

I'm tired of talking to the suckers
I'm tired of talking to the wealthy
I wanna talk to men and women
Who haven't got anything left

Do I have to hit you over the head with it?
Do I have to hit you over the head with it?

Carry me down to the water
Where I used to play when I was five
Let me go, let me go down to the water
Don't bring me back alive

Do I have to hit you over the head with it?
Do I have to hit you over the head with it?

ΔΔΔ

The concluding number on *On Juhu Beach* is one of the best pure folk songs I've ever written, from a musical perspective—a little recurring riff on the high strings, a little blues walk down on the lower ones. As with the other songs on this EP, I have a special affection for it. Some people remember the wild times they had in college fondly. I remember the times I chased a story nobody was ever going to care about until it gave up its secrets, which were all the more magical precisely because they were secrets.

23 · COLOR IN YOUR CHEEKS

She came in on the red-eye
to Dallas–Forth Worth, all the way
from sunny Taipei
skin the color of a walnut shell
and a baseball cap holding down her dark hair

and she came here after midnight
the hot weather made her feel right at home
come on in, we haven't slept for weeks
drink some of this—it'll put color in your cheeks

He drove in from Mexicali,
no worse for wear
money to burn
time to kill
but five minutes looking in his eyes
and we knew he was broken pretty bad
so we gave him what we had

we cleared a space for him to sleep in, and we let
the silence—that's our trademark—make its graceful presence felt

come on in, we haven't slept for weeks
drink some of this—it'll put color in your cheeks

They came in by the dozens,
walking or crawling
some were bright-eyed
some were dead on their feet

and they came from Zimbabwe
or from Soviet Georgia—
East St. Louis—or from Paris—
or they lived across the street,

but they came, and when they'd finally made it here
it was the least that we could do
to make our welcome clear
come on in, we haven't slept for weeks
drink some of this—this'll put color in your cheeks

ΔΔΔ

Although there's an internal plot here that requires a little teasing out—an actual physical house to which the visitors arrive—I would hope that its broader purport is obvious enough. The travel details were almost certainly inspired by a plane ticket for a journey I wouldn't take until much later, one that took me from Des Moines through Dallas, Los Angeles, Taipei, and Kuala Lumpur to Perth. It's a long story. I slept like a child at the end of it.

24 · STORE

In the five minutes' worth of lost time that I had
When I was passed out on the supermarket floor

I saw you at the head of the heavenly chorus
And I heard your song ringing all through the store

In the five minutes when my broadcast got pre-empted
I saw you touch down—you were no longer dead
I was happy to see you, I had lots of questions
And I put my hand to the wound in your head

Ah, the blood!
All of that blood!
All of that warm blood,
Flowing freely from you!

In the five minutes when I was dead to the world
In a place far away from my friends and my home
I saw you with a smile on your radiant face
Amidst all the cans, and the glass, and the chrome

And in those five minutes my signal was jammed,
And the frequencies that I received were so pure
That I almost believed that the sight of the hole in your skull
Was a thing that my heart could endure
Ah, the blood!
All of that blood!
All of that warm blood,
Flowing freely from you!

ΔΔΔ

I have several songs in which people have epiphanies in grocery stores. As epiphanies go, this one's a little bloodier than most, which is how you know it's legit.

25 · JEFF DAVIS COUNTY BLUES

After three nights in jail,
I head north from Toyahvale—
switch to 285 in Pecos, and head up to Red Bluff.
My walk's real steady, and my eyes are real cold
but I feel like I'm all of sixteen years old—
lost in the Travelodge,
with the television on with the sound down,
I don't feel so tough.

Old issues of *Sunset* magazine to read.
Sleep for twelve hours. Dream about home.

I have no place to go, so I drive up to New Mexico.
Fix my eyes in the rearview
when I cross the state line.
And I panic, I guess, and, although it's quite late,
I take the first exit to 128.
I am coming back to Midland, and I hope you won't
mind.

Polaroids of the two of us
scattered on the passenger's seat.
I drive slowly, and evenly,
and I dream about home.

ΔΔΔ

Toyahvale is an unincorporated municipality that makes Colo, Iowa, look like a bustling metropolis; it used to have a rail stop but they trimmed the line back to Saragosa in 1971. They do not have a jail. Our speaker's story begins somewhere a little earlier, but he doesn't want to bring us in on that part. It doesn't matter what he was in jail for. It does matter that he was in jail.

26 · YOGA

We had our passports out and the kits to fix them up with,
and the hurricane lamp cast our shadows on the ceiling.
I watched them box with one another up there—Punch and Judy.
It was lovely, it was awful, it was that kind of feeling

When you said
it was real sure
there was nothing standing in our way,
and the lie
ran off and hid itself in the alleys all across Bombay.

I saw you knock the lamp over while reaching for the scissors,
and I wondered how we'd ever get by without it,
and you fell into my arms then. Sweet and gentle.
Poison in the water, little doubt about it

And you said
that one of us
would be all alone someday.
And the truth of it
echoed inexhaustibly
up and down the thoroughfares all across Bombay.

ΔΔΔ

This, as I think is clear enough from the storyline, was something written for *The Coroner's Gambit*, but its home on a one-sided 12″ EP was more fitting. As the opening number of a stage musical, this would foreshadow a sad ending; as a scene in a film, it would be in black and white, and would be directed by Michael Curtiz, who was born Manó Kaminer in Budapest on the twenty-fourth of December, 1886. The chances that this film gets out of turnaround are slim unless we unattach Curtiz, but I am standing firm.

27 - ABSOLUTE LITHOPS EFFECT

After one long season of waiting,
after one long season of wanting
I am cracking open.

My insides are pink and raw,
and it hurts me when I move my jaw
but I am taking tiny steps forward.

And I
I feel
sure that my wounds will heal
and I
will bloom
here, in my room

With a little water,
and a little bit of sunlight
and a little bit of tender
mercy
tender
mercy.

The big trucks come up the highway,
and the big wheels rattle my windows
and night,
night comes to Texas

After one blind season alone in here—
after one long, sweltering summer—
I
I'm going
to find the exit.

And I
will go
to the house of a friend I know
And I will let
myself
forget
with a little water
and a little bit of sunlight
and a little bit of tender
mercy
tender
mercy.

ΔΔΔ

I am at this point almost ten years removed from *Taboo VI: The Homecoming*, and my range has increased: Some of the songs I write are just songs, and some are songs that might have been poems, and some are still poems disguised as songs. Although the tune of "Absolute Lithops Effect" is more complex than anything I might have attempted on the early tapes, I'd put its lyric in that third category, with an added chance element, which pleases me—I don't think "waiting" and "wanting" were both in the original draft. I think I wrote down one, and saw on the page that it might also be the other, and said to myself: "Let's keep them both." Accidents are my favorite strategy. You can always rely on an accident.

28 - INDONESIA

The summer came in carrying spring in its
  mouth
held it up for everyone to see
This is the time when all our plans and schemes
melt down into listless anarchy—

historically, anyway, that's been the case
but this year there's a new pink sheen on your face

Like the color of a secret flower
that grows tall and moist and incorruptible
In Indonesia, Indonesia.

The season tunneled forward, like a moth through grain
its hunger was an all-consuming, mindless thing
And you slept for twelve to fourteen hours at a stretch
I wondered what the weather in the fall was going to
bring
and then you said you'd dreamt of cowboys that were
zombies in disguise—
I knew fall was never coming, it was written on your eyes

Like a mist that hangs there in the air
On the mountainside where rare and nameless flowers
grow
In Indonesia, Indonesia

ΔΔΔ

"Indonesia" didn't make the cut for *All Hail West Texas*—it's a bonus track on the CD reissue—but pieces of it stick to my ribs. "Everyone to see" / "listless anarchy"—I've worked with songwriters who can pull that sort of thing off routinely, but for me it's a plum. "Rare and nameless flowers"? The Mountain Goats I'm fondest of finds a way to work in some rare and nameless flowers, especially ones growing on a misty mountainside. I think of this lyric like a static-interrupted dispatch from the post-*Tallahassee* future, when romantic relationships in lyrics are taking a backseat to elliptical angles and arcane equations.

29 - INSURANCE FRAUD #2

Bag full of oily rags,
fifty cent lighter
dreams of retirement in Cancun
burning ever brighter
there's a lot of ways to make money in this world
but I can't recommend insurance fraud

Burned out shell of a Volkswagen
bloodstains on the driveway
torn up Mercedes
by the side of the highway
big plans, big plans
let me tell you something sister
you will never get away with it

You were sitting in the recliner
with the TV on
when you said something evil
and then you were gone

Explosives in the water main
a blown fuse
college graduation photograph
splashed all over the six o'clock news
I won't be cashing in your policy
'til I find out what it is you're trying to do to me

ΔΔΔ

You could, if you were so inclined, divide these lyrics into categories—"songs about animals," "songs referencing historical events," "love songs (people)," "love songs (addiction)," "love songs (trees)." When there's paranoia in a song, it's usually not my personal paranoia, but I can locate a pretty convincing paranoia if I close my eyes and just believe. This is near the top of the list of "guy who thinks he's marked for death" songs, which, for many people, is a top Mountain Goats song category. "Insurance Fraud #2" also cross-categorizes into the "songs featuring televisions" folder, which bulges with entries, but sits suspiciously alone in the "songs about insurance fraud" file.

30 - SOFT TARGETS

You cry when you get drunk,
and I can't find the right things to say.
Sooner or later you'll start breaking plates
And I'll do what I can to get out of your way.

There is nobody innocent here—
I've got more blood on my hands than you do.
It's you and it's me, and the baby makes three.
Ah, but we've got our love to carry us through.
We've got our love to carry us through.

I cry when I'm hungry.
Something is wrong with my brain.
And the ghost of our future's awake in the attic.
He moans and he wails as he rattles his chain.

We embrace on the floor in the kitchen,
emissaries from neighboring lands.
When I hunt down the vampire that did this to us,
I will rip out his heart with my hands.
I will rip out his heart with my hands.

ΔΔΔ

I suspect but can't prove that this song predates *Tallahassee*. There's a child involved in the story; that makes it partner to "Poltergeist," and to "Letter from a Motel," songs in which the warring couple risk greater collateral damage than usual. These songs draw some of my better vocal takes out of me, because—well, you know, "collateral damage." It's a phrase you've maybe had occasion to contemplate in quiet hours. Or maybe you haven't, depending on your luck.

MAY

1 - TWELVE HANDS HIGH

I know you never asked for my opinion,
but I'd say that horse is crazy
I know what I think doesn't matter any more,
but I'd say his mind is gone
And I know you know what I know,
even though you'd rather die than say it
I know you feel the same way
or you wouldn't be sleeping on the lawn

I heard the hooves crack the window,
saw the body come through
Saw the big brown eyes flashing,
I fell all over you
I got pressure bearing down on me

There was a reason why I came here,
but I guess now it doesn't matter
I had a good, good, good, good reason,
but I guess now you couldn't care
There is a certain kind of feeling that you get
when you're totally helpless
And there's a different world waiting for me
when I lift my head up from your thick dark hair

I heard the hooves crack the window,
saw the body come through
Saw the big nostrils flaring,
I fell all over you
I got pressure bearing down on me

ΔΔΔ

This song originates in a dream I had in or around December 1988. In this dream, a horse came crashing through the wall of a hardware store while two people were ballroom dancing inside it after-hours. Middle of the night, doors locked, lights out, moon through the window, ballroom dancing, horse crashes through the wall. The wall doesn't open onto the street; it divides the hardware store from whatever business it adjoins. This image inspired a sequence of poems I called *Songs from Alpha Privative*, my second poem cycle; I was enamored of Berryman and wanted to do something ambitious. It featured two characters drinking their way toward an inevitable divorce. Over the next fourteen years I would develop, abandon, and habitually revisit these characters. From them I learned how to let a story germinate and how to follow its tendrils where they go. All from a dream I had one night whose central image seemed worth remembering in song.

2 - OLD COLLEGE TRY

From the housetops to the gutters
from the ocean to the shore
the warning signs have all been bright and garish
far too great in number to ignore

From the cities to the swamplands
from the highway to the hills
our love has never had a leg to stand on
from the aspirins to the crosstops to the Elavils,

but I will walk down to the end
with you
if you will come

all the way down
with me.

From the entrance to the exit—
that's longer than it looks from where we stand
I want to say "I'm sorry" for stuff I haven't done yet
things will shortly get completely out of hand

I can feel it in the rotten air tonight—
in the tips of my fingers, in the skin on my face
in the weak last gasp of the evening's dying light
in the way those eyes I've always loved illuminate this place

like a trash can fire in a prison cell
like the searchlights in the parking lots of Hell

I will walk down to the end
with you
if you will come
all the way down
with me.

ΔΔΔ

So what happened was the storied English label 4AD called me in Iowa asking: "What do think you'd want to do if you made an album with us?" And I said, well, I used to write all these poems and songs about this divorcing couple, and when I wrote the last song in the series I was relieved, because I'd been torturing them for several years, but if they could have their own album, it would be kind of like I was doing right by them. As it turned out, there was rather a lot more torture in the offing, but I hadn't even written one of the songs yet. It was just an idea in the air. This one I imagined as the overture, the lyric that sets the scene for the great big catastrophe.

3 · TALLAHASSEE

Window facing an ill-kept front yard
Plums on the tree, heavy with nectar
Prayers to summon the destroying angel
Moon stuttering in the sky like film stuck in a projector,

and you: you.

Twin-prop airplanes circling loudly overhead
Road to the airport, two lanes clear
Half the whole town gone for the summer
Terrible silence coming down here,

and you: you.

There is no deadline, there is no schedule
There is no plan we can fall back on
The road this far can't be retraced
There is no punch line anybody can tack on

But there are loose ends by the score
What did I come down here for?

You. You.

ΔΔΔ

But the song that ended up opening the album was the title track, this one. *Tallahassee* marked a radical departure in my writing method, though I didn't mark it at the time—nor, really, until just now. Prior to this album, when I sat down to write, I'd just pull something from the air and see if it had enough substance to become a song. There are countless songs in notebooks that never got there: things originating in a stray phrase or image that couldn't sew enough clothes around themselves to make a suit. But here, I knew what I was going to be writing about every time I picked up a pen. These people. Their house. Their lives. I didn't know it at the time, but the album was teaching me how to write a novel.

4 - FIRST FEW DESPERATE HOURS

Bad luck comes in from Tampa
bad luck comes in from Tampa
on the back of a truck
doing ninety up the interstate

We have bad dreams the night he rolls in
we have bad dreams the night he rolls in
and we try
to keep our spirits high

but they flag, and they wane
when the truck pulls up
in the light spring rain
and they sag like withering flowers
let the good times roll on
through these first few desperate hours

The driver drops his cargo at the curb
The driver drops his cargo at the curb
and the sun peeks in
like a killer through the curtain

And when cloven hoofprints turn up in the garden
Yeah, when cloven hoofprints turn up in the garden
we keep up the good fight
to keep our spirits light

but they drop like flies,
and there's a stomach-churning shift
in the way the land lies
and they lean like towers
on a hillside struggling to stand
through these first few desperate hours

ΔΔΔ

The advantage, the tremendous advantage I should say, to revisiting characters and storylines you spent a long time developing and then laid to rest is that you know them intimately when you return to them, if you do return to them. A central plot point of the *Songs from Alpha Privative* poems had been that they flee California and drive all the way to Florida, where they run out of road. (They sojourn in Las Vegas first, a plot point not explored on *Tallahassee*.) Do they drive a U-Haul? No, I didn't think so, I figured they'd splurge and hire a moving truck. Then, when their stuff shows up, it's clear that they've failed to leave their old selves behind.

5 - SOUTHWOOD PLANTATION ROAD

I've got you
you've got whatever's left of me to get
our conversations are like minefields
no one's found a safe way through one yet

I spend a lot of money
I buy you white gold
we raise up a little roof
against the cold

on Southwood Plantation Road
where at night the stars flow like milk across the sky

where the high wires drop
where the fat crows fly

All night long,
you giggle and scream
your brown eyes
deeper than a dream

I am not going to lose you
we are going to stay married
in this house like a Louisiana graveyard
where nothing stays buried

on Southwood Plantation Road
where the dead will walk again
put on their Sunday best
and mingle with unsuspecting Christian men
la la la la la

ΔΔΔ

As we observed earlier, there is no standing rule of the printed "la la," or at least not one that can be legally enforced. But here, certainly, it's the character who's saying "la la la la la," not me, and so the "la la" is preserved. Why does he, or she, la? Well, because she must, I think, or because it can't be helped. And indeed: When the time of the la la comes, you know it's truly come because it can't be helped.

6 - THE HOUSE THAT DRIPPED BLOOD

Look beyond the broken bottles
past the rotting wooden stairs
root out the wine-dark honeyed center
not everyone can live like millionaires

Look through the air-thin walls
Tear up the floorboards, strip the paint
Go over every inch of space
With the patience of a saint

Grab your hat. Get your coat
The cellar door is an open throat

Look past the kitchen cabinets
Go through the chest of drawers
Scrutinize the casements
Rip the varnish off the doors
And dig up the laughing photographs,
They're here somewhere or other
Take what you can carry
But let me tell you, brother:

Still waters go stagnant
Bodies bloat
And the cellar door is an open throat

ΔΔΔ

There's this famous scene in the *Agamemnon* of Aeschylus, the "carpet scene," lines 783–974. Agamemnon, returning triumphant from Troy, is invited by Clytemnestra to enter his house via the red carpet (which is not actually a carpet but elaborate and expensive robes spread on the floor). Agamemnon resists—"To trample ornate beauty is / For me a thing I'd be afraid to do" (tr. Andrew Wilson)—but only for a page or two, and then tramples the ornate robes right into the house of Atreus, which will devour him, because those aren't rugs or robes, they're the hungry tongues of Tantalus. The house in *Tallahassee* isn't a palace in Argos, but it still has an appetite. In its original draft, this was called "Blood Song," and while I'm usually not too interested in drafts, there are some struck-through lines in the second verse that had promise: "gun the motor, head directly north"; "the house is hungry / someone's gonna have to feed it"; "put down your weapon." Weapon? Did somebody say "weapon"? I'm intrigued!

7 - OCEANOGRAPHER'S CHOICE

Well: Guy in a skeleton costume
comes up to the guy in the Superman suit
runs through him with a broadsword

I flip the television off
bring all the bright lights up
turn the radio up loud

I don't know why I'm so persuaded
that if I think things through
long enough and hard enough
I'll somehow get to you

and then you reached up, and you reached out
you kicked the ashtray over as we came toward each other
I stubbed my cigarette out against the west wall
quickly lit another

look at that! would you look at that?
we're throwing off sparks
what will I do when I don't have you
to hang on to in the dark?

Yes: Everybody's going to need a witness
everybody's going to need a little backup
in case the scene gets nasty

You throw the attic window open
and I throw myself all around you
and then night comes to Tallahassee

I don't know why it's gotten harder
to keep myself away
I thought I'd finally beat the feeling back
it all came back today

and then we fell down, and we locked arms
we knocked the dresser over as we rolled across the floor
I don't mean it when I tell you
that I don't love you any more

look at that, would you look at that?
the way the ceiling starts to swerve—
what will I do when I don't have you,
when I finally get what I deserve?

ΔΔΔ

One fun exercise for me is to take the songs from *Tallahassee* and imagine them with no context, no storyline—which is of course how most people who hear them at all hear them, but requires intention if you already know the plot. This, removed from the story, becomes much sadder for me—there is irreparable damage here. The sadness is mitigated for me by the speaker's complicity: It took two people to make this mess. Nothing left to do now but watch TV and squeeze whatever carnal pleasures are left out of each other.

8 - SEE AMERICA RIGHT

I was driving up from Tampa when the radiator burst
I was three sheets to the wind

a civilian saw me first
and then there was the cop
and then the children standing on the corner
your love is like a cyclone in a swamp,
and the weather's getting warmer

I was getting out of jail, headed to the Greyhound
you said you'd hop on one yourself
and meet me on the way down
I was shaking way too hard to think
dead on my feet, about to drop
I went and got the case of vodka from the car,
walked the two miles to the bus stop

Got on the bus half-drunk again
the driver glared at me
met up with you in Inglis
thumbed a ride to Cedar Key
If we never make it back to California
I want you to know I love you
but my love is like a dark cloud full of rain
it's always right there up above you

ΔΔΔ

Peter played the drum: We turned a kickdrum on its side and he played sticks on it. I think he overdubbed it onto our extant guitar-and-bass live take. We compiled the vocal take from four discrete passes, most of it probably from the best one—but the "I" and the "was" are from two different takes. It's the two-mile walk to the bus stop from jail with a case of vodka in hand that defines the action here. We will never know what he was doing all the way down in Tampa.

9 - ALPHA RATS NEST

Ah the lengthening hours, and the refinery
belching fire into the sky
we do our best vampire routines
as we suck the dying hours dry
the night is lovely as a rose
if I see sunlight hit you,
I am sure that we'll both decompose

Ah the fitful sleep, and the fire engines
that I dream of, when I dream
someday we'll both wake up for good
I will try hard not to scream
the evening wind will shake the blind
you're stirring from your slumber,
we've got something hateful on our minds

O sing! sing! sing!
for the dying of the day
sing for the flames that will rip through here,
and the smoke that will carry us away
sing for the damage we've done
and the worse things that we'll do
open your mouth up and sing for me now
and I will sing for you

ΔΔΔ

The house does not burn down. They think about it a lot, and they see fire everywhere, but the house in *Tallahassee* doesn't burn down. I like to imagine them actually trying to make it happen: first with matches, then with bundles of newspaper, finally with flamethrowers. In the end it's a love story. What is a love story without immense columns of flame rising into the Florida night?

10 - NO CHILDREN

I hope that our few remaining friends
give up on trying to save us
I hope we come up with a fail-safe plot
to piss off the dumb few that forgave us
I hope the fences we mended
fall down beneath their own weight
and I hope we hang on past the last exit
I hope it's already too late
and I hope the junkyard a few blocks from here
someday burns down
and I hope the rising black smoke carries me far away
and I never come back to this town again, in my life.
I hope I lie, and tell everyone you were a good wife,
and I hope you die.
I hope we both die.

I hope I cut myself shaving tomorrow
I hope it bleeds all day long
our friends say it's darkest before the sun rises
we're pretty sure they're all wrong
I hope it stays dark forever
I hope the worst isn't over
and I hope you blink before I do
I hope I never get sober
and I'd hope, when you think of me, years down the line,
you can't find one good thing to say
and I'd hope that if I found the strength to walk out
you'd stay the hell out of my way

I am drowning
there is no sign of land
you are coming down with me

hand in unlovable hand
and I hope you die
I hope we both die

ΔΔΔ

This is one of the two best-known songs I'll ever write, most likely, and its beginnings are now lore: how I heard "I Hope You Dance" while driving to the airport and, hating it, changed its chorus to "I hope you die"; how I wrote the idea down on the paper envelope that holds the plane ticket and somehow got home from either Athens, Georgia, or Tallahassee with the envelope miraculously still in my possession. That envelope used to be somewhere among my notebooks, but I haven't seen it in a while. The draft that proceeded from it is presently on my lap, in a red Mead notebook. It took me four pages to get it right. "Rolling guitar figure," it says in the upper left-hand corner of the first page; the song's in 6/8, so I followed that direction. The original first verse through chorus read:

Cut my hand washing some dishes
bled all over the sink, and the countertop too
I'd missed the tendon by a quarter of an inch
washed it under the faucet, and I thought about you

I hope you die

After this, there's about eleven lines that don't go anywhere; and then

there will be no children
in this house
there will be only the sound of the wind in the door
when we get through

The second page has the whole first verse and chorus, with chords, and then wanders off into the weeds again. The third page has "I hope we never get sober" and five more verses that didn't get used, and then, marked "(save)," the "I am drowning" bridge, exactly as it came out. The remainder of the lyric along with several more unused verses are on the fourth. Of them, I like these lines best, from just above that "(save)":

I hope we never get sober
I hope we never get well
I wish I knew where we were headed
I wish there were some way to tell

It was a busy day in Iowa.

11 - (UNTITLED)

red-hot corrugated steel walls
glowing bottles bursting on the shelves
this is not another vision
this the coming-out party for our true selves

let the vivid colors rise
let me see them dancing on your eyes

~~I'm going to hold you in my arms~~
~~because my love for you is powerful and terrible~~
~~but it's almost all used up by now~~
~~as the heat becomes unbearable~~

~~we pour the good stuff straight into our mouths~~
~~as we start whooping like a pair of cranes~~

~~deny the stinking flesh~~
~~let the spirit take the reins~~

we lurch and stumble up and down the aisle
our choreography is terrible
our love is truly almost all used up
and then the heat becomes unbearable

we crack open high-end bottles and we laugh
tip our hats and tap our canes
deny the stinking flesh
let the spirit take the reins

step light
I will show you what you mean to me tonight

ΔΔΔ

Before we leave *Tallahassee*, this, which I found in a grey Mead notebook still on my shelf with all the other old notebooks, twenty-three years after the fact. The first song in the notebook is “Idylls of the King”; the second one is “Alpha Chum Gatherer”; then “Alpha Rats Nest,” and then this. No title, enough revision to suggest I meant to finish it. I think I was trying to pull back from tell-not-show lines, trying to avoid having the characters speak in expository proclamations, but I have to say, today for rhythm I’d make it “the coming-out party for our own true selves,” combine the excised lyrics (here, the ones in strikethrough) with their revision into something more satisfying, and hit record—there’s an aggression in this that, for me, with respect to these characters, really hits the spot.

12 · CUT OFF THEIR THUMBS

We sprawl out on the bed or we lean against the wall
down among the dregs out where the yellow spiders crawl
the telephone is broken and the drapes have all been closed
hands up, who doesn't know exactly where this story goes?

I'm going to kill everybody in this room
I'm going to kill everybody in this room

How has it come to this? well, I haven't got a clue—
You looking up at me, and us two glowering down at you
Wind shakes the palm trees with an escalating fury
Face the judge, or take your chances with the jury

I'm going to kill everybody in this room
I'm going to kill everybody in this room

Let's have a little music on this hazy afternoon
Let's hope the tension in here finds its resolution soon
Radio on the windowsill, old white moon above
God watches over children and he cares for fools in love

I'm going to kill everybody in this room
I'm going to kill everybody in this room

ΔΔΔ

I saw a movie at some point—maybe *Dog Day Afternoon*, I'm not sure—where a cop remarks that only an idiot takes hostages, because once you've taken a hostage there's no good way out. This idea festered in me, because it seemed self-evidently true, and it also seemed that the moment at which the hostage's luck goes sour is when their captor realizes this is true. By the time I write this I've had a gun pulled on me several times and have kept the company of people who later ended up in prison—but in earlier years. By now I'm living safely, like a normal person, but I'm remembering a few rooms that nobody would confuse with a normal person room. I'm exaggerating them for effect, but only in the way that you might describe the worst possible outcome of a snakebite. The venom's there whether it killed you or not.

13 - DESERTERS

The neighbors are cloning themselves
we found their cocoons in the garbage
and we'll either stay high forever, or crash in an hour
or two
sleeping the sleep of the blessed
picking through trash cans with you

The guy on TV is a prophet
you just have to look in his eyes
and we'll either turn our lives over to Christ, or we'll just
drift off
trying to better ourselves
giving up after one or two tries

The high school's a front for Yakuza
everyone, everyone knows it
and we will all shortly be richer than God if we'll just
hold on
As long as we play all our cards right
As long as nobody here blows it

I've drawn up a map of Rialto
the holding tank's full for the night
I heard all about it on citizens band, it's a brand-

new day
we'll be awake until Thursday
the future's disarmingly bright

ΔΔΔ

This, a B-side that exists only as a home recording, didn't make the master list for the *We Shall All Be Healed* sessions, but it's kind of a key player: All the images were gathered by me, harvested by hand during my years using hard drugs; just a handful of years, really, but productive years, in a manner of speaking. I met a lot of guys who were right on a cusp of a really big score back then, but to the best of my knowledge none of them ever crested the cusp.

14 - SNAKEHEADS

Weather cell from northern Canada
due in before the afternoon is over
brown cows in the fields
eating their way slowly through the clover

And the canopy of apple trees before us
symmetrical and pure as a pagoda
me and Lee Chong from Chicago in a U-Haul
headed out through western Minnesota

headed for the islands
headed for the islands

Our load is heavy, and you can hear it shifting
say what you like, I'm never gonna stop
everyone will eat when we've arrived
white apple blossoms soften up the blacktop

Two days from now we'll get to where we're going
the western sky will pitch-correct its whining
our cargo's gonna spill out from the cabin
and rub its eyes, and see the silver lining

headed for the islands
headed for the islands

ΔΔΔ

We Shall All Be Healed is an aggressive album with pockets of tenderness; on the studio version of this song, my vocal take misreads which side of the line it needs to be on. The track ended up as a B-side. It's about human smuggling—"snakeheads" are gangs from Fujian who smuggle their customers into the Western countries. I had almost certainly read about them in the *World Press Review*, a magazine that aggregated newspapers and magazines from around the world; I had a subscription. Like its *We Shall All Be Healed* brethren, this song is cold-eyed. Or realistic, depending on where you're standing.

15 · DUANE ALLMAN SLEPT HERE

bag of sweet red licorice bits in my coat pocket
Kate's phone number breaking up and blurring in my brain
I have to find myself a doorway to rest in
up for three days smoking rock cocaine

I got an idea to head down to Cable airport
maybe steal a little two-seat plane
maybe put the fear of God on my old friends down below
up for three days smoking rock cocaine

I caught five minutes' sleep, it was an accident
my eyes look like grapes, sticky and overripe

I get the dates and times wrong all the time,
    I'm too young to get the dates and times wrong
up for three days, lips around the pipe

I will come to see you, it's inevitable
some wood may warp, but you probably can't change the grain
I'm not who you think I am—the person you thought you knew
  is gone
up for three days smoking rock cocaine
up for three days smoking rock cocaine

ΔΔΔ

I have no idea when I wrote this; it's from the *We Shall All Be Healed* notebooks. "Kate" is a composite, but the song is otherwise a fairly accurate description of a week I had around the summer of 1987. As with a number of lyrics from the time when the songs began to get more autobiographical, the reason I didn't set music to it until much later was because it nested a little too close to the bone. I had a car, so the doorway is perhaps a gilding of the lily. A reverse gilding and a different sort of lily, but, you know how it is—you can only knock it once you've tried it.

16 - BEAT THE DEVIL

hauling peanut butter crank through Arizona
gotta keep the glowstick babies fat and happy
cactus standing taller than Goliath
all the vultures come directly at me

we stack them in between some bales of lumber
on flatbeds coming in from Colorado
I don't know what you're doing down in Memphis
all winter you've been incommunicado

take a picture
do it fast
for the good times
that won't last

hot sun peels the paint down to the primer
overheating engine spits and whines
try to keep our minds on what we're doing
try to keep the wheels between the lines

the feeling when the cop car flips its lights on
the near-electric tension bubbling here inside the truck
the lack of any word from you in Memphis
the sound of someone running out of luck

take a picture
do it fast
for the good times
that won't last

ΔΔΔ

As we approach *We Shall All Be Healed*—an album especially close to my heart, as the gentle reader can probably guess from the attention I'm giving the B-sides and castaways—we'll note the ongoing presence of the noble vulture. I want to say "I am the vulture," and in one sense that's true, but in another sense the vulture is that presence toward which one can only aspire. That he will necessarily be the last to leave the party is only one of his virtues. To make an exhaustive list of all these virtues would, and will, require a lifetime.

17 · GOOD MORNING TO ALL VULTURES

Good morning to all vultures, high up in the trees
Good morning to all vultures, of high and low degrees
Good morning to all vultures, near and far
High above the sea,
Or right here where we are

Good morning to all vultures atop the temple gate
Good morning, sleepy vulture, trying to fly straight
Good morning to the vulture with the great big beak
We hope today you find
The carrion you seek

It's hard sometimes to be a vulture today
And so we say "Good morning" just to start you on your way

Good morning to all vultures high above this town
Don't let anybody try to bring you down
Circle 'round the cemetery way up high
Anyone would be proud to know so much of the sky

ΔΔΔ

We Shall All Be Healed goes down into the mire and stays there, by design, and it's good, while we're in it, to come up for air midway through. This is a song I wrote, years later, for my son, when he was a toddler: when my desperate years were specks in the rearview. I found him a vulture stuffie at a bookstore, and we played with it, and I wrote this. It's unreleased, because I have a whole very tiresome schtick about how I didn't wanna be the guy who becomes a dad and is suddenly making wholesome music for children. But at home, in private, after I became a dad? Please trust that I wrote a whole album's worth of children's songs and several of them stand among my best work.

18 - SLOW WEST VULTURES

breaking the signal 'til it's totally unreadable
drinking the dregs, eating the utterly inedible
we do what we do
all for you
all dressed up, black hat and white cane
slowly circling the drain

ready for the future
ready for the world about to come

shooting the sequel before the treatment's even finished
sanding numbers off the Monojects as our slight returns
diminish
we are what we are
get in the God damned car

ready for the future
ready for the world about to come

ΔΔΔ

What's "funny" to me about this one is that I think it's ground zero for me becoming preoccupied by the future, by the phrase "the future" and by the idea of the future and by the way the future is always a moving target, one that assumes any number of shapes, depending on who's taking aim, and how clear a shot they have at it. It's also being written from the perspective of my younger self, who didn't believe there was going to be any actual future at all—for whom "the world about to come" doesn't include me.

19 · ALL UP THE SEETHING COAST

I eat a couple Milky Ways for breakfast
I take my coffee light and sweet
Show up for dinner when you tell me to
I heap the sugar high and white on everything I eat

Carry an apple in my pocket
I write reminders on my skin
Clip meaningless pictures from old magazines
I tape them to the walls
It's a bad place I'm in

And nothing you can say or do will stop me
And a thousand dead friends can't stop me

I go back to places I remember
See what's been going on without me
Stare down the strangers at the bus stop
Pretend they've been gossiping about me

White sugar by the spoonful
Cantaloupes and grapes and watermelons
I force it down like it was medicine
Anybody asks, you tell them what you want to tell them

But the best you've got is powerless against me
and all your little schemes break
when they come crashing up against me

ΔΔΔ

There's a legendary bit in Richard Pryor's *Live on the Sunset Strip* where he talks about freebasing. At the climax of the piece, he's talking to his pipe. "Fuck all your appointments," the pipe says to him. "Me and you are just going to hang out in this room together." You get real intimate with a room when you feel like leaving it would be a tactical error; but when you've started framing simple errands of daily life in tactical terms, the error is already some considerable distance behind you. Tactics are for generals, but in the room, you only have the specifics.

20 - LINDA BLAIR WAS BORN INNOCENT

Gentle hum of the old machines
here we come, scrubbed and scoured
patches on our jeans
when the drone sounds in the cool night wind
we pick up the call
kick all the traces in

hungry for love
ready to drown
tie down the sails
we're going downtown

Great big drain on the power grid
you may not like Tate's methods,
but you've got to admit she's a real nice kid
we walk light
down the wires
higher than weather balloons
empty hearts on fire

hungry for love
ready to drown
so tie down the sails tonight
we're going downtown

ΔΔΔ

I love Tate because she only turns up as an aside delivered by a speaker who assumes you already have an opinion about her. According to my personal poetics, "everybody else already knows most of the details" is a terrific starting point, a few beats down the line from *in medias res*. Even today, if you go downtown, you might find a few staples with yellowed paper clinging to them stuck in an old utility pole, or an empty Cricket lighter wedged into a crevice on a fire hydrant. The things Tate left in her wake, the things that goad you to remember her name later and then you probably get it wrong. Possibly. Possibly not.

21 - BUTTER TEETH

We spilled out through the front door
into the blinding late light
sun reflected on the storefront windows
tremendously bright

We were Norwegians come down from the north
attacking the walls of the fortress
I was permanently at the point of exhaustion
you were gorgeous

Who's here? just us—
nobody else around
stray electrical currents
trying to find the ground

We haunted the walls of the pharmacy
artlessly shoplifting random things
painkillers, cough syrup, tiger balm
bubblegum, cigarettes, and shower curtain rings

We were Portuguese warships cresting the waves
cannons raised, ready to dock
you were counting down the hours and the minutes
I was trying to find a way of stopping the clock

Who's here? just us—
nobody else around
stray electrical currents
trying to find the ground

ΔΔΔ

Here's a thing about this *We Shall All Be Healed* B-side that feels like a voice speaking to me from the other side of the veil, or like a message from inside the crystal ball, or like some graffiti on a wall in a foreign city that was waiting for me, specifically me, to read it: It takes up space. For me only, but it takes up space. It claims more territory than has in reality been deeded to it. A phrase from the lyric will occur to me, and I'll hear the chords in my head, and I'll think: "Oh, yeah, that song. We've played that song a million times." We played it five times in total, most recently in 2004. That's it. Hardly anyone has ever heard it, and yet, when the phrase "Who's here? Just us" pops into my mind, I have a sense memory, a physical echo, an akashic impression of having sung it to hundreds of audiences over the years. Sharing the feeling. Seeing the same things. In my bones I feel like it's been a whole thing, dozens of times. But: five.

22 - HOMMEL WEST

And then we came to the part of the story where the corners
started getting tight
ears pressed up against the motel wall
listening to disembodied voices all night
all night

Lamp on the chintzy end table
beer bottle full of cigarette butts
knock at the door, and then silence
answer it if you've got the guts, if you've got 'em

Smoke, and dust, and spiders
hot exhaust, and grime, and mosquitoes, and you
like a boy scout
brave, loyal, and true

if they'd come with their colors all out on display,
that'd be one thing, all right?
but when they dress themselves up like the Latter-day
Saints
we let them in and lock the door tight, lock it up tight

when we project our black-and-white films on the wall,
you can hear their stomachs turn
your eyes on mine, and my eyes on the door,
and everybody in here's going to burn. Everybody

Smoke, and dust, and spiders
hot exhaust, and grime, and mosquitoes, and you
like a boy scout
brave, loyal, and true

ΔΔΔ

Somewhere in the process of writing *We Shall All Be Healed* I did this, which I've only played live once, but whose melody sticks with me, and whose words, I have to say, constitute one of the darkest stories in the catalog. The climactic image probably has its roots in the trailer for Paul Schrader's *Hardcore* (1979), where George C. Scott, in a dark theater, cries out for the projectionist to stop screening a pornographic film of his daughter. There's a lot of film and videotape in *We Shall All Be Healed*; possibly only one photograph, two at most, survive from the years on which I based the songs. I don't look like a Boy Scout in these pictures, but I do look like I'm trying very hard to be brave.

23 - LETTER FROM BELGIUM

Martin calls to say he's sending old electrical equipment
That's good: We can always use some more electrical
equipment

In the cold clear light of day down here,
everyone's a monster
that's cool with all of us,
we've been past the point of help since early April

Susan and her notebook
freehand drawings of Lon Chaney
blueprints for geodesic domes
recipes for cake

Yeah, we're all here, chewing our tongues off
waiting for the fever to break

when we walk out in the sunlight, we tell everyone we know it
hurts our eyes, when the real reason we don't like it is that it
makes us wonder if we're dying

And Martin's found an old trunk full of stage makeup in the
basement
and he's sending it along! We can always use more makeup—
more

creams
and powders

And Carrie's got the feeling
that the people next door
will close in like a wolf pack
should we make one small mistake

Yeah, we're all here, chewing our tongues off
Waiting for the fever to break

ΔΔΔ

This song is about people who use meth intravenously, among whose numbers I once counted myself, which is the sort of thing that, if you're going to write about it, you have to decide what you're going to foreground. The rush? The crash? The milieu? I'm trying for the trifecta here.

24 - YOUR BELGIAN THINGS

The men were here to get your Belgian things
they'll store them for you in an airplane hangar
there's guys in biohazard suits,
mud caking on their rubber boots
they've come to keep your pretty things from danger

The men were here to get your Belgian things
they'll spend the whole day hauling them downstairs
I shot a roll of thirty-two exposures
my camera groans beneath the weight it bears

I can see you in my sleep
playing the points for all you're worth

walking gingerly across
the bruised earth

The men were here to get your Belgian things
they waltzed right through the door and went fluorescent
their boots were black and shiny and your treasures gleamed like stars
bones from deep down in the fertile crescent

The arteries are clogging in the mainframe
there's too much information in the pipes
I saw the mess you left up in the east bedroom
A tiger's never gonna change its stripes
I guess, I guess
but Jesus, what a mess
One way in, no way out

The men were here to get your Belgian things
and I alone was here to see them do it
I wish you had a number where you are
it's hard with no one here to help me through it

I can see you in my sleep
playing the points for all you're worth
walking gingerly across
the bruised earth

ΔΔΔ

Even if the people you knew in your lost years emerge intact, there's a sense in which you never see them again. You can't. Either they metamorphose and leave their toxic carapace behind, or they don't make it. Rephrase that: Either you metamorphose and leave your toxic carapace behind, or you don't make it. Do it again: Either I metamorphosed and left my toxic carapace behind, or I didn't make it. This song works out as many versions of this sentence as I can tolerably stand.

25 - MOLE

I came to see you up there in intensive care
they had handcuffed you to your bed
there were tubes going into you and out from you
bright white gauze bandages at your head

I am a mole
sticking his head above the surface of the earth
I am a mole
sticking his head above the surface of the earth

And then they said "Lights out,"
and it was lights out
and they gave you your medication
I know what you want, you know what I want
Information. Information.

I am a mole
sticking his head above the surface of the earth
I am a mole
sticking his head above the surface of the earth

Out in the desert we'll have no worries
out in the desert, just you and me
I came to see you up there in intensive care
out in the desert we'll live carefree

I am a mole
sticking his head above the surface of the earth

I am a mole
sticking his head above the surface of the earth

ΔΔΔ

This is a song about the time I woke up handcuffed to a hospital bed because I'd become violent after they administered an opiate antagonist to save my life. The facts of its origins sort of render further explanation superfluous. I still have questions about whether I could actually have just slept it off, but I'm better now.

26 - HOME AGAIN GARDEN GROVE

Wipe down the windshields and roll down the windows
let's go where the jackals are breeding
wrap this bandanna around your head
don't let anyone see that you're bleeding

Fire up the scanner and keep your eyes on it
don't speak unless someone speaks to you
hands in your pockets and sun on your face
the warm love of God coursing through you

Home again, home again
Garden Grove, Garden Grove

I can remember when we were in high school
our dreams were like fugitive warlords
plotting triumphant returns to the city
keeping TEC-9s tucked under the floorboards

Now we are practical men of the world
we tether our dreams to the turf

and cruise down these alleys for honey to feed them
jellyfish riding the surf

Shoving our heads
straight into the guts of the stove
home again
Garden Grove, Garden Grove

ΔΔΔ

Never had a TEC-9, never rode with anybody who was bleeding from the head, never had a scanner: Much of this song is cinematic fantasy, except that the town where I've set it is a place whose alleys I spent a little time in once. Twice, three times. I hope the alleys are less active now, but, thank God, I wouldn't know.

27 - PIGS THAT RAN STRAIGHTAWAY INTO THE WATER, TRIUMPH OF

You're going to send me back to where I came from
please don't send me back to where I came from
let me go
where the white magnolias grow

You're gonna fit me for that orange jumpsuit
please don't fit me for that orange jumpsuit
let me ride
where the dragonflies glide

Yeah, but you're going to do
what you wanna do
No matter what I ask of you
You think you hold the high hand
I've got my doubts
I come from Chino where the asphalt sprouts

Big bus headed southeast from the courthouse
but I'm not headed southeast from the courthouse
let some mysterious chunk of space debris
puncture the roof and set me free

And even if I have to go to Claremont—
well, I guess I'll just have to go to Claremont
let me go
let me lie low

Yeah, but you're going to do
what you wanna do
No matter what I ask of you
And you send your dark messengers to tempt me
I come from Chino, so all your threats are empty

ΔΔΔ

However many dark corners you've lingered in, you want to get out of the album on an up note, right? Sometimes, anyway. There was dancing in the studio while we were tracking this one. Sometimes you come from Chino whether you actually come from Chino or not, and you need to dance about it.

28 - AGAINST POLLUTION

When I worked down at the liquor store
guy with a shotgun came raging through the place
muscled his way behind the counter
I shot him in the face

This morning I went down to the Catholic Church
because something just came over me

forty-five minutes in the pews
praying the rosary

When the last days come,
we shall see visions
more vivid than sunsets
more brighter than stars
we will recognize each other
and see ourselves for the first time
the way we really are

Decorative grating on my window
gets a little rustier every year
I don't know how the metal gets rusty
when it never rains here

A year or so I worked at a liquor store
and a guy came in
tried to kill me, so I shot him in the face
I would do it again. I would do it again.

When the last days come,
we shall see visions
more vivid than sunsets
more brighter than stars
we will recognize each other
and see ourselves for the first time
the way we really are

ΔΔΔ

It's a song about making peace with your choices; it's also a gloss on this passage from C. S. Lewis's *Mere Christianity*, a book I'd read about a decade earlier:

We see only the results which a man's choices make out of his raw material. But God does not judge him on the raw material at all, but on what he has done with it. Most of the man's psychological make-up is probably due to his body: when his body dies all that will fall off him, and the real central man, the thing that chose, that made the best or worst out of this material, will stand naked. All sorts of nice things which we thought our own, but which were really due to a good digestion, will fall off some of us: all sorts of nasty things which were due to complexes or bad health will fall off others. We shall then, for the first time, see every one as he really was. There will be surprises.

29 · ROSE QUARTER DRIFTING

Left home in a blur, arrived in the light
everything's going to be all right
came back to the place where it all flared out
just to check if the reservoir still bore the mark of the drought
up to 13th and Taylor, check my pulse
you weren't there, and neither was anybody else
stared down demons, came back breathing
no real point in ever leaving
Tracy, and Ivory, and Brad, and me, too
we will see some great miracle
before the night is through

Slipped in through the entrance, stood in the hall
left my fingerprints on the elevator wall
went down to my old room, stood outside it a minute
wondering if parts of me were still there in it
who can say? it won't be me
you are gone now, and I am free—
Wesley, and Quinn, and Devon, and you

we will all be fixed up
good as new

and I stared at the number 10 on my old apartment's door
that's one ghost that can't bite me any more

and someday we will all feel at home in our new skin
and someday we will all never be alone again
when the sun comes up and the night has passed
we shall all be healed
at last, at last, at last

ΔΔΔ

This song is unreleased, and was unfinished until several years after the album that shares a title with a line from its last verse. It's a true story. When I go back to Portland I go to the places where, by rights, I ought to have died, and commune with the memories of some people who did.

30 - COTTON

This song is for the rats
who hurled themselves into the ocean
when they saw that the explosives in the cargo hold
were just about to blow
this song is for the soil
that's toxic clear down to the bedrock
where no thing of consequence can grow
drop your seeds there—let them go
let them all go

This song is for the people
who tell their families that they're sorry

for things they can't and won't feel sorry for
and once there was a desk
and now it's in a storage locker somewhere
and this song is for the stickpins and the cottons
I left in the top drawer
let them all go
let them all go

I want to sing one for the cars
that are, right now, headed silent down the highway,
and it's dark, and there is nobody driving
and something has got to give
I saw you standing by the roadside
you didn't know that I was watching
now you know
let it all go
let it all go

ΔΔΔ

I'm the "you," of course, and probably also the "I," and probably also the people, and the rats, too. I will wonder about the eventual fate of the desk until the day I die, and I will never get an answer, but I kept my things there for the season of my life that eventually crystallizes in this song.

31 · PORCILE

When I wake up, I crawl on all fours to the kitchen
and I admire myself in a dish of water on the floor
these summer mornings—they can't last forever, you know
there's going to come a day, come a day
        when no one here can stand it any more:

The stench, and the overwhelming noise
Pull the truck up to the front
Drive 'em in, boys! Drive 'em in, boys! Drive 'em in

So when I hear them coming, I try to stand up, but I fall
down
and I smash my nose against the counter as I go—
blood splashes on the tiles
And I want to clean it up, but there is no time to clean it up, is
there?
Things are bad for us right now
Things are going to be bad for a while

Yeah, the stench, and the overwhelming noise
Pull the truck up to the door
Drive 'em in, boys! Drive 'em in, boys! Drive 'em in

ΔΔΔ

Porcile is a film by Pier Paolo Pasolini, a director I knew about through my stepfather and, later, through digging up his poetry in the Honnold Library and the Huntley Bookstore. "Porcile" means "pigsty" in Italian; the VHS edition of this film sports an arresting image from the film, that of a young man with a hog's head where his own head ought to be, his finger raised to his snout in the universal gesture for "shhh." I rented this VHS from Visart Video in Durham not long after moving to North Carolina from Iowa, and later bought the house in which I presently stand typing through a real estate agent who had, before it closed, owned Visart. It was not the first lyric I'd written about a man who believes he is a pig, but it's the only one anybody's ever heard.

All this detail matters because these details constitute a subsection of the circumstances that would lead to me writing *The Sunset Tree*, the album that came after *We Shall All Be Healed*. "Porcile" occurs in that fertile space.

JUNE

1 - 60% WOLF

Among the Douglas firs so tall and proud
in the shade of the forest with my head bowed
feeling something dying deep down at my core
sinking into the quiet warm forest floor
let's get our work boots on
and let's get down to business before the moment's gone
I am 60% wolf
60% wolf

And down there in the center where the light died away
all the greater little darknesses came on out to play
and graceful as an elk, I rose up to my feet
I had sugar in my blood. I was quivering in the heat
gaudeamus igitur
this is what they make you take the medication for
I am 60% wolf
60% wolf

ΔΔΔ

This song predates *The Sunset Tree* by several years; I wrote it in Colo, and stylistically it shows the manicured care I gave to smaller songs in those days—compact compound adjectival phrases, granular focus on a single moment in its narrator's imagined life. It's "not about anything." It's "just a story." It's a trifle, it's an outtake, it's something I didn't release. But if I were a dream analyst in charge of John Darnielle's file, I'd see *The Sunset Tree* predicted by this one. "Let's get our work boots on"—yes, let's, for when the moment really does arrive a few years from now.

2 · YOU OR YOUR MEMORY

I checked into a bargain-priced room on La Cienega
gazed out through the curtains at the parking lot
went down to the corner store just before nightfall in my bare feet
black tarry asphalt, soft and hot
and when I came back, I spread out my supplies
on the counter by the sink
looked myself right in the eyes:

St. Joseph's baby aspirin
Bartles & Jaymes
and you, or your memory

I ducked behind the drapes when I saw the moon begin to rise
and I gathered in my loose ends, and I switched off the light
and down there in the dark I could see the real truth about me
as clear as day; Lord, if I make it through tonight,

I will mend my ways,
and walk the straight path to the end of my days.
St. Joseph's baby aspirin
Bartles & Jaymes
and you, or your memory

ΔΔΔ

This is the first song on *The Sunset Tree*, our best-known album and the first one that will be mentioned in my obituary. Here in the month of June we'll be devoting ourselves almost exclusively to it, and to some songs ancillary to it—written during the same period, or connected otherwise to it. This song is written from the point of view of a guy who, just three years before, lived in the house where most of the rest of the album takes place. That guy is me, for better and worse.

3 - ABANDONING MY FATHER TALKING BLUES

It was 9 a.m. when the U-Haul came,
and I heard my mama call my name—
my dad taught English at Cal Poly S.L.O.,
he was at work that day. It was time to go. We were moving.

I was five years old and my sister was three;
I was wondering what'd likely become of me.
My sister looked sad, and I tried to be strong,
but it was hard just to get up and move along. We were moving.

But by five in the afternoon, we were gone,
And my stepfather welcomed us with open arms.
We strolled right through that apartment door,
I had never lived in an apartment before.
It was weird.

I'll probably never know what it was like that night
For my dad, but I'd wager it was pretty bad.
My sister and me, we stayed up late,
Talking in the dark and not feeling so great:

We were moving
out of our house
Into somebody else's place
Into a two-story
apartment complex
With a swing set and a sandbox in the middle of a parking lot
And a laundry room
with four glistening washing machines
And two dryers
Keep the home

fires
burning

ΔΔΔ

The studio version of this didn't make the album—we weren't really equipped as a band to play country music yet, and I was writing above my skill set, and Scott Solter was kind enough to say so plainly, directly. I'm grateful for that; learning one's limitations is the beginning of growth. Otherwise, to explain this song is just to restate the story it tells. When children get to any new place—an apartment, a motel, a duplex—they are excited; they usually can't immediately tell how their new home differs from the old one. We lived in the apartment for, I think, the remainder of first grade. It's a little blurry, and sometimes less blurry than you'd want.

4 - DANCE MUSIC

All right: I'm on Johnson Avenue in San Luis Obispo,
and I'm five years old, or six, maybe
and indications that there's something wrong with our new house
trip down the wire twice daily
I'm in the living room watching the Watergate hearings
while my stepfather yells at my mother
launches a glass across the room straight at her head,
and I dash upstairs to take cover

lean in close to my little record player on the floor
so this is what the volume knob's for
I listen to dance music
dance music

OK so look: I'm seventeen years old
and you're the last best thing I've got going

but then the special secret sickness starts to eat through
you
what am I supposed to do? No way of knowing,
so I follow you down your twisting alleyways
find a few cul-de-sacs all my own.
there's only one place this road ever ends up,
and I don't want to die alone

let me down, let me down gently.
When the police come to get me,
I'm listening to dance music
dance music

ΔΔΔ

My stepfather was dead. Peter and I were on tour. Long drives, bad sleep, constant grind. We had a radio session to do at Abbey Road's Maida Vale 4 for John Peel. We didn't have anything planned. I didn't want to just play songs from the album we were promoting. I had been writing lyrics in my notebook the whole tour; something in me was breaking open. There was a draft of this on a page, so I knocked it into shape and made up a quick chord progression; Peter and I worked it up and they rolled tape.

Four songs that made the album happened that way on that day; none of them had existed prior to that morning: April 8, 2004. Thanks for the opportunity, John Peel. These songs might never have made it out of the notebook otherwise.

5 - SONG FOR MY STEPFATHER

You have got that look in your eye
in the pinprick place where kindness goes to die
I'll be six years old next year
you erase me

You'll be sorry, you always feel sorry later on
when you come around to say so, I will be gone
and in my place, meet my letter-perfect body double
you erase me

and a few years later,
I set out on my own
learned to take the reins up all by myself
dug the spurs in clean down to the bone

But all that comes later
now there's only you and me
and the replica where my body used to be
go ahead and hit him—he feels no pain at all
you erase me
you erase me

ΔΔΔ

I didn't record it because I wasn't sure I wanted to share it with anybody; I played it a few times on tour in 2004 as a way of connecting myself to the story I hoped to tell on the album we were going to make. Songs can do so many things, can come from so many places; there isn't one way to make a song, there are no rules of what they are or aren't for. But, for me, they are usually not places for working through trauma like this. I sometimes play it anyway, in case some good might come from it, but to make it a regular occurrence would seem gauche to me. Even my harder stories manage to locate a little joy somewhere in them, something we can celebrate together. This, pointedly, does not.

6 - MAGPIE

Feed the kittens in the kitchen
set food out for the strays

try hard to do your best
the magpie will have his way

Fill your mouth with berries
by the full light of the moon
work all night if you have to
the magpie comes at noon

Shore up the crucifixes
above the archways and the doors
the magpie will come at midday
and you will go down on all fours

And when the cherry's white with blossoms
be ready and be brave
and remember what we had here
when there was something left to save

ΔΔΔ

Also written on the floor of Maida Vale 4—entirely written, I think, lyrics and music; some of the other stuff from that day was in draft when we reported for duty. Formally, this bears a debt to A. E. Housman, though there are metrical substitutions he would have fixed before publishing. The cherry, white with blossoms, is directly from "Loveliest of Trees," a Housman poem I've loved since my father gave me a copy of the collected poems in my early twenties. A yearning for my father is kind of the ghost note of *The Sunset Tree*.

7 · HAST THOU CONSIDERED THE TETRAPOD

You are sleeping off your demons
when I come home
spittle bubbling at your lip

fine white foam
I am young, and I am good
it's a hot southern California day
if I wake you up
there will be Hell to pay

and alone in my room,
I am the last of a lost civilization
but I vanish into the dark
and rise above my station
rise above my station

But I do wake you up, and when I do,
you blaze down the hall, and you scream
I'm in my room with the headphones on
deep in the dream chamber
and then I'm awake, and I'm guarding my face
hoping you don't break my stereo
because it's the one thing that I couldn't live without
and so I think about that, and then I sort of black out

held under these smothering waves
by your strong and thick-veined hand
but one of these days
I am going to wriggle up on dry land

ΔΔΔ

The headphones were Radio Shack—Nova 30s. Consumer grade over-the-ears. More than enough. I plugged them into a Marantz receiver that my father gave me after he upgraded his own rig. I would have been listening to prog-era Genesis, or to Ian Hunter, or possibly to Renaissance's *Live at Carnegie Hall*. Or *Hell Comes to Your House*. Or Lou Reed. There was a poster of Lou Reed on the wall by my bed; he was bathed in a purplish light, playing an acoustic guitar. There weren't so many pictures around of Lou Reed playing an acoustic guitar, but there was one on the wall of the bedroom where this song takes place.

8 - BROOM PEOPLE

'36 Hudson in the garage
all sorts of junk in the unattached spare room
dishes in the kitchen sink
new straw for the old broom
friends who don't have a clue
well-meaning teachers
but down in your arms, in your arms
I am a wild creature

Floor three-foot-high with newspapers
white carpet thick with pet hair
half-eaten gallons of ice cream in the freezer
fresh fuel for the sodium flares
I write down good reasons to freeze to death
in my spiral ring notebook
but in the long tresses of your hair
I am a babbling brook

ΔΔΔ

Peter Hughes grew up in Chino, in a house very different from my own; this, for me, makes his work on this song all the more remarkable. When he drops to the tonic on the rising high note with which I conclude the song, he pedals triplets that triumphantly express the song's meaning: the memory of the sheer joy of having located, in a person who cared about me and who saw my circumstances more clearly than I did, a life raft. Not everybody gets a first serious girl- or boyfriend who rises to the occasion, but during this time of my life, when my luck wasn't often great, I have to say—and had to say, here, in song—I lucked out.

9 - SCAVENGER BABIES

Wake up all the birds of prey
dig your tools out from the clay
seal the exits of your room
watch the cactus flowers bloom

And send my regards to the boys down on the corner
send my regards to the boys down on the corner

Build a house from sticks and mud
listen to the poison singing in your blood
pull yourself a tall cool drink
carve your initials in the bathroom sink

And send my regards to the boys down on the corner
send my regards to the boys down on the corner

The city of Norwalk, in my dreams,
rises like Atlantis from a watery grave
burn the things you have to burn
save all the people you're supposed to save

and send my belongings to the drop box in Tijuana
and send my regards to the boys down on the corner

ΔΔΔ

This B-side predates all the stuff on *The Sunset Tree* but is something of a study for the work I didn't yet know lay ahead: The corner boys are old friends from Portland, most of them now dead. The cactus flowers bloomed once in my Norwalk room years after all that but a few different years before this. It's a codex of images, in the old style, but the images connect to specific points both in my life and in the map of the world by which my consciousness navigates its way through space and experience. Bands should make a practice of giving their better songs to the B-side, and I'm glad I did so here; B-sides get to cherish a little obscurity. "Build a house from sticks and mud / listen to the poison singing in your blood" is as close to giving advice on writing as I ever expect to come.

10 - DILAUDID

The reception's gotten fuzzy
the delicate balance has shifted
put on your gloves and your topcoat
let's pretend the fog has lifted

now you see me
now you don't
now you say you love me
pretty soon you won't

If we get our full three score and ten
we won't pass this way again,
so kiss me with your mouth open
turn the tires toward the street
and stay sweet

All the chickens come on home to roost
black bodies blotting out the sky
you know it breaks my heart in half
when I see them trying to fly

Because you just can't do
things your body wasn't meant to
hike up your fishnets
I know you

If we live to see the other side of this
I will remember your kiss
so do it with your mouth open
and take your foot off of the brake
for Christ's sake

ΔΔΔ

This song is three years after "Broom People." Three years is a long time when you're young, no matter what else you may have going on in your life. When I was seventeen, the word was that if you were going through withdrawal and couldn't score, Dilaudid was one of the better replacement meals available. A friend and I, in this song, share this word as if it held the secret to life itself.

11 - CIGARETTES

Our beat-up little family has taken on water
there's a leak in the bottom of the boat
I've taken up smoking—here's hoping
the poison eats holes in my throat

The past is dead, and the present is murky
but the future's becoming real clear
I am a freshman in high school
I will be dead by this time next year,

and I don't love Jesus
I don't love Jesus

I don't love Jesus
Jesus doesn't love me

My heart's a swamp by a nuclear reactor
I give off a phosphorescent glow
my friends all tell me I've got to get out of here
where is there for me to go?

Things are bad, and it's worth some reflection
to think how much worse they might get
my stepfather
isn't quite done with me yet
get me out of here, get me out of here
give me a cigarette

I don't love Jesus
I don't love Jesus
I don't love Jesus
Jesus doesn't love me

ΔΔΔ

There is no music to this one. It was written as a lyric and I read it to a couple of audiences while we were touring during the span of time that led us to Prairie Sun studios in Cotati, California, where we'd make *The Sunset Tree*. The lyrics that didn't make the album share a hopeless quality, I think, and that's certainly true here.

12 - FROM TG&Y

Out behind the Safeway
just before the flood
huffed some cans of spray paint
and began to vomit blood

one more night in this town
is going to break me, I just know
hang on to your dreams
'til someone makes you let them go

Stumbled on down Indian Hill
tail between my legs
sick taste in my mouth,
Folger's crystals and hard-boiled eggs
if I can't run away tonight,
I don't know what I'll do
hang on to your dreams
'til someone beats them out of you

Do what you have to do
go where you have to go
when the time comes to loosen up your grip,
you'll know

I called my friend in New York,
three thousand miles away
halfway through her metamorphosis
nothing I could say
hoard my small resentments
like rare and priceless gems
hang on to your dreams
until there's nothing left of them

ΔΔΔ

During my time in Portland, when my father could infer by my silence that things were not well with me, I got a letter from a guy who, for one summer and maybe two, had been a boarder at my dad's house. He was a friend of the family through one of Dad's colleagues and had been trying to establish himself in the world; but he was young, and reveling in it. He was writing me from jail: his third drunk driving arrest. I'd known him when I was thirteen or fourteen. I was nineteen now. I'm reasonably certain that my father asked him to write me—that he asked him, as a favor, to write and caution me about the road I was on. But I had already been on that road for three years. I liked the scenery. This song sketches some of that scenery. People who aren't in trouble would be less attracted to such views, but I was in trouble.

13 · RESCUE BREATHING

Soothing sound of traffic from the freeway
bright white Pomona moon
that triple zero that we got in Costa Mesa
turning golden as a sunrise on the spoon

it was the warmest feeling in the world
when the ghost rose in my throat
it matched the sweetest song you'd ever heard
note for note

you came down to meet me on the floor
splashing that cold water on my head
holding my eyelids open with your thumbs
bringing me back from the dead

it was the warmest feeling in the world
a crystal-clear signal ringing from the station
there was no tenderness, no goodnight kiss
just mouth-to-mouth resuscitation

I had a blanket wrapped around my shoulders
you had a dream of all the oceans in your eyes

no thing on earth could quite nail our coffin shut
every time that we went under, we would rise

it was the warmest feeling in the world
and you were the warmest thing to walk its surface
easing me   painlessly
all the way down to the furnace

ΔΔΔ

I found this in a notebook while I was planning out and rehearsing for a January 2020 solo stand at San Francisco's Swedish American Hall. As with "Cigarettes" and "Came Home Late" (June 27), it sort of stunned me; here was something from ten or more years earlier, from before I had children. When I wrote it, it was from an earlier life; when I unearthed it, it was from a *previous* life. It is a true story about an overdose at which I was present, except that I've flipped the "I" and "you," which is something I do a lot. We live in an indiscreet age. One has to row against the tide here and there.

14 - YOU WERE COOL

This is a song with the same four chords I use most of the time
when I've got something on my mind,
and I don't want to squander the moment
trying to come up with a better way to say what I want to say.

People were mean to you,
but I always thought you were cool
clicking down the concrete hallways
in your spiked heels
back in high school.

It's good to be young, but let's not kid ourselves,
it's better to pass on through those years and come out the other side
with our hearts still beating,
having stared down demons and come back breathing.

People were mean to you,
but I always thought you were cool
clicking down the concrete hallways
in your spiked heels
back in high school.

You deserved better than you got
someone's got to say it sometime because it's true.
People should have told you you were awesome
instead of taking advantage of you.

I hope you love your life now
like I love mine;
I hope the painful memories only flex their power over you
a little of the time.
We held on to hope of better days coming,
and, when we did, we were right.
I hope the people who did you wrong have trouble sleeping at night.

People were mean to you,
but I always thought you were cool
clicking down the concrete hallways
in your spiked heels
back in high school.

ΔΔΔ

The first performance of this was partially improvised from some notes I had, and so of course nobody knew the song, and its emergence that night felt potent. I have never recorded it in the studio because that moment of communion felt like part of the song itself. It's for a girl I knew in high school: a friend then and a friend now, a strong person and a powerful witness for whose presence in my life I'm deeply grateful. I'm not sure that further analysis of this song is really possible: It's as plain-spoken as I've really ever been.

15 - THIS YEAR

I broke free on a Saturday morning
I put the pedal to the floor
Headed north on Mills Avenue
And listened to the engine roar

My broken house behind me and good things ahead
A girl named Cathy wants a little of my time
Six cylinders underneath the hood crashing and kicking
Aha, listen to the engine whine

I am going to make it through this year if it kills me
I am going to make it through this year if it kills me

I played video games in a drunken haze
I was seventeen years young
hurt my knuckles punching the machines
the taste of scotch rich on my tongue

And then Cathy showed up, and we hung out,
trading swigs from the bottle, all bitter and clean
locking eyes, holding hands
twin high-maintenance machines

I am going to make it through this year if it kills me
I am going to make it through this year if it kills me

I drove home in the California dusk
I could feel the alcohol inside of me hum
pictured the look on my stepfather's face
ready for the bad things to come

I downshifted as I pulled into the driveway
the motor screaming out stuck in second gear
the scene ends badly, as you might imagine
in a cavalcade of anger and fear—
there will be feasting and dancing in Jerusalem next year

I am going to make it through this year if it kills me.
I am going to make it through this year if it kills me.

ΔΔΔ

My favorite story about this song is that I considered it unfinished—I like choruses with rhyme lines, I'm never aiming for an anthem. I emailed it to Peter while I was working toward the album session—hot off the presses, so to speak—and mentioned to him that I expected to revise the chorus, give it a little more body. Peter, choosing his words carefully so as not to elicit a defensive response, said that I could do as I pleased, but it seemed good to him the way it was, and that I might consider just letting it stay that way. I've said this before, but thanks, bud.

16 - UP THE WOLVES

There's bound to be a ghost at the back of your
  closet
no matter where you live

there'll always be a few things, maybe several things
that you're gonna find really difficult to forgive

There's gonna come a day when you feel better
you will rise up free and easy on that day
and float from branch to branch, lighter than the air
just when that day is coming, who can say? who can say?

Our mother has been absent
ever since we founded Rome
but there's gonna be a party when the wolf comes home

We're gonna commandeer the local airwaves
to tell the neighbors what's been going on
and they will shake their heads, and wag their bony fingers
in all the wrong directions, but by daybreak we'll be gone

I'm gonna get myself in fighting trim
scope out every angle of unfair advantage
I'm gonna bribe the officials, I'm gonna kill all the judges
it's gonna take you people years to recover from all of the damage

Our mother has been absent
ever since we founded Rome
but there's gonna be a party when the wolf comes home

ΔΔΔ

I resist writing "going to" as "gonna"—it feels like an affectation—but the "going to"s here are decidedly, emphatically "gonna"s. As to the song, I tracked it in the concrete room Tom Waits once favored at Prairie Sun. I was isolated in there while the band played live in the adjacent studio—playing in isolation didn't fit the energy I wanted, so I asked Mooka, the studio owner, to come sit with me while I played vocals and guitar live together. He sat directly facing me, listening thoughtfully to a song nobody outside of camp had ever heard before. An indelible memory for me of a session we could not have known would become such a part of us in the years ahead.

17 - PSEUDOTHYRUM SONG

Why do you treat me this way?
and why do you try so hard
to break my spirit?
I think someone was mean to you
when you were little, that's what I think.
I think someone was mean to you.

Why do you cling to such petty points of contention?
And why can't you allow me
one or two small victories, now and then?
I think someone was mean to you
when you didn't deserve it, that's what I think.
I think someone was mean to you.

But I—I am not that guy,
can you get that straight?
I am a completely different person
from the one you have in mind.

Why do you stand by the things you say
long after you don't mean to hurt anybody any more?
I think someone was mean to you
for a long, long time, that's what I think.
I think someone was mean to you.

ΔΔΔ

I wrote this in 1999; when I sing it, it surprises me, because it's really quite levelheaded. I'm proud of my work and think it's good, but "levelheaded" is not a term I'd usually attach to it. This song applies to many relationships, it's an observable phenomenon, but of course I was thinking partly of my stepfather—how he loved to argue until the argument stopped being fun for anybody. How he could not help himself. People like this didn't get that way on their own. In the environments that shaped them, they learned. This is, to understate the case by rather a lot, a sad thing, and this is a sad song.

18 - OLYMPIC AUDITORIUM NIACIN BLAST

we hit the freeway a little past five
took the ten to Grand Avenue
dined like kings down the street at the Pantry
we were our own special tag team, me and you

found our seat on the north side of the ring
fifteen rows up
we were the only two guys in the building
drinking hot coffee from Styrofoam cups

and when the undercard got underway
you leaned over and gave me the play-by-play

and the night rolled in deep, and the heat rose
sky cyc lights and Roscolux gels, red and blue
the bad guys beat up on the good guys
three hours on a school night, just us two

when we come through the last of the storm
and the time to remember's upon us

it's easy to play up the bad times
but we ought to be honest

you were an evil man
much of the time
but in our best hours,
we were partners in crime

ΔΔΔ

This was a completed song, or nearly so; the chords to the verses are on the top of the page in the notebook. I consider it a study for "Pale Green Things" (June 19), whose position as the last song on *The Sunset Tree* holds weight; it is the last word by design. Lots of people who grew up like I did struggle when explaining to others that abusive households aren't haunted houses. They're complex systems of relation. When my stepfather wasn't terrorizing his family, he was often teaching me things, laughing with me, and educating me in values I still hold to this day. This is an important thing for me to understand, and had no place on an album in which I spoke freely, for the first time, about the bad times, in the hopes that my own clarity might be a little contagious somewhere down the line.

19 · PALE GREEN THINGS

Got up before dawn
went down to the racetrack
riding with the windows down
shortly after your first heart attack

We parked behind the paddock
cracking asphalt underfoot
and coming up through the cracks,
pale green things, pale green things

We watched the horses run their workouts
you held your stopwatch in your left hand
and a racing form beneath your arm
casting your gaze way out to no man's land

Sometimes I'll meet you out there,
lonely and frightened
flicking my tongue out at the wet leaves
pale green things, pale green things

My sister called at 3 a.m.
just last December
and she told me how you'd died at last, at last
and that morning at the racetrack was one thing I
  remembered

and I turned it over in my mind
like a living Chinese finger-trap
seaweed and Indiana sawgrass
Pale green things, pale green things

ΔΔΔ

I don't remember writing it. It takes place a couple of years after the rest of *The Sunset Tree*. My stepfather was trying to reestablish a connection to the family he'd lost. I did not want to deny him this. We were never going to reach any place of full healing and restoration; in an important sense, there had never been something whole that might have been restored. There is more to say about all this than I could say in song or in prose, but this one allows me to place my hand against something dense and alive, and to hold my hand against it while I for a moment am able to partially sound its depths.

20 · THE DAY THE ALIENS CAME

I will wake up at 6 a.m. again
and I will find my way to the front door
like a soldier crawling through the smoking carnage
smoldering bodies at my feet
I'd love to stick around, but I've got someone to meet
and I will put my best foot forward
and I'll thank God I made it out of there
on the day when
my new friends come

I will present myself in my nice white tuxedo jacket
and I will look out at the day through my dark sunglasses
and take in the scene:
the house behind me, and the people in it
will all go up like steam in just a minute
there's gonna be a redefining of some borders
and I will receive my orders
on the day
when my new friends come

The rooftops and the sidewalks
will all melt like plastic
And O friends—old friends—dear friends,
I'm gonna look fantastic

There won't be any reason left to cry
because there won't be any people left to cry for
my memory's going to vaporize itself
and my Italian shoes, well, they will be to die for
I believe I can fly
why don't you look up at me and wave goodbye

on the day
when my new friends come

ΔΔΔ

Life being what it is,
we all dream of revenge.
—KAKI KING, "Life Being What It Is"

21 - WHON

The garbage man is never going to come
the cans out at the curb will bloat and stink
the rot will work its way through cracks in the foundation
the water will go stagnant in the sink
and you, you will know
where it is that memories go

The migratory birds will not come back
the charms that summer held will all turn sour
and from the treetops when the wind stops
sweet blossoms will rain down and you will stand beneath the shower
and it will be so clear
you will never quite escape last year

The wind will blow or else it won't
sometimes you just move on and sometimes you just don't
you think the matter through, you try hard not to think
the water all goes stagnant in the kitchen sink
and you will know, and I will too
what it was I might have left to you

ΔΔΔ

The notebook remnant predates *The Sunset Tree* by several years; when I stumbled across it, the couplet "and it will be so clear / you will never quite escape last year" sounded like something with its eye on the future. Given that it was neither released nor, to the best of my knowledge, ever played live, it's surprising how well I remember the melody, and where the changes are. But what I remember wrong, every time, is the last line. In my mind, it's "meant." On the page, it's "left." These are two very different words—even more different in this context! Something more about this song's prophetic half existence rests in this phenomenon.

22 - (UNTITLED)

you in your white shirt
head full of dreams
I got my eye on you
deep in the crossbeams
me and my long hair
poised at the door
butcher knife in my fist
shadow stretching across the floor

all dead, all dead, all dead, all dead

sirens and children
sing in the street
the sky's looking overcast
I turn up the heat
our habits possess us
they've taken the reins

I'm coming in with a baseball bat
to knock out your brains

all dead, all dead, all dead, all dead

and inside, in your bedroom
you've gotten undressed
all of the young waves
ready to crest
everyone's waiting
there's nowhere to go
my big plans like seaweed
rushing back through the undertow

all dead, all dead, all dead, all dead

ΔΔΔ

I chose not to record, nor even title, the song I wrote about one of several nights I spent doing the math in my head about how things would play out if I tried to kill my stepfather in his sleep. It is a vivid and unpleasant memory. Upper right on the page it says "Cars song in C," so the idea was that it be snappy and mid-tempo. The next song in the same notebook is "This Year."

23 - NEW LOVERS REGGAE

I bite my lower lip
dig my nails into my hand
clench my fist
as hard as I can
and shut my eyes
real tight

paring knife in my pocket
safely tucked away
wait til everyone's asleep
make sure everything's OK
hop through the window
tunnel toward the light
and if I starve to death, well, that may be
but you all have seen the last of me
and that's enough
and that's enough
and that's enough

window open wide
I sneak a cigarette
I may get a-
way with this yet
I keep cool
breathe deep
I listen to the noises
out in the hall
ear pressed up
against the wall
until the whole house drifts off to sleep

my whole family's crazy
and I
am fourteen years old
ready to die

ΔΔΔ

This is an unfinished draft, transcribed here verbatim, from the notebook that contains the original drafts for "Up the Wolves," "You or

Your Memory," "Song for Dennis Brown," and "Lions Teeth." It's a mess; I'm telling a story and trusting myself to tighten the prosody later. Because I don't date my notebooks, I can't tell you whether this pre- or post-dates "Came Home Late" (June 27). If the former, it means I remembered this line while writing a song that felt like a good home for it. If the latter, it means I knew I wasn't going to sing "Came Home Late" to anybody, but wanted to save at least this one line. Drafts are organ donors, most of the time. This one had a couple of functioning kidneys. But in the end its real use was to get me thinking about Dennis Brown.

24 - DESIGN YOUR OWN CONTAINER GARDEN

I took to the highway,
went out to Pico-Crenshaw
old friends, old friends
I took to the highway,
the highway took to me
like a second skin
rolled around in the evening,
circling like a buzzard
trouble in mind
excavating
the space we left behind

Yes I took trinkets with me,
left them by the crater
"Here, ghosts, old ghosts"
smelled all the chlorine,
I took the low road
where the light
was just right
crawled around in the glowing, all-embracing wreckage

sunburned and snow-blind
excavating
the space we left behind

ΔΔΔ

I wrote this sometime in the *Tallahassee* span of time, and my home recording of it served as a B-side for the first single on our new label, 4AD. It is not part of the *Tallahassee* cycle. It's a study for "You or Your Memory"; the bargain-priced room on La Cienega was actually in the Pico-Crenshaw district (and was not, truth be told, on La Cienega at all). I was working weekends in Pico-Crenshaw and staying at a motel overnight so as not to tax my car's engine. Time alone in a motel, as we'll see in July, can take you some places when the elements align.

25 · SONG FOR DENNIS BROWN

On the day that Dennis Brown's lung collapsed,
spring rain was misting down on Kingston;
and down by the harbor, local cops
had intercepted an inbound shipment;
And for a while there it was chaos,
as they handcuffed and then roughed up some sailors.
On the day my lung collapses,
it's not going to be much different.

On the day that Dennis Brown's habits caught up with him,
schoolchildren sang in choirs;
and out behind the Chinese restaurants,
guys were jumping into Dumpsters
and the stench was overbearing,
but they were past the point of caring.
On the day my habits catch up with me
I'll be down among the jumpers.

And when the birds come home in spring,
we will fill them full of buckshot;
and jets of contaminated blood
will cloud the rivers and the lakes.
It took all the coke in town
to bring down Dennis Brown.
On the day my lung collapses,
we'll see just how much it takes.

ΔΔΔ

The most metaphorical song on *The Sunset Tree* is also one of my favorites; formally it's of a piece with "The Last Day of Jimi Hendrix's Life," but turning inward and with a lot more road behind me. It's one of three songs on the album whose vantage point is from a little farther down the line; of those three, this one is nearest to what I'll hesitantly call the action, maybe two years after getting out of the house. Loose internal ends were fraying within me just as anybody might have predicted, with predictable, if spectacular, results.

26 · TYLER LAMBERT'S GRAVE

Steal west across the country
under moonlight soft and wet
and let the dead of night
hide you from things you can't forget
spend daylight in dark tunnels
where the demons rave
one day closer every day
to Tyler Lambert's grave

Shoplift when you have to
keep your visor low
and if your hunger shames you,

never let them know
feel your sadness lifting
ride it like a wave
that sets you gently down beside
Tyler Lambert's grave

Fall into a pattern
never get unstuck
anyone who can't relate
should thank God for his luck

Young man in a yellow tie
hair gel in his hair
no context for the picture
just kind of standing there
try to step outside the shadow
of your great catastrophe
dream all night of freedom
never wake up free

ΔΔΔ

Tyler Lambert was Dana Plato's son (see February 17); Plato struggled with addiction from an early age, like many child entertainers. She was twenty years old when she became a mother. She lost custody of her son, Tyler, in divorce proceedings, when he was six; nine hard years down the line, in her Winnebago RV parked outside her manager's mother's house, she died of an overdose. Tyler was fourteen. A decade on he took his own life with a shotgun. "These past ten years have been pure Hell," his grandmother told *People* magazine. This is a sad story of people trying without success to break free from the past, of compulsions and apparitions. It is a song about the desperate feeling you get when you have run out of hopeful synonyms for "try."

27 - CAME HOME LATE

munitions-grade plutonium dealer
came through town in his eighteen-wheeler
I crawled out from underneath
by the skin of my chipped front teeth
College Avenue near first
where the demons did their worst
when the sun shines through the glaze
I remember awful days
        poison candy puff cream cloud
        all the good air leaking out

tortured stucco architecture   of the
uncompleted parking structure
got ready for my burst of glory
and climbed up to the second story
college avenue near first
call the coroner, book the hearse
my whole God damned family was crazy and i
was just 14, and ready to die
        strike while the iron's still nice and hot:
        you people can stay here but I will NOT

crawled up on the railing there
ran my hand through my long brown hair
looked down at the railroad track
felt the cool wind on my neck
cloudy poison candy cream
had a girlfriend named Marci Dehm
she was going to be mad as hell
when they scraped my brains up from the stairwell
looked down maybe a minute too long:
who's strong today, and who's not so strong?

train crossing tolling: ding-dong bell
back to the castle where the monsters dwell

ΔΔΔ

Written in the dressing room of a club in Amsterdam during the *We Shall All Be Healed* tour that led to the Peel Session at Abbey Road. I was, by the time of its writing, deep within myself: grieving, I say now, not having said so about that time prior to this very moment but knowing, now, that it's the right word. All capitalization and line-spacing preserved as nearly as possible from the handwritten draft. I wrote music for it in that dressing room, too, and I can still remember the verses, but this is too private to take it further, and I record it here only to give the *Sunset Tree* songs their proper context. It is a true story about a day when I wanted to kill myself and could not. Later that day I put my fist through the window of my bedroom. I was just a kid, I know now, but I could not imagine, on that day, ever getting any older.

28 - ATTENTION ALL PICKPOCKETS

In comes you:
not the same person I knew
looking roughly the same
but something hungry getting restless in your brain

So there I go
not the same person that you used to know
peeking through
the fish-eye lens at you

And the cornet blows
where the oleander grows
and us two:
not the same people that our old friends knew

And so down the street you head,
in the high summer heat
white long-sleeved Oxford
pushed up to just before your elbows

Black pumps, and a medium-length black skirt
eating a path through the dark damp earth
I hope they've got
plenty of money where you're going

And the cornet blows
where the oleander grows
And us two:
not the same people that our old friends knew

ΔΔΔ

Astrid Lindgren, the author of *Pippi Longstocking*, once gave a reading at the library where my mother worked; when it came time for questions, the children all asked variants of the same question. Is Pippi real? Is Tommy real? Is Annika real? Is Villa Villekulla real? "Oh, yes," Lindgren replied to each question with grandmotherly patience. "Pippi is real, Tommy and Annika are real." In the spirit of that legendary villa, so are the black pumps, and the long-sleeved Oxford, and above all the need for some money to keep the transformation engine humming on its way to where it's headed.

29 · KEEPING HOUSE

You clean out your junk drawer
you mop up some blood
while the first of the new creatures
rises from the mud
cursing the moment

that saw him draw breath
the ghost on your doorstep
is starving to death

You spray down the windows
you wipe them all clean
and you douse your old clothing
with fresh gasoline
and the ghost on your doorstep
is soaked wet with rain
and he clutches his stomach
and howls at the pain

And you can stay busy all day;
he's never going away

So let all the lights blaze
keep your heart light
play really loud music
all hours of the night
and when you set the table,
set it for two
the ghost on your doorstep has to eat,
same as you, same as you

ΔΔΔ

We can have our disagreements about the existence and nature of ghosts but on one question I will give no ground, ever: They feel pain. Even in their insubstantial bodies they experience pain like what they felt while still corporeal. If they don't eat, they get pangs. What they eat and how they eat it, about this we can all have our little opinions. But it hurts to be a ghost. That is why they try to make themselves known. So you'll notice.

30 - GOING INVISIBLE

When I rose from a heavy sleep
I was stepping lightly
and I put on my grey suit
and the matching fedora
ready to face the world
fairly nearly ready
came down the hallway
looked in the mirror

I'm going to break something
I'm going to break something today
and sweep all the pieces away

And I stood before the mirror then
like I was waiting for a phone call
squinting like a lost traveler in a thick fog
but nothing clear came into view
except for you
just off in the distant horizon
something hidden in your hand

I'm going to break something
I'm going to break something today
and sweep all the pieces away

And so I pulled my hat brim
down over my eyes
and preened and posed and tried
my new self on for size

Then I was out the door
in the faint winter sunlight

just a number in the crowd
Smiling at everyone
ah, but who'd smile back
at a face like that?

I'm going to break something
I'm going to break something today
and sweep all the pieces away

ΔΔΔ

This is the one that got away, one of my favorites of the *Get Lonely* bunch. We did not manage to better the demo in the studio. That's the yardstick: Studio version beats the demo or the song doesn't make the record. At some point I shared that demo online; had I not done so on the day I did that, it'd be lost forever, most likely, since the laptop from which I shared the demo is now dead. Those studio sessions still exist, though; they're on two-inch reels in my dark basement, magnetic particles slowly shedding, seeking their destiny. Going away. Going invisible.

JULY

1 - OX BAKER TRIUMPHANT

I will rise from the swamp
where they dumped my private plane
I'll be clutching a life preserver
in my teeth
and I will find the highway
and I will flag down a truck
worry lines on my forehead
big smile underneath

And when I come back to town
I'm going to cast my burden down
a little worse for wear
practically walking on air

I will thank my ride
and crawl my way back inside
to the guts of the building, where my enemies
hide in the dark like roaches
and I will signal the camera crew
and everyone will do what he's been trained how to do
sweat dripping from my face
as my moment approaches

click your heels, count to three
I bet you never expected me
a little worse for wear
practically walking on air

ΔΔΔ

I made a bunch of hand-drawn little booklets while I was writing *We Shall All Be Healed*—they were like homemade comic books, sort of, and they were called *Chavo Guerrero Is Champion of the World*. Doing these and thinking about the Olympic Auditorium while writing *The Sunset Tree* got me meditating about pro wrestling, which I'd been absolutely marked out for when I was eleven and twelve years old. Ox Baker came to LA once and said he was going to kill Chavo Guerrero. I believed him then and I believe him now. Rest easy, Ox. Your ability to scare the shit out of me was without any earthly peer.

2 - IF YOU SEE LIGHT

When the villagers come to my door,
I will hide underneath the table in the dining room,
knees drawn up to my chest.

When the villagers come to my door,
I will breathe shallow breaths from high up in my stomach:
ah ah ah ah ah ah ah

waiting for the front door to splinter
waiting all winter

When the villagers come to my door,
I'll be all tucked away with my face to the floor
and my eyes closed.

And no one knows how to keep secrets round here,
they tell everyone everything, soon as they know
and then where is there left for poor sinners to go?

waiting for the front door to splinter
waiting all winter

ΔΔΔ

I don't, *ever*, sit down and say: "What am I doing next?"—I just work; that is my process, to just start writing and see where it goes. *The Sunset Tree* was considerably more successful than anybody expected, I think it's fair to say. I am proud that my natural impulse was to follow up with an album that digs itself a dark tunnel underground and builds a little bunker inside it. The songs on *Get Lonely* are closer to the poems-set-to-music standard I'd aspired to early on, but with the advantage of more mileage on the tires.

3 - MAYBE SPROUT WINGS

A bad dream shook me in my sleep
and I woke up sweating
ran through the dark to the shower
already forgetting

Try to think good thoughts
trying to find my way clear
let the room fill with steam
traced pictures on the mirror:

ghosts, and clouds, and nameless things
squint your eyes and hope real hard
maybe sprout wings

I clawed my way to the living room window
stood there in the cold
the last bits of my dream like figures in the distance
hard to hold

I thought of old friends, the ones who'd gone missing
said all their names three times
phantoms in the early dark
canaries in the mines

ghosts, and clouds, and nameless things
squint your eyes and hope real hard
maybe sprout wings

ΔΔΔ

The canary in the mine saves you from what killed the canary when you released it into the mine, but you also don't get to see the inside of the mine. That is the trade-off.

4 - HALF DEAD

It was raining outside,
so I cleaned house today
spent half of the morning
throwing old things away

Try not to get caught up
try to think like a machine
focus in on the task
try not to think about what it means

Can't get you
out of my head
lost without you
half dead

Took my spot at the window
looked out at the road

dots and dashes of traffic
like a message in code

And whole boxes of memories
wrapped up at the curb
I sang songs to myself
that didn't have any words

Can't get you
out of my head
lost without you
half dead

Stole out to the backyard late last night
pine trees frozen in the silvery moonlight
rising like giants from the cold earth
what are the years we gave each other ever going to be worth?

Can't get you
out of my head
lost without you
half dead

ΔΔΔ

Anybody who knows me spots that this is pure fiction from its first line, which, if it were me speaking, would begin "It was raining outside / so I complained about that and then played video games all day," but this is the advantage to storytelling instead of self-disclosure: Instead of repeating things you already know about yourself, you end up with a line like "what are the years we gave each other ever going to be worth?" I will take this bargain every time.

5 - GET LONELY

I will rise up early
and dress myself up nice
and I will leave the house
and check the deadlock twice

and I will find a crowd
and blend in for a minute
and I will try to find
a little comfort in it

and I will get lonely, and gasp for air
and send your name up from my lips
like a signal flare

and I will go downtown
stand in the shadows of the buildings
trying to stay strong,
spirit willing

and I will come back home
maybe call some friends
maybe paint some pictures
it all depends

and I will get lonely, and gasp for air
and look up at the high windows,
and see your face up there

ΔΔΔ

I always picture, in my mind, the front door of the house in which I wrote this song, and myself dead bolting it, even though I was never lonely in that house once—it was a house of love and shared growth and shared struggle and change, all the things that loneliness is not. And so I think, when I sing it: This is the mark loneliness leaves on you, to warn you against finding anything romantic in it. Once known, forever remembered.

6 · MOON OVER GOLDSBORO

I went down to the gas station
for no particular reason
heard the screams from the high school
it's football season

Empty lot the station faces
will probably be there forever
I climbed over the four-foot fence
I was trying to sever the tether

Moon in the sky
cold as a stone
spend each night in your arms
always wake up alone

I lay down in the weeds
it was a real cold night
I was happy 'til the overnight attendant
switched on the floodlight

Walking home, I was talking to you under my breath
saying things I would never say directly
I heard a siren on the highway up ahead
kind of wished they'd come and get me

Frost on the sidewalk
white as a bone

try to get close to you again
always wake up alone

And as I was crossing our doorstep,
I hesitated just a moment there
remembered the day we'd moved into our small house
'til the vision got too vivid to bear

You were almost asleep,
halfway undressed
I lay right down next to you
held your head against my chest

And a guy with any kind of courage
would maybe stop to think the matter through
maybe hold you still and raise the question
instead of blindly holding on to you

But we crank up the heat,
and you giggle and moan
spend all night in the company of ghosts
always wake up alone

ΔΔΔ

I never did anything like this and I don't smoke any more, but at the same time, the guy who goes down to the gas station to buy smokes on a winter night and then lies down in a vacant lot he had to climb a fence to get into, that guy is me in every actually important way; if you want to find me in physical space then you have to get the coordinates, but if you want to locate me spiritually you just have to look for the guy on his back in the vacant lot by the gas station. In this sense the song is pure autobiography, but in no other sense.

7 - WOKE UP NEW

On the morning when I woke up without you for the first time,
I felt free, and I felt lonely, and I felt scared
and I began to talk to myself almost immediately
Not being used to being the only person there

The first time I made coffee for just myself, I made too much of it.
but I drank it all, just 'cause you hate it when I let things go to waste
and I wandered through the house like a little boy lost at the mall,
and an astronaut could've seen the hunger in my eyes from space

And I sang:
Oh, what do I do?
what do I do?
what do I do?
what do I do without you?

On the morning when I woke up without you for the first time,
I was cold, so I put on a sweater and I turned up the heat
And the walls began to close in, and I felt so sad and frightened
I practically ran from the living room out into the street

And the wind began to blow, and all the trees began to bend,
and the world, in its cold way, started coming alive
and I stood there like a businessman waiting for the train
and I got ready for the future to arrive

And I sang:
Oh, what do I do?
what do I do?
what do I do?
what do I do without you?

ΔΔΔ

I have this theory about songs—that the best ones live in the air but die on the page: or, if they don't die, have a different life on the page, one that can only be fully realized in the air. My theory is often wrong. "Get Lonely," for example, is really its own man on the page: different but not less than its fully clothed self, and in some ways more; its individual phrases have more air to breathe when they're not bound by the constraints of the song's running time. But "Woke Up New" is the case for the prosecution. It exists precisely within the span of its allocated length. The breaths that divide its phrases are part of it, but the page can't preserve this. I love this about songs so, so much—they alone can mark the reaches of the printed page as finite, they alone can take it a step further.

8 - SONG FOR LONELY GIANTS

No one washed behind my ears—high in the trees, alone for years. Practicing my solitary scales 'til they rise like balloons, and watching them go where they will go.

Face in the leaves, song in my throat. Fall through the air hoping to float. Practicing my solitary scales until they grow heavy, too heavy to carry. Watching them go where they will go.

ΔΔΔ

Even the least astute reader will note that I'm rendering this as a sort of prose poem, instead of with line breaks. Most of the songs in the *Coroner's Gambit* notebook also appear there in this format—as paragraphs rather than verse—but of them only "Family Happiness" gave me pause. Here, there are breath breaks in the delivery that might suggest an on-page presentation like something by A. R. Ammons, but if I do it in sentences, it reads like a page from somebody's diary that they absolutely never intended for another living soul to see. That's the mood I was trying to strike on this album, and these technical questions are the kinds of things I think about to flesh out that mood.

9 - WILD SAGE

I leave the house as soon as it gets light outside
like a prisoner breaking out of jail
and I steal down to Business 15-501
like I had a bounty hunter on my tail
and somebody stops to pick me up
but he drops me off just down the block

and along the highway
where the empty spirits breed
wild sage growing in the weeds

Walk down the soft shoulder, and I count my steps
headed vaguely eastward, sun in my eyes
and I lose my footing, and I skin my hands breaking my fall
and I laugh to myself. I look up at the skies,
and then I think I hear angels in my ears
like marbles being thrown against a mirror

and along the highway
where unlucky stray dogs bleed
wild sage growing in the weeds

on some days I don't miss my family
on some days I do
on some days I think I'd feel better if I tried harder
most days I know it's not true

I lay down right where I fell, cold grass in my face
and I could hear the traffic like the rhythm of the tides
and I stare at the scrape on the heel of my hand
until it doesn't sting so much—until all the blood's dried
and when somebody asks me: "Are you OK?"
I don't know what to say

and along the highway
from cast-off, innumerable seeds
wild sage growing in the weeds

ΔΔΔ

In my nursing days I worked with people who got lost. Lost to their families, lost to themselves, lost to the world. At a forty-hour job you get to know these people well, and to see through their eyes a little, if you're paying attention. We err when we consider life as a continuum headed one way or the other—every life has seasons, or stations; the narrator here isn't doomed. He needs help. Everybody on *Get Lonely* is in need of help. The nylon-string acoustic is played on the track by Franklin Bruno, who also, I think, fleshed out the song's chords to have the sevenths that give it the character it needs—I think I sang live as he played; the original version was an up-tempo shuffle. We tried it some in studio. Thank God for producers like Scott Solter who'll tell you to your face when you're not doing justice to the song.

10 - SWAMP CREATURES OR NEW FRIEND

Calling to ghosts down among the dry leaves
between subdivisions I found a few trees
where the apartments rise up from the mud
like alien invaders subsisting on blood
wire high and transcontinental

here's where we expected to see something jump from the
shadows
and here's where the long shadows end
here's where the mosquitos would breed in the pools on the
concrete
make straight the path for my new friend

ΔΔΔ

This is an unfinished draft from a notebook that contains: my notes to myself for a presentation I'd give to the New York offices of 4AD introducing them to the *Get Lonely* album; an early draft of "So Desperate" (July 22); several songs that would end up on *Undercard* by the Extra Lens, née Glenns, sometimes under different titles ("Cruiserweights" began life as "Quick Tillis Goes Through the Ropes"; let's please note that Tillis actually fought at heavyweight, sixty-five fights, forty-two wins with thirty-one by knockout); at least two attempts at the still uncompleted as of 2025 "Great Roman Families," a song about Primo Carnera; and the song title "The Sorcerer Self-Immolates in a Distant Clearing," corrected on the page from "The Sorcerer Bursts into Flames," a song that got no further than its title, but was followed, on the same page, by the following quotation from Elfriede Jelinek: "They remain at the edges of things, not because they're afraid of the light but because the light, understandably, is afraid of them."

Heretic Pride would be next.

11 · MICHAEL MYERS RESPLENDENT

I am ready for my close-up today
too long I've let my self-respect stand in my way
now the prom queen's
caught in the high beams
and the strings keen
it's a big scene

but when the house goes up in flames
no one emerges triumphantly from it
when the scum begins to circle the drain
everybody loves a winner

I spent eight hours in my make-up chair
waxed my chest and shaved off all my hair
now the fire's bright
and the frame's tight
try to get right
while we've still got light

but when the house goes up in flames
no one emerges triumphantly from it
when the scum begins to circle the drain
everybody loves a winner

ΔΔΔ

Years later, in *Devil House*, I addressed this theme again: The hero is the character whose presence in the story defines the story. You are rooting for him whether you like it or not and whether you want to or not. This is not a problem with people but with heroes, which, I'd argue, gives meaning to the quotation marks around the word on the cover of David Bowie's *"Heroes,"* quotation marks about which I have been idly musing for at least two-thirds of my life; if you get me started on them you'll lose at least ten minutes to the subject; we'll stop here.

12 - AUTOCLAVE

Hand me your hand, let me look in your eyes
as my last chance to feel human begins to vaporize

maybe it's the heat in here, maybe it's the pressure
you ought to head for the exits. The sooner the better

I am this great, unstable mass of blood and foam
and no one in her right mind would make my home her home
my heart's an autoclave
my heart's an autoclave

When I try to open up to you, I get completely lost
Houses swallowed by the earth, windows thick with frost
And I reach deep down within, but the pathways twist and turn
And there's no light anywhere, and nothing left to burn

and I am this great, unstable mass of blood and foam
and no emotion that's worth having could call my heart its home
my heart's an autoclave
my heart's an autoclave

I dreamt that I was perched atop a throne of human skulls
on a cliff above the ocean—howling wind and shrieking seagulls
and the dream went on forever, one single static frame
sometimes you want to go where everybody knows your name

and I am this great, unstable mass of blood and foam
and no one in her right mind would make her home my home
my heart's an autoclave
my heart's an autoclave

ΔΔΔ

In my general experience, trying to marry your practice to your environment is a doomed effort. Go spend a week at the beach and try writing about the ocean, and watch your writing come up short of its theme. Tour diaries fail to capture the energy and chaos of touring; food writing is best done by people who haven't eaten yet. But I was in a subbasement two floors beneath ground level in a Stockholm hotel when I wrote this, and I hadn't seen daylight in at least twelve hours, so maybe there's something to the Environmental Theory of Poetics, which I just made up.

13 - IN THE CRATERS ON THE MOON

If the strain proves too much, give up right away
if the light hurts your eyes, stay in your room all day
when the room fills with smoke, lie down on the floor
in the declining years of the long war

well, the blood's in the water, and the shark's going to come
and we swim in the dark until our bodies are numb
blind desert rats in the moonlight, too far from shore
in the declining years of the long war

empty room with a lightbulb swinging where the phone starts to
ring
everybody gets nervous, nobody says anything
next day someone's initials show up carved on the door
I think I'm going to crack, can't live like this any more
ugly things in the darkness, worse things in store
in the declining years of the long war

ΔΔΔ

One of the several songs written in that Stockholm hotel room two stories below ground, not just lacking daylight but aggressively insulated from the daylight—see also "Autoclave" (July 12). With the stipulation that I personally am not the speaker in either song: The latter is a call for help, and this one is what happens after nobody answers.

14 - SEPT 15 1983

Long dinner with some friends
way out, way out in Portmore
servants of the pharaoh
slip in through an open door:
all business
bearing knives and zipguns
so get on the floor now
every last one, every last one

the heat drifts across the land
if I forget you, Israel, let me forget my right hand

And on the floor, Michael James Williams
feels his fingers start to freeze
and the whole scene's like a movie
paramedics on their knees
try try your whole life
to be righteous and be good
wind up on your own floor
choking on blood

the heat drifts across the land
if I forget you, Israel, let me forget my right hand

And the house still smells like onions
when the ambulance arrives
Gabriel in postal blue
loads up the car and drives
to Spanish Town,
about three miles away
where will the wicked run to
on that last day, on that last day

the heat drifts across the land
if I forget you, Israel, let me forget my right hand

ΔΔΔ

It's from Psalm 137:1, the "by the rivers of Babylon—there we sat down and there we wept when we remembered Zion," one of the most beautiful poems in any language up until its last lines, at which point it becomes a fantasy of nightmarish violence. This song is about the murder of Prince Far I, whose body of work is some of the greatest music ever made. He loved the psalms while he lived, and I'd hazard that he loves them still.

15 - TIANCHI LAKE

Children by the water banks
laughing long and loud
Changbai's high fine western peaks
just beneath the clouds
currents in the water
churning in their course
body of a sea lion,
head just like a horse

Preacher in the soft brown sand
begins to speak his piece
high winds in the treetops,
low flying winter geese
no one taking pictures
everybody still
and then the water sought its course again
the way that waters will

No one at the lakeside now,
moon up in the sky
night birds in the dragon spruce
moaning long and high
backstroking on the surface,
moonlight on its face,
floats the Tianchi Monster,
staring into space

Out around the temple now
narcissus in bloom
censers packed with sandalwood
send smoke into the room
children in the sand outside
on their hands and knees
sketching pictures all day long
of stranger things than these

ΔΔΔ

Zheng said that when they climbed to the top of the mountain above Lake Tianchi at about 10 a.m., it was covered with thick fog that suddenly gave way to bright sunshine. The water emerged as clear as a mirror, ideal for photography. Zheng's film lasts almost a minute, and in it a black object can be seen emerging from the water in the same place three times, each time lasting just a few seconds, before it finally vanishes and does not reappear. —HE NA, *China Daily*, July 11, 2005

16 · HERETIC PRIDE

Well, they come and pull me from my house
and they drag my body through the streets

and the sun's so hot I think I'll catch fire and
  burn up
in the summer air so moist and sweet

And the people all come out to cheer
rocks in the pathway break my skin
and there's honeysuckle on the faint breeze today
with every breath I'm drawing in

I want to cry out
but I don't scream and I don't shout
and I feel so proud to be alive
and I feel so proud when the reckoning arrives

Now the crowds grow denser by the second
as we near the center of the town
and they dig a trench right in the main square, right there
and they pick me up and throw me down

And I start laughing like a child
and I mark their faces one by one
transfiguration's gonna come for me at last
and I will burn hotter than the sun

I've waited so long
and now I taste jasmine on my tongue
and I feel so proud to be alive
and I feel so proud when the reckoning arrives

ΔΔΔ

Every good Catholic has pinups of the martyred saints on the dorm room wall of his mind, and no matter how many years ago you stopped going to church, you probably never left the Church. Indeed, when you stopped on the path, the moon high above you, thinking you'd heard something by the side of the road in the dark—what shone in the light of your torch? Only leaves, and branches, and the Church.

17 · WIZARD BUYS A HAT

Shuffled up Sixth Street in the rain
kept my head down as I looked past the people
and in the department store
I found what I was looking for
This is the church, this is the crucible

They come out to Broadway and they look for me
I'm on the red steps smoking a cigarette
easy to recognize
black bandages on my eyes
This is the church, these are the congregants

Sun sets on the broad square and lights come up
feel like this town's gonna put a quick end to me
but if I came here to drown,
I'm going to take a few people down
This is the church, occupied by the enemy

ΔΔΔ

Should I live to be one thousand years old, and write every day, and pursue my craft like an assassin on the trail of his quarry, tireless, my vision narrowed to take in only the object before it, viz., to write a better title than "Wizard Buys a Hat," yet do I know that it will never, ever happen; I will never peak, but, as titles go, "Wizard Buys a Hat," for me, is it, the grail toward which my titling days aspired, and every song after it ought to have gone nameless, or, better, to have been titled using a numbering system: 1+WBaH, 2+WBaH, et cetera. Just trying here to be honest with you about how I feel about the title of this song, which, in case you missed it, is "Wizard Buys a Hat."

18 - SARCOFAGO LIVE

We were hungry,
there was no food
we were restless,
there were too many things to do
so we gathered
in a concrete room
eyes up
at you

And in a small room in Brazil,
we were waiting
and in a small room in Brazil,
we were waiting

We were howling
like dogs
we were feeling
the full brunt of the age
guys from our neighborhood
looking down at us
all of you, all of you
rage! rage! rage!

And in a small room in Brazil, we were waiting
and in a small room in Brazil, we were waiting

ΔΔΔ

The self-released *Satanic Messiah* EP is, like *Oh Juhu Beach* or the three one-sided 12″s, a weird outlier from a time of transition, and so it is also naturally one of my favorites in the catalog. I like the notion of an artifact that, exhumed by archaeologists millions of years in the future, would invite close scrutiny and elaborate theories to explain it—or that would otherwise invite no attention at all. Sarcofago is and was a Brazilian thrash band from the eighties. They're "important," a word I try to avoid, but it applies. They were just kids when they made a mark on the world. That mark, like all marks, will go invisible over time, but it was there.

19 - SATANIC MESSIAH

I saw the posters popping up around the city
pale blue and washed-out red
I went down to the arena pushing through
hoping I'd run into you
sweet freshly scrubbed smell of the crowd
all the excitement in their eyes
we were all made young when he stepped onto the stage
like an animal escaping from his cage

Raise the trumpet
sound the drum
he whom the prophet spoke of long ago has come

All of us too dazed to leave when it was over
dawdled by the vendors for a minute
gathered underneath a summer sky
I was hoping you'd pass by
but though I didn't see you that day or the next,

I'm pretty sure that you were there
making your way among the young and happy horde
headed down to your reward

Raise the trumpet
sound the drum
he whom the prophet spoke of long ago has come

ΔΔΔ

I've said this before but the most personal songs aren't the ones that recount actual moments from an extant past, not the ones that can fairly be called "confessional." The personal songs are the ones whose hurt is cloaked inside a story that hides it from the world. I wrote and recorded this not as I emerged from one of the most painful seasons of my entire life, but right in the middle of it. I had begun playing the piano because it made me feel better. It's certainly possible to interpret this song as political allegory but the better tack is to apply dream logic to it, because it emerged from me as a dream might: unbidden but welcome, just something that happened inside me once.

20 - MOSQUITO REPELLENT

All day, all day
sweeping out the shards
do what I have to do
try to start anew, but I

thought of you twice
couldn't help myself
I don't know what I need
clutching and fingering the rosary beads

and I try, try, try, but I know
I can't let go

TV upstairs
leave it on all night
do what I have to do
add, subtract, and divide by two, but my
eyes light up
at cops-and-robbers time
I hope the bad guys win
I hope the good guys get their skulls bashed in

and I try, try, try, but I know
I can't let go

ΔΔΔ

During that desperate time alluded to in the "Satanic Messiah" entry, I left a note on a dressing room wall thanking the guitarist and songwriter Kaki King for her music, which was, at that time, a tonic needed twice daily for me. She wrote me from that same dressing room a month later, and we made an EP together. She sent me a piece of music that sounded like a person trying to solve a puzzle that would open a locked door, growing increasingly desperate; I was where I was and how I was, and I wrote these words for it.

21 - THANK YOU MARIO BUT OUR PRINCESS IS IN ANOTHER CASTLE

I waited here all by myself
the room was dark and it smelled like sulfur
I heard the screams from way down in the darkness
felt pretty sure my life was over

I kept my hat on just for luck
sang simple tunes the whole night through
I wondered if I'd wake to find myself in flames
as I waited here for you

Yeah when you came in,
I could breathe again

I saw some guys dressed up like sorcerers
blue robes that flowed above the ground
they came and went and I was frightened for my life
I tried not to make a sound

just when my solitude was closing in
I heard a howl like screeching tires
and I told you the one thing I know how to say
through the bright ringing drone of 8-bit choirs

yeah when you came in,
I could breathe again

ΔΔΔ

It's a simple song about how Toad must feel inside when Mario beats Bowser, which is to say, it's a song about being surprised to see someone whose absence from your life has been a total catastrophe: personally, physically, spiritually, emotionally, practically, vertically, horizontally, Game Over. Unless it's not actually Game Over, which is the cruel hope of the home console: that the new beginning will never end, until it does.

22 - SO DESPERATE

We were parked in your car
In our neutral meeting place, the Episcopalian churchyard.

I had things I'd been meaning to say;
but in the dazzling winter sun that late,
I could feel them melt away,

And through the warm radio static,
I couldn't hear my stage directions.
And the fog on the windshield
obscured our sad reflections.

I felt so desperate in your arms.

We were parked near some trees,
and the moonlight soaked the branches in ever-deepening degrees.
Had my hand in your hair.
Trying to keep my cool 'til it became too much to bear

When we cracked the windows open,
well, the air was just so sweet.
We could hear the cars ten feet away
out there on the street.

I felt so desperate in your arms.

ΔΔΔ

Can I forget you, being as ye were
So beautiful among the pleasant fields
In which ye stood? Or can I here forget
The plain and seemly countenance with which
Ye dealt out your plain comforts? Yet had ye
Delights and exultations of your own.
—WILLIAM WORDSWORTH, *The Prelude*, BOOK 1, lines 501–506

Wordsworth was addressing some cottages in a field; and yet.

23 - BLACK PEAR TREE

I dug a hole and filled it up with compost
rested on the cool grass for a minute
I saw the future in a dream last night
there's nothing in it

I set the sapling in the hole
started gently tamping down the dirt
I saw the future in a dream last night:
somebody's gonna get hurt, somebody's gonna get hurt

I hope it's not me
but I suspect it's going to have to be

I dug my heels in for the winter
and I waited for the snow
but something was stuck up in the clouds, something was stuck
up there
they couldn't let go

and when its time came, I could see it happen
blossoms black and sweet as Texas crude
I saw the future flowering like a ruptured vessel
somebody's gonna get screwed

it won't be me
someday I am going to walk out of here free

ΔΔΔ

I have told, repeatedly, the story of how, between sound check and stage time, I wrote this song in a Stockholm emergency room because I was having pains in my chest and was afraid. It is from a span of time during which my songs fairly nakedly described my inner landscape. That this span seems, to my eye, also to mark a pronounced increase in economy of expression and vividness of imagery—well, it's frustrating to me, to be honest, because I would rather not lend fuel to the "art comes from pain" fire. Still, what interests me most here is the "they" in "they couldn't let go." The snow won't come. They're not going to let it happen. In my older songs it would certainly have snowed. Now, though, they're making me wait for it.

24 - SUDDEN OAK DEATH

Lose a little feeling in my fingers
gain an edge of panic in my face
search for some sign to tell me just how long I've been here
overturn the place

Feels like each time my efforts fail,
the whole hillsides disapprove
feel like a man whose veins have frozen overnight,
lying there trying to move

When the crack sounds in the wood
you will know that I'm down for good
when the crack sounds in the wood
you will know, old friend, that I'm down for good

I want to try to stand my ground
dig my heels into the hills
hope someone will come to right my balance
no one will

Feels like when I try to stretch my legs
everyone around me's trying, too

so ready just to fall down,
just to fall down, and to stay down
I don't want to spoil the view

When the crack sounds in the wood
you will know that I'm down for good
when the crack sounds in the wood
you will know, old friend, that I'm down for good

ΔΔΔ

In Christopher Guest's *A Mighty Wind*, the folk singer Mitch Cohen, an earnest heart-on-sleeve guy from his earliest days on the scene, documents the collapse of his life in the titles of two solo albums: *Cry for Help* and *Calling It Quits*. The first album's cover depicts him in a straightjacket; the latter finds him digging his own grave. The albums are only visible on the screen for a quick second. I laugh just remembering them. I'd like to dedicate July 24 to Mitch Cohen, from a singer-songwriter who recalls a time in his life when he was having a real Mitch Cohen moment.

25 - SURROUNDED

Cold white moon shine down on Colorado
hide my dirty secrets down here in the shadows
where the quaking aspens tremble in the snow
haul me up the hillside, hold me high and let me go

let me fall right through my own roof like a meteorite
let the world and all its wonders leave me to my toys tonight,
and my ninety-six-inch television screen
let me die, let me die
surrounded by machines

high winds knocked the power out last night,
but I've got my own supply here
all my windows blaze with light
and the light falls through the window
to the empty plain below
finds nothing but some trees
and six fresh feet of snow

and I find a broadcast station that's signed off for the night
and the static floods the speakers in glorious black and white

on my ninety-six-inch television screen
let me die, let me die
surrounded by machines

ΔΔΔ

The lead-off track on the EP *Moon Colony Bloodbath*, a collaboration with the great John Vanderslice recorded by Chris Stamey at his home studio. Concept albums are well-known, but only the brave in spirit assay the concept EP. Yet we dared! To tell, in song, a story about the organ-harvesting colonies on the moon, and the profound seclusion in which its astronaut laborers live during their off cycles on Earth. Readers who remember July 24 may wonder if there's a metaphor here, too, maybe? But my lips, while not exactly sealed, have flapped enough.

26 - SATORI IN DENVER

Speed down 24
toward the city for supplies
technically out-of-bounds
roll my window down,

hear my tires sing to the asphalt
and drink in the highway sounds

O solitude, friend of the friendless
light in the dark night coming on
grab what I want without saying a word
and drive through the dark 'til dawn

Track lights blur together,
anklet buzzing on my leg—
thinking up lies to tell
and this may be the time
I get banished from the palace
to seek out some smaller cell

O solitude, friend of the friendless
light in the dark night coming on
grab what I want without saying a word
and ride through the dark 'til dawn

ΔΔΔ

It's the secluded astronaut breaking protocol to make a run to a convenience store, but also it's anybody who ever made a 3 a.m. run to a convenience store because they had to: just had to, for whatever reason, and found themselves out in the world, feeling like a visitor in a place where they once were a resident.

27 · GOING TO LUBBOCK

He drove north out of Dallas on a Tuesday afternoon
and the summer wind was sweet in his mouth
as the engine whistled a solitary tune
ran out of gas in the middle of nowhere

among the rocks and the tumbleweeds and the dust
he popped the trunk, and he pulled out the shovel
punched the dull blade through the earth's tough
  crust

When he dug up the human skull
that was bigger than a basketball
he took one step back
he took one step back
into the sunlight

He stood there by the roadside
underneath the clear blue sky
and ancient stories ran through his mind
as a certain detail caught his eye
there was a pronounced depression
along the skull's occipital bone
his eyes burned in the dry June sun
and his forehead dripped like an ice cream cone

he laid the skull down gently in the backseat
and in his mouth, the summer wind was sweet
he took one step back
he took one step back
into the sunlight

ΔΔΔ

Several of my very best numbers from the early days went to the Extra Glenns, where Franklin Bruno would help them realize a potential I was often trying to bury under tics and detritus, just to make it harder to find. This one, which, like its July 26 predecessor in this volume, features a guy who just gets in a car and drives somewhere, originates in a cover story from the *Weekly World News* claiming that the skull of Goliath had been found. The internet tells me that story ran on June 1, 1993, so this song was probably written on or around June 2, 1993. We did not brook delays in those early times.

28 - NEW ZION

There were signs up in the sky
when we gathered by the garden wall
everybody on his best behavior
listening for the altar call
high priest of Salem in his robes
ranting at the coming of the day
ravens at the gates
frightening all the visitors away

I lay down by the water
dreamed a dream of where I come from
old things made new
waiting for you

There were wooden wind chimes rustling
in the trees along the hillsides in the dunes
on the high wind we could hear them
old, familiar tunes
that little bit of faith we had once
like the memory of a movie
that got burned up in the great fire
reassembling itself, slowly but surely

I lay down by the water
dreamed a dream of where I come from
old things made new
waiting for you

ΔΔΔ

Two things: First, this is kind of a riff on "Dover Beach," right? I think you could go through my extended body of work and find a pretty decent handful of things that are versions of, or responses to, Matthew Arnold's "Dover Beach"; second, "the great fire" is specifically the 1965 MGM studio fire, about which I should probably write a novel, but, knowing me, it will instead be a chapbook of poems that lives on my hard drive but only two people know about from screenshots I very occasionally and quite excitedly send them of the poems themselves, often in the middle of the night. The hard drive dies with me and the poems vanish into the ether. It's nature's way!

29 - LOVECRAFT IN BROOKLYN

It's going to be too hot to breathe today
but everybody's out here on the streets
somebody's opened up a fire hydrant
cold water rushing out in sheets

Some kid in a Marcus Allen jersey
asks me for a cigarette
companionship is where you find it
so I take what I can get

Hubcaps on the cars like funhouse mirrors
stick to the shadows when I can
Lovecraft in Brooklyn

When the sun goes down, the armies of the voiceless,
several hundred thousand strong,
come out without their bandages
their voices raised in song

and when the streetlights sputter out
they make this awful sizzling sound
I cast my gaze towards the pavement
too many bloodstains on the ground

Rhode Island drops into the ocean
no place to call home any more
Lovecraft in Brooklyn

Head outside most every day
to try to keep the wolves away
imagine nice things I might say
if company should come

Woke up afraid of my own shadow
like, genuinely afraid
headed for the pawnshop
to buy myself a switchblade

Someday something's coming
from way out beyond the stars
to kill us while we stand here
it'll store our brains in mason jars

And then the girl behind the counter
she asks me how I feel today
I feel like Lovecraft in Brooklyn

ΔΔΔ

My coming to New York had been a mistake; for whereas I had looked for poignant wonder and inspiration in the teeming labyrinths of ancient streets that twist endlessly from forgotten courts and squares and waterfronts to courts and squares and waterfronts equally forgotten, and in the Cyclopean modern towers and pinnacles that rise blackly Babylonian under waning moons, I had found instead only a sense of horror and oppression which threatened to master, paralyze, and annihilate me.

—H. P. LOVECRAFT, "He"

Lovecraft hated Brooklyn for all the wrong reasons—his racism was septic, it teemed within him—but the image of a guy who finds himself alone and paranoid in a Red Hook apartment in 1925, his wife having hightailed it to Ohio not from estrangement but for work, that's the good old Mountain Goats vintage source text material right there. A guy waiting for his chances to improve, learning on the fly about how chance really works.

30 - SAX ROHMER #1

fog lifts from the harbor
dawn goes down to day
an agent crests the shadows of a nearby alleyway
piles of broken bricks
signposts on the path
every moment points toward the aftermath
yeah

sailors straggle back
from their nights out on the town
hopeless urchins from the city gather around
ships from imperial China
wash in with the tide
every battle heads toward
surrender on both sides

and I am coming home to you
with my own blood in my mouth
I am coming home to you,
if it's the last thing that I do

bells ring in the tower
wolves howl in the hills
chalk marks show up on a few high windowsills
and a rabbit gives up somewhere,
and a dozen hawks descend
every moment points toward its own sad end
yeah

ships loosed from their moorings
capsize, and then they're gone
sailors with no captains watch a while, and then move on
and an agent crests the shadows
and I head in her direction
all roads lead toward the same blocked intersection

I am coming home to you
with my own blood in my mouth
I am coming home to you,
if it's the last thing that I do

ΔΔΔ

One of the great clichés of the promotional cycle is a band claiming that they're getting back to their roots, which in our case is hard to do: Our roots are a boom box in an empty apartment. We don't live there any more. But formally and thematically, *Heretic Pride* is much nearer to the early days than to the albums that preceded it. Images come fast and loose; words packed tight and quivering together like popcorn kernels in oil; image after image after image. It's the rabbit who gives up somewhere by which you can measure the distance from those earlier songs to now. That rabbit seems to have been running for quite some time at this point! Whatever will happen to him? One hates to consider it.

31 - SUPERGENESIS

In the twinkling of an eye, my sentence gets passed
and I drop to the ground and I go slithering through the grass
carving out
the battle lines
as I crawl

Find a hollow branch to rest in, slip inside
Wait for mice to poke their heads in, jaw hinged open wide
Hang by
my tail
listening for the call

someday, someday
the call will sound
and we all, we all
are going to get up from the ground

Feel the wet leaves pressed against me cling like drowning men
try to hoist myself upright: again. Try again
hold on
to the memories
all night

And where my legs and arms once sprouted, skin is smooth and slick
Rub the smooth spots on some rough rocks, I feel cold and sick

Hold on
to the battle plan
hold tight

'cause someday, someday
the call will sound
And we all, we all
are gonna get up from the ground

ΔΔΔ

In the song I say "'cause someday, someday," but I have an aversion to abbreviating "because" on the page—almost every instance of "'cause" can be replaced in print with "because"—or aloud, for that matter, but in this case no. This may seem a small sticking point, but I think it's actually near the center of how I think about songs on the page: The page is not the song; it's an echo of the song, or a wobbly mirror of it, or a clarification of its position. They are different, and one is not the other, and for this cause there shall be no 'cause beyond the great cause, viz., learning to walk again when we have been made limbless, which was kind of my situation at the time I wrote the song, cf. the album we'll be looking at next month.

AUGUST

1 - ROMANS 10:9

Wake up sixty minutes after my head hits the pillow,
I can't live like this
And in the shower, I am a sailor,
Standing, waiting, ready for the ship to list
Everything looks burned up
I'm too scared to look around
Don't feel like going on, but come on:
Make a joyful sound

If you will believe in your heart, and confess with your lips,
surely you will be saved one day.

Try to think of ways to fix myself,
But everything ends in a cul-de-sac
The beast broke from the barn while we were sleeping
Face it, face it, he's not coming back
Don't see what the point is
In even trying to fight
Look for the bigger picture
When I close my eyes at night

If you will believe in your heart, and confess with your lips,
Surely you will be saved one day.

Look for the sign of Daniel—
Consider the clues
Wait as long as we have to for good news

Wake and rise and face the day
And try to stop the day from staring back at me
Busy hours for joyful hearts,
And later maybe head out to the pharmacy
Won't take the medication,
but it's good to have around
A kind and loving God
Won't let my small ship run aground

If you will believe in your heart, and confess with your lips,
surely you will be saved one day.

ΔΔΔ

The first Bible reference on a Mountain Goats record dates back to *Taboo VI*, and there'd been several songs along the way whose titles were chapter and verse citations ("Genesis 19:1–2" and "1 Corinthians 13:8–10," just going from memory), but people still seemed a little shocked when the tracklisting for *The Life of the World to Come* was announced. All Bible, all the time. In retrospect it would have been an even more aggressive move to call the album *All Bible, All the Time*, but the whole matter was pretty serious to me back then; I was having a hard time of things, and I couldn't see my way out of the dark, and I did go get a prescription that I never filled. This song is, therefore, fairly autobiographical, and the chorus is meant both as bitter irony and as an actual cry of hope. "Both are true" is a mast to which I will still be happily tied on the day the ship finally goes down.

2 - 1 SAMUEL 15:23

I became a crystal healer,
and my ministry was to the sick.
Creeping vines would send out runners
and seek me in their numbers.

I sold self-help tapes.
Go down to the netherworld.
Plant grapes.

And as word spread of my power,
they would seek me far and wide
All sad faces at my window.
I would welcome them inside.
I sewed clothes for them,
cloaks and capes.
Go down to the netherworld.
Plant grapes.

My house will be for all people
who have nowhere to go.
My supply of shining crystals
a shield against the snow.
There's more like me where I come from.
Mark our shapes.
Go down to the netherworld.
Plant grapes.

ΔΔΔ

The chorus refers to *Odin Sphere*, a game whose intricate plot can fairly be described as "convoluted" but features an arc in which a character finds himself in the netherworld, transformed into a rabbit. One of the game's mechanics is that characters can pick vegetables from the ground, to either eat them or have them cooked into dishes for restoring health. Playing this game one day, I was struck by how this mechanic still applied in Hell, and that grapes require cultivation. As a child of nineties postmodernity I fetishize ambiguities, but being who I am I can seldom fully embrace them: but in this song's narrator, a huckster who is nonetheless protective of his clientele, I approach the ideal.

3 - ISAIAH 45:23

If my prayer be not humble, make it so.
In these last hours, if the Spirit waits in check,
help me let it go.
And should my suffering double,
let me never love You less.
Let every knee be bent,
and every tongue confess.

And I won't get better,
but someday I'll be free.
I am not this body that imprisons me.

I read the magazines somebody brought.
Hold them near my failing eyes
until my hands get hot.
And when the nurse comes in
to change my sheets and clothes,
the pain begins to travel,
dancing as it goes.

And I won't get better,
but someday I'll be free.
I am not this body that imprisons me.

If my prayer goes unanswered, that's all right.
Should my path fill with darkness,
and there is no sign of light,
let me praise You for the good times—
let me hold Your banner high.
Until the hills are flattened
and the rivers all run dry.

And I won't get better,
but someday I'll be free.
I am not this body that imprisons me.

ΔΔΔ

This story pretty clearly has its roots in my time working in hospitals and in home care, but it won't surprise you to learn that this is also me: not dying, not hospitalized, but at home, unable to sleep through the night because of a couple of chronic health matters that had descended on my house in 2008 and liked the view well enough to stay. Of all our albums, *The Life of the World to Come* comes closest to confessional folk, the very genre whose existence led me to call my act the Mountain Goats as a distancing tactic. Sonically it's careful, curated; polite, even, for the most part; but lyrically it's raw like uncooked meat. It was attached to a living creature just a little while before you saw it.

4 - HEBREWS 11:40

Masks hanging on the tomb walls
where the coven grieves
witches hiding in the brambles
ground level down where the dry leaves

blow, and burn slowly
no ground is ever going to hold me

White candles in the manor
where the curse takes hold
bodies reassembling down where the worms crawl
make your own friends when the world's gone cold

it gets dark, and then
I feel certain I am going to rise again
If not by faith, then by the sword,
I'm going to be restored

Build fires to keep the beacon flashing
where the earth lies flat
blood calls to blood as the hours draw down
invent my own family, if it comes to that

hold them close, hold them near
tell them no one's ever going to hurt them here

Steal the treasure and try to leave town
fight my way back down
don't want to hurt anyone
probably gonna have to before it's all done

Take to the hills, run away
I'm gonna get my perfect body back someday
if not by faith then by the sword
I'm going to be restored

ΔΔΔ

The physical scene being described is from *Black Sunday* by Mario Bava (1960), but the song that grows out of these images is one of the most personal things I've ever written—about feeling ownership of my body and my self, about tending to and caring for the things within myself that are soft and good; about growth. It is, therefore, pretty opaque, because I don't have any artistic interest in just speaking these things out plainly. For me the magical transformative power is in the image, and in the transformation of idea into image. I haven't read Jung but I suspect thinking this process through is more his domain than mine. My job is to occasionally write songs where it happens, and to otherwise write songs whose tension resides in a kind of resistance to the whole process.

5 - 1 JOHN 4:16

In the holding tank I built for myself,
it's feeding time
and I start to feel afraid,
because I'm the last one left in line
the endless string of summer storms
that brought me to today
began one afternoon with you
long ago and far away

And someone leads the beast in on his chain
but I know you're thinking of me,
because it's just about to rain
so I won't be afraid of anything ever again.

In the cell that holds my body back,
the door swings wide
and I feel like someone's lost child
as the guards lead me outside
and if the clouds are gathering,
it's just to point the way
to an afternoon I spent with you
when it rained all day

And someone leads the beast in on his chain
but I know you're thinking of me,
because it's just about to rain
so I won't be afraid of anything ever again.

ΔΔΔ

Really, it's a simple song about how, when things are hard, you can locate a point or person in your past and fix your attention there, and then hold on for dear life. It is a hopeful song. But because I'm the guy writing it, I have, of course, set the action inside some nonspecific imperial Rome–like arena, where the narrator expects to be eaten by a wild animal as soon as he's done talking. It looks grim! But in the broader and more personal sense, this narrator seems still to not be done talking, so our wild animals will have to wait a while longer. One bright day, they will be fed, no doubt. But until then!

6 - GENESIS 3:23

House up in Clear Lake
where I used to live
picked the lock on the front door
and felt it give

Touch nothing, move nothing, stand still
keep my ears open for cars
see how the people here live now
hope that they're better at it than I was

I used to live here

Pictures up on the mantle—
nobody I know
I stand by the tiny furnace
where the long shadows grow

Living room to bedroom to kitchen
familiar and warm

hours we spent starving within these walls
sounds of a distant storm

I used to live here

Fight through the ghosts in the hallway
duck and weave
stand by the door with my eyes closed
when it's time to leave

Steal home before sunset
cover up my tracks
drive home with old dreams at play in my mind
and the wind at my back

Break the lock on my own garden gate
when I get home after dark
sit looking up at the stars outside
like teeth in the mouth of a shark

I used to live here

ΔΔΔ

There are several Mountain Goats songs in which the narrator goes back to a house where he used to live, figures out a way to get inside, and then looks around in there, trying to establish some connection between the person he was when he lived there and the person he is now, elsewhere. My explanation for this theme is deeply esoteric and hermetic: It's because I have, on several occasions, gone back to a house where I used to live, figured out a way to get inside, and then looked around in there, trying to establish some connection between the person I was when I lived there and the person I am now, elsewhere, which is to say, here.

7 - DEUTERONOMY 2:10

The sun above me and the concrete floor below
scratch at the chain links, maybe bare my teeth for show
fed twice a day, I don't go hungry any more
feel in my bones just what the future has in store
I pace in circles so the camera can see
look hard at my stripes
there'll be no more after me

Laze by the shoreline while the sailors disembark
scratch out a place to sit and rest down in the dark
smell something burning downwind just a little ways
they set up camp and sing and sweat and work for days
I have no fear of anyone—I'm dumb, and wild, and free
I am a flightless bird,
and there'll be no more after me

In Costa Rica in a burrow underground
climb to the surface, blink my eyes and look around
I'm all alone here as I try my tiny song
claim my place beneath the sky, but I won't be here for long
I sang all night—the moon shone on me through the trees
no brothers left,
and there'll be no more after me

ΔΔΔ

The Tasmanian tiger, the dodo, and the golden toad are all extinct. People sometimes say they saw a Tasmanian tiger—in their yard, out in the bush, crossing a road. But the last footage of a known Tasmanian tiger was through the bars of the cage in which he died, more than a hundred years ago. You can watch that footage online if you like: It is hard to watch. Say whatever nice things you may about human beings, but the trail of destruction we leave in our wake is littered with blameless beings who were in our way.

8 - MATTHEW 25:21

They'd hooked you up to a fentanyl drip
to mitigate the pain a little bit.
I flew in from Pennsylvania
when I heard the hour was coming fast.

And I docked in Santa Barbara;
tried to brace myself.
But you can't brace yourself when the time comes.
You just have to roll with the blast.

And I'm an eighteen-wheeler headed down the interstate,
and my brakes are going to give,
and I won't know 'til it's too late.
Tires screaming when I lose control.
Try not to hurt too many people when I roll.

Find the Harbor Freeway, and head south.
Real tired, head kind of light.
I found Telegraph Road; I'd only seen the name on envelopes.
Found the parking lot and turned right.

I felt all the details carving out space in my head:
Tropicanas on the walkway, neon red.
Between the pain and the pills trying to hold it at bay
stands a traveler going somewhere far away.

And I am an airplane tumbling wing over wing;
Try to listen to my instruments, they don't say anything.

People screaming when the engines quit.
I hope we're all in crash position when we hit.

And then came to your bedside—
and as it turns out, I'm not ready;
and as though you were speaking through a thick haze,
you said hello to me.

We all stood there around you,
happy to hear you speak:
The last of something bright burning, still burning
beyond the cancer and the chemotherapy—

And you were a presence full of light upon this earth,
and I am a witness to your life and to its worth.
It's three days later when I get the call,
And there's nobody around to break my fall.

ΔΔΔ

A song for Nancy Chavanothai, who was born in 1948 in Sibley, Iowa, and who died on the second day of October 2007, in Ventura, California, surrounded by the family she loved.

9 - MATTHEW 11:14–19

"He who casts the stone can't ever do so on his own.
It takes a crowd to drown a witch"—
So he said to us when he'd wriggled free and got the gun from me,
Standing before us, his cracking voice rising in pitch,

And then the blood that's been spilling from his eyes
Soaks through the bandages that are wrapped around his face,

And just before he walks backwards through the wall,
He pivots 45 degrees to face us all, and he says:

"Let him who has eyes to see
Take a good look at me
I'm a Mylar sheet hanging in the sun"

Claude Rains in all his glory
was not arrayed like these
Who have come to walk before us,
Rising from their knees,

Fighting back against their captors,
Calling down the curse—
Like this man, whose substance is malleable,
Screaming out chapter and verse

And then the blood that's been spilling from his eyes
Soaks through the bandages that are wrapped around his face,
And just before he walks backwards through the wall,
He pivots 45 degrees to face us all, and he says:

"Let him who has eyes to see
Take a good look at me
I'm a Mylar sheet hanging in the sun"

ΔΔΔ

The Life of the World to Come is a very emotional album, but this song, from the demos but not on the album, cloaks its emotional core in a story that's pretty hard to follow and is littered with references that call for a score sheet, which is to say, it's an old-school song I wrote while composing a new-school album. *Life* could be reimagined as a collection of songs beginning with "Matthew 11:14–19" and branching out from there to bizarre and allegorical territories closer to *Heretic Pride* than to the confessional, shirtless-to-the-waist album we made. This imaginary alternate *Life* is called *Descendit ad Inferos*—"He descended into Hell"—and no release date has been set as of this writing.

10 - ENOCH 18:14

I saw some old friends as I came to the city gate;
they asked me where I'd been of late.
I hadn't been anywhere, but what was I going to say?
Two hopeful people, looking at me that way.

You and your brother, you both escaped the curse.
You can't comprehend what it's like!

We stood in the sunlight, and they asked me where I'd been—
held the gate open, and told me to come on in.
I saw the damp green grass, so nice, on the other side.
Couldn't explain myself to them, but I tried:

You and your brother, you both escaped the curse.
So you can't comprehend what it's like!

The ground was dry but giving, the sky was nearly black;
I saw some old friends when I looked back.
Remember my old home—haven't forgotten yet.
What happens on the day when I forget?

You and your brother, you both escaped the curse.
You can't comprehend what it's like!

ΔΔΔ

Further exposition on the action of the game *Odin Sphere* (August 2). Much of the game takes place in Hell, really. In this sense, it's less a game than a philosophical essay.

11 - BRISBANE HOTEL SUTRA

From the crooked road that took me north
and brought me home again;
From the pit of writhing serpents
out to the lion's den;
Where the labyrinth is lightless
and the faithless wander crazed—
let the light rise from the darkness.
Let His name be praised.

From the sunrise of my childhood
to its premature demise;
From my mother's best intentions
to my stepdad's seething eyes.
From the hidden self-inflicted wounds
that flowered in later days:
To the folly of their learning,
let His name be praised.

In the holes the worms have eaten
through all once treasured things;
From the wet mouth of the vulture
to the red tips of his wings;
In the dazed eyes of the penitent
emerging from the maze—
In his wordless explanations,
Let His name be praised.

ΔΔΔ

This was written for *All Eternals Deck* but is too pious to live there. The All Eternals Deck is thirteen face cards and all of them are people. This song is about God. There is no God card in the All Eternals Deck. Everybody knows this.

12 - USED TO HAUNT

Tunnel down to the core
climb through the trap door
soft pink sky full of rumpled clouds
radio up loud

There's a pop in the speakers
where I hear your voice come through,
so brave and true;
when did I lose sight of you?

Come and rattle your chain all you want.
You're always going to be welcome
here in the hallways that you used to haunt.

Ride the sentimental rodeo
down to where the shadows grow
long while since I felt this way
stand by the window, wait for day

There's a pop in the speaker
where I hear your voice come through,
so brave and true;
let me never lose sight of you.

Come and rattle your chain all you want.
You're always going to be welcome
here in the hallways that you used to haunt.

ΔΔΔ

The piano in this one, recorded by Scott Solter at New York's Mission Sound, sounds unbelievably good; as a ballad of longing, I like the song, too. But there were already two piano ballads on the second side of *All Eternals Deck*, and both of them were more complex, lyrically and musically, and side two is where you have the luxury of complexity. On side one you bang the drum, and then on side two, as a reward, you get to complicate things. You know the phrase "I don't make the rules"? It doesn't apply here, because I made this rule.

13 - CATHERINE ANTRIM'S KID

Brush all the dust of Kansas off of my special shoes
when the coach lets us out at the corner store
Mom was coughing like an old man,
shivering like a cold man

and I found some trouble to get into
and the admiration was mutual
split my winnings with mom 55/45
but it didn't keep her alive

I got lost out there in New Mexico
nothing to lose, nowhere to go
I got lost
when my lucky stars crossed

that night I dreamt about Fort Stanton
though I didn't know to call it that yet

and the night wrapped me up
in its long dark embrace
I had that same expression on
as that one picture of my face

which was all anyone would ever know about me
after my visitors got done with me
I lay down singing on the porch
blood streaming from my mouth
sounded kind of like Paul Westerberg, to tell you the truth

I got lost out there in New Mexico
nothing to lose, nowhere to go
I got lost
when my lucky stars crossed

ΔΔΔ

Henry McCarty was born in New York City in either September or November of 1859; his younger brother, Joseph, in 1863. When their father died, his mother, Catherine, moved, with her sons, to Indianapolis. There she met William Antrim; in 1870, they all moved together to Wichita. Antrim and McCarty were married three years later. By this time they resided in the New Mexico Territory, in Santa Fe. A year later, she contracted tuberculosis and died. William didn't stick around to see what would become of the kids.

In the short span of Henry's life he'd moved all the way across the country, and now he was an orphan. He's known as Billy the Kid in the popular imagination, and only one photograph of him survives, though a second disputed image surfaced in 2010. In any case, he did not live to see twenty-two. This song visits him for the second time in my catalog. Lots of us find trouble to get into when we are young. But few of us do so in such a way that our names live on forever, even when the known details of our lives are murky, and uncertain, and contradictory. Of those few, even fewer succeed in largely vanishing into the icon they've left behind.

14 - ROTTEN STINKING MOUTHPIECE

Lob some spit at the window
watch it run down the pane
it's only the guilty who concern themselves
with clearing their names

You bring tidings of hope: false tidings
when you come here
there's two friends who did me wrong that you're
  protecting
it's so clear

And when you speak, it's those two who
speak through you;
who'll speak for me?
The burning and the electricity.

Sun goes down, San Francisco
friends are hard to find
chew them up just as quick as I can find them
try to clear my mind

remember hours at the table
gauze white light easing through
if there's one thing that I'm not going to do tonight,
it's die for you

'cause when you speak it's those two who
speak through you;

who'll speak for me?
The burning and the electricity.

ΔΔΔ

I have this abiding idea about the "pure" song, even knowing that all notions of purity are nonsense—but allowing the conceit for the moment: The pure song does not exist on the page, and exists only by default in the recorded artifact. The pure song can only exist in the air, where its phrases do and don't have punctuation: We hear the breath pauses and intuit commas, semicolons, question marks, et cetera, and share these momentary inflections in the space of the song, but that's the only space where the meaning of the song can be fixed. "Fixed" here is no less difficult than "pure"—can something be fixed if it's strictly temporal by definition? "Rotten Stinking Mouthpiece" describes the action of *Indestructible Man*, starring Lon Chaney Jr., a 1956 Hollywood curiosity mainly memorable for Chaney Jr.'s silence throughout most of the film—he's said to have been recovering from surgery, necessitating a rewrite of his character, a betrayed criminal who rises from the dead to seek revenge. As a song, it approaches my absurd standard for what constitutes "purity," valiantly resisting the siren call of the printed page, where its best effects—the drawn-out "hours," the "those two who / speak through you" quadruple rhyme, the breath-pauses in the chorus—simply vanish; and for this, I am exceedingly fond of it, and it holds, for me, a place of high privilege among all my songs.

15 - FOR CHARLES BRONSON

catch a lucky break / try to make it last
rig a blanket curtain up between / the present and the past
play my lucky numbers / for most of what they're worth
lie about my age right down to my last day on this earth

set your sights on good fortune
concentrate
pull back the hammer
try to hold the gun straight

hit the gym each night / stay cool and seldom speak
keep the heart of a champion
never let them see you're weak
and whatever they say / on your page 3 mention
focus on the parts that make you feel good
be grateful for the attention

set your sights on good fortune
concentrate
pull back the hammer
try to hold the gun straight

try to hold the gun straight, and true, and steady
let the frame find you
when the cameraman's ready

work until I drop / float from place to place
Ehrenfeld, Pennsylvania
scratched into my face

set your sights on good fortune
concentrate
pull back the hammer
try to hold the gun straight

ΔΔΔ

The slashes: They were in the original document when I dug it up for this book. The text itself I like a lot, but at the moment I am more interested in the slashes, because I'm pretty particular about how lines sit on the page. I don't abbreviate "yr" for "your"—I avoid shorthand almost everywhere. Most likely I did it here to fit the whole thing on one page, and possibly I will, in my future but your past, get a polite letter from my editor asking politely if we might adopt a similar strategy for other lyrics that run long. To this I will reply, just as politely: No, we might not. Charles Bronson rose from poverty most of us can't even contemplate to study under Strasberg. To him alone do I dedicate this song, slashes in its working draft and all.

16 - THE AUTOPSY GARLAND

One clear shot or else he gets away.
Red sun high in the sky tonight.
Look west from London, down toward Hollywood—
Remember the first days in California.

You don't want to see these guys without their masks on.
You don't want to see these guys without their masks on.

Fat rich men love their twelve-year-olds.
Deco cuff links and cognac by the glass.
Look west from London toward the Emerald City.
Remember Minnesota.

You don't want to see these guys without their masks on.
You don't want to see these guys without their masks on,
or their gloves.

Sweet spearmint and bitter tangerine,
bedside decked with roses.
Look west, look west—look west, and look away
from old familiar faces.

You don't wanna see these guys
without their masks on
You don't wanna see these guys
without their masks on

ΔΔΔ

I've told this story before: I was no older than five, and possibly only four, when I announced to my parents that I knew who I would marry when I grew up: Judy Garland. They exchanged a "he doesn't know" look, and as gently as they could told me she was dead. I cried; then as now I cry easily. Her story is a story of child exploitation and mine isn't, but I share with her knowledge of the sound a mask makes when it slips from its wearer's face and hits the floor. *All Eternals Deck* is, like *Heretic Pride*, an album in which I reached out to figures whose stories I carry with me. Hers is one of the oldest, and dearest, to me.

17 - BEAUTIFUL GAS MASK

Come hard through the fog
blindfolded and bound
'til we stand at the edge
of a hole in the ground

We hold hands, and we jump
and as we fall we sing
paupers hammering the walls of the castle
going to meet the king

Never sleep, remember to breathe deep
never sleep, remember to breathe
breathe deep

Crash in from deep space
shot birds falling fast
who will be there to catch us in his jaws
when we arrive, alive at last?

I can't hear you in the dark
wish I knew where you'd gone
know you're there, off in the shadow somewhere
try to soldier on

Never sleep, remember to breathe deep
Never sleep, remember to breathe
breathe deep, and breathe humbly
secure your mouthpiece when you can

Toxic shapes adorn the walls
as we rise from our knees
someone's coming to reward us, you wait and see
or crush us both like fleas

Never sleep, remember to breathe deep
never sleep, remember to breathe
breathe deep

ΔΔΔ

Prior to outlining this book I hadn't realized there were two songs involving masks on *All Eternals Deck*; had I noticed it while writing, all its songs would have featured a mask, and I would have tried to title the album *Mask 2*, since Bauhaus already has an album called *Mask*. My manager and Merge Records, then, would likely have raised the following objections: First, that although *Mask 2* redirects, on Wikipedia, to a forgotten sequel called *Son of the Mask*, it's still a sequel to a Jim Carrey movie, and people who own the rights to Jim

Carrey movies tend to have armies of lawyers just itching for work. Second, that there was also a Peter Bogdanovich movie called *Mask*, about a disfigured teenager named Rocky, who dies at the end of the movie, and that people therefore might take *Mask 2* as a tasteless joke. Preemptively and retroactively I wish to reject both objections and suggest that the real reason *Mask 2* is rejected involves the failure of *Taboo VI* to chart when it was released. This is cowardly thinking. *Mask 2* is an entirely different record.

18 - LIZA FOREVER MINNELLI

There's the part you've braced yourself against, and then
there's the other part.
Steal up inclining northward streets with some
weird sickness in the dark.
Saw your name on the sidewalk, saw your brave face in my
mind.
If you want to sit next to the dealer, you have to bet blind.

Never get away, never get away
I am never ever going to get away from this place.
Lay down in the street, my eyes toward the sun,
your star next to my face.

The compasses I came into this world with
never really worked so good.
Gentle shadows sliding down the hills
up on Mulholland at Ledgewood.
Turn back, turn back! Find someone to tell your secrets to.
Dream past an old hotel on Ivar, and seconds later I saw you.

Never get away, never get away
I am never ever going to get away from this place.

Lay down in the street, my eyes toward the sun,
your star next to my face.

Let the camera track me from the footlights to the wings.
Let me set aside an hour or two in memory of sweet things.

Regrind the lens again, and again, but still the picture flips.
Anyone here mentions "Hotel California"
dies before the first line clears his lips.

Never get away, never get away
I am never ever going to get away from this place.
Lay down in the street, my eyes toward the sun,
your star next to my face.

ΔΔΔ

A fairly in-the-moment confessional song from when I had to let our tour bus go on ahead of us for a couple of days in 2009 while I stayed behind in Los Angeles, trying to get over some ghost malaise I couldn't shake. I lay down on the sidewalk to take a picture of myself next to Liza Minnelli's star on the Walk of Fame. In the picture, my eyes are closed, and I'm thinking about a club not far from there where I spent time in the 1980s. Bowie's "Life on Mars?" was envisioned as a song for crooners to sing, and this is my version of that: an openly sentimental song with room for a big voice and heavy chops. To date, either the crooners haven't noticed it, or they're just chicken.

19 · AGE OF KINGS

Halls of the stone tower in the foothills
why should we hide from anyone?
held you in my arms for the first time that day
felt like God's anointed when you didn't push me away

Gold light shining on so many things
in the age of kings.

Lean on the concrete walls in shadow
why should we wait to throw the switch?
Felt your name burn in like a tattoo into my skin
rain on the clay tiles all night, your head nestled beneath my chin

Gold light shining on so many things
in the age of kings:

In the lost age
where the jewels hide
and the sword sticks
in the waiting stone, still warm.

Small chambers shrinking til they vanish
wolves in the hallways gaining ground
reach down to the moment when I should have said something
true
shadows and their sources stealing away with you

Gold light shining on so many things
in thc age of kings

ΔΔΔ

After 1997 the love songs thin out a little as I become attracted to knottier themes—death, struggle, alienation—and after *Tallahassee* they complete their journey from common to uncommon to rare. They're like desert rain with me now, but when I wrote love songs all the time I had multiple defenses of the form in reserve in case anybody wanted to argue the point with me. This title germinated in my notebook for several years, from around the time of *Get Lonely*, waiting for its moment.

Its earliest draft was a song in memory of the Aurora monster models of the 1970s, and it rhymed "moon" with *Creature from the Black Lagoon*, but only the foolish would imagine it was any less a love song.

20 · BIRTH OF SERPENTS

Let the camera pull back 'til the fullness of the frame
is clear and plain
peer into the screen until you see it all
like a vision in a crystal ball
    let it fill all of a sudden with smoke
    is this somebody's idea of a joke?

Let the fixer work until the silver's washed away
take the picture from the tray
look hard at what you see and then remember you and me
let the truth spring free
    like a jack-in-the-box
    like a hundred thousand cuckoo clocks

From the Oregon corners to the Iowa corn
to the rooms with the heat lamps where the snakes get born

Crawl through the tunnel
and follow, follow the light northwest
see that young man who dwells inside his body
like an uninvited guest
    see the tunnel twist
    clutch your birthright in your fist

Let the camera do its
dirty work down there in the dark

sink low, rise high
bring back some blurry pictures to remember all your darker
moments by
permanent bruises on our knees
never forget what it felt like to live in rooms like these

From the Oregon corners to the Iowa corn
to the rooms with the heat lamps where the snakes get
born

ΔΔΔ

I was in Portland; I looked up Quinn, who I'd been told by a hairdresser was still alive. He was not. Back in my hotel, I wrote this in the middle of the night without an instrument to hand, just writing something for later. I remembered Quinn, visiting me in my apartment on the other side of the river in late winter of 1986. Just casual friends getting to know each other a little better. Pictures of Quinn from that time exist but of me there is only one. We were not terribly close but I felt his absence, and the distance from then to now, and I traced a little of that distance on the page: as I say—for later.

21 · FOR DENISE MATTHEWS

Stay down when something strikes me down
head off the hounds of chaos at the pass
self-medicate through all my waking hours
gulp down venom by the glass

Head down into the cave
where the white smoke swirls
B-movie demon faces
frighten little boys and girls

But I am not afraid,
and that's what's wrong with me
I am not afraid, I am not afraid
I am not afraid when I should be

Crash hard against any surface that will take me
each time the pain gets worse, increase the dose
hear darkness winging like a falcon sent from hell
stand my ground against it, end up comatose

Jump wild-eyed into the river
pockets full of stones
miss the set call, tear the phone out of the wall
I'm going down alone

But I am not afraid,
and that's what's wrong with me
I am not afraid, I am not afraid
I am not afraid when I should be

ΔΔΔ

A version of this was tracked in Boston at the session where we captured the "High Hawk Season" men's chorus, but it's unreleased. Denise Matthews was better known to the world as Vanity, Prince's protégé from the pre–*Purple Rain* days; strikingly beautiful and intensely charismatic, she found, in fame and success, something darker and more dangerous than the life she'd hoped for. Another way of putting this is to say that Nikki Sixx of Mötley Crüe remembers Matthews as the person who taught him how to freebase cocaine. In 1994, after a kidney transplant following several overdoses, she found her way free from addiction and devoted her life to Jesus Christ. In a clip from 2001, on the Trinity Broadcasting Network, she says, with great passion: "I praise the Lord because He lifted me up from the dead." "If you're going through Hell, keep going," they sometimes say in rooms where survivors gather. And so we do.

22 · SOURDOIRE VALLEY SONG

Bang the small rocks on the big ones
until the small ones are sharp and clean
catch something, kill something
new blade cuts real keen

And then the grass grows up to cover up
the firepit and the forge
half a world away from
the Olduvai Gorge

Chew these roots for a toothache,
chew these ones for atmosphere
dream the pleasant dreams that people dream
when they grow up down here

And then the grass grows up to cover up
the firepit and the forge
half a world away from
the Olduvai Gorge

Take care of the old man
see if he's in pain
have somebody stay with him
comfort him when he complains

Keep to ourselves mostly
few friends and fewer closer friends

lead a long life, if you're lucky
hope it never ends

And then the grass grows up to cover up
the firepit and the forge
half a world away from
the Olduvai Gorge

ΔΔΔ

I know that the life of the Neanderthal was perilous, and hard, but I also know that if the world of the Neanderthal does not in some way call to something very near your core, then you and I are cut from different cloth. My cloth is embroidered along its hem with an *N*, which, do I need to spell it out, stands for "Neanderthal."

23 - AMY AKA SPENT GLADIATOR 1

Do every stupid thing that makes you feel alive
do every stupid thing to try to drive the dark away
let people call you crazy for the choices that you make
find limits past the limits
jump in front of trains all day and stay alive
just stay alive

Play with matches if you think you need to play with matches
seek out the hidden places where the fire burns hot and bright
find where the heat's unbearable and stay there if you have to
don't hurt anybody on your way up to the light and stay alive
just stay alive

People might laugh at your tattoos
when they do get new ones in completely garish hues

I hide down in my corner, because I like my corner
I am happy where the vermin play
make up magic spells, we wear them like protective shells
landmines on the battlefield
find the one safe way and stay alive
just stay alive

ΔΔΔ

Transcendental Youth began life as *For the Demons*, which I only know because that's the name of the folder on my laptop in which the original lyric sheets reside; after that it was *Infernal Youth*, until I discovered that there was an English band with that name. This song, as its title suggests, was written in response to Amy Winehouse's needless death. I mark that, by contrast to pretty much all of *All Eternals Deck*, it's a near-naked credo of faith: But *AED* concluded on a similarly direct and confessional note with "Liza Forever Minnelli." That's entirely by chance, but don't tell anyone that.

24 - HARLEM ROULETTE

Unknown engines underneath the city
steam pushing up in billows through the grates
Frankie Lymon's tracking "Seabreeze" in a studio in Harlem
it's 1968

Just a pair of tunes to hammer out
everybody's off the clock by ten
the loneliest people in the whole wide world
are the ones you're never going to see again

Feel so free when I hit the avenue
nothing like a New York summer night

every dream's a good dream, even awful dreams are good
  dreams
if you're doing it right

Remember soaring higher than the clouds
get pretty sentimental now and then
the loneliest people in the whole wide world
are the ones you're never going to see again

    And four hours north of Portland
    a radio flips on
    and some no one from the future
    remembers that you're gone

Armies massing in the dusky distance
ghosted in the ribbon microphone
leave a little mark on something maybe
take the secret circuit home

Nothing in the shadows but the shadowhands
reaching out to sad young frightened men
the loneliest people in the whole wide world
are the ones you're never going to see again

ΔΔΔ

Frankie Lymon got very famous when he was young, and struggled to find his way in the world when that fame ran out. Dana Plato, Judy Garland, Denise Williams—I have returned to this theme many times. I'll think I'm done with it, and then I'll hear a story of someone who rose high in their craft only to lose sight of themselves, and I'll feel a sharp ache about it, and write something to address that ache. What it means that this theme called to me before I'd accrued anything resembling a measure of fame is, I think, more for the reader to say than the author.

25 - "STAY TRUE"

Scan the playfield, everything looks broken
want to walk away, want to leave things where they lie
want to get numb want to get numb want to stay numb
but every living creature loves the moonlight in July

The rot creeps through the floor, you can't sleep safely any more
secure your tiny corner, wait for brighter days to come
it would be so easy just to let the darkness take you
but every living creature loves its brief walk in the sun

Stay true
to who
you are
stay true

Lose touch with all your friends, wonder where they went
notice where they're missing   all that empty space
hope they'll be back someday trace their names up in the night sky
every living creature loves the starlight on its face

To the souls in prison: get free someday
to ghosts gone hungry: one day you won't be hungry any more
practice all your notes, because the binding spells are breaking
every living creature hides a song down at its core

ΔΔΔ

This is in the *For the Demons* folder inside a subfolder named "Incomplete Demons." It is a riff on the American Music Club's divine, essential "Who You Are," from *The Golden Age* (2008). To my ear it's audibly of a piece with "Amy aka Spent Gladiator 1": There's not a lot of secondary meaning to tease out—formally I can hear in my head how some of its phrases would "spring" in the Hopkinsian sense, and where some key breath pauses would happen to make the meter work ("To the souls"—beat—"in prison"—beat—"get free someday"). As to why it went missing, it is probably that I forgot it existed, which remained true until just now, though I have remembered over the years that I was working on an "every living creature loves" thing I never finished.

26 - UNTIL I AM WHOLE

Sunset on Snohomish
burn the treeline down
hold my hopes underwater
stand there and watch them drown

Fishing out their bodies
from the bathroom sink
leave them in a bucket
'til they start to stink

I think I'll stay here until I feel whole again
I don't know when

Trout swim past the fishing lines
sky gets dark and close
cars start up and make
their nightly exodus

On a picnic bench alone
I watch the lake go dark
dig my nails into my hands
hope it leaves a mark

I think I'll stay here until I feel whole again
I don't know when

ΔΔΔ

Fair to say that when I write about the Pacific Northwest I get a little dark. I'm very proud of this lyric, which surely owes a little to Richard Hugo on days when he looked over his shoulder instead of out through the window; and although I should strive to be better than a man who sets up a blinking sign above a good rhyme, "dark and close" / "exodus" is me punching at least one class above my weight.

27 - LAKESIDE VIEW APARTMENTS SUITE

Downtown north past the airport,
a dream in switchgrass and concrete.
Three grey floors of smoky windows
facing the street.

Michael pulls the blinds back up,
stares blankly down at the intersection:
watching for the guy who's got the angel dust.
Crystal clear connection.

Days like dominoes, all in a line.
We cheer for the home team every time.
Lakeside View
for my whole crew.

Most nights now, sleep in the kitchen.
Keep my face cool on the floor
And John, John comes by to drop off his envelopes—
still playing postman after all these years.

Pull down my army surplus jacket.
Dig through some drawers to find the keys.
Emerge transformed in a million years
from days like these.

Under each eye, little greasepaint smudge.
You can't judge us: you're not the judge.
Lakeside View for my whole crew.

And just before I leave, I throw up in the sink.
One whole life recorded in disappearing ink.
And Ray left a message thumbtacked to the door.
I don't even bother trying to read them any more.
Lakeside View for my whole crew.

ΔΔΔ

During the time when many of my friends anticipated that I'd die young, there was a short stretch when it felt like half the people I met were named Michael. I can still see several of the Michaels in my mind's eye. One of them is very pretty and has piercing green eyes, like shards of glass from 7UP bottles. He is not actually in the crew, and I hope he never even met the crew. The crew is to be avoided where possible. Only when avoiding them is no longer possible should one consider joining up with the crew; but, having said that, we have evidence from the ones now outside that you could do worse.

28 - IN MEMORY OF SATAN

Got my paint box out last night.
Stayed up late and wrecked this place.
Woke up on the floor again
cell phone stuck to the side of my face.

Dead space on the other end.
Perfect howl of emptiness.
Cast my gaze around the room:
Someone needs to clean up this mess.

Tape up the windows.
Call in a favor from an old friend.

Make some scratches on my floor.
Crawl down on my hands and knees.
In old movies, people scream,
choking on their fists, when they see shadows like these.

But no one screams, because it's just me.
Wrapped up so tight in myself. Never going to get free.

Something sacred, something blue.
Cannons in the harbor dawn.
I crawled down here to dig for bones.
One more season then I'm gone.

Black drapes over the crosses.
Call in a favor from an old friend.

ΔΔΔ

All notions of the album as form are conjectural—there isn't any one way an album works, but there are ways of thinking about them that help make their shapes more visible. I think of albums as usually having a single gravitational point, like a star, around which the other songs orbit like planets. The notional sun will rarely be the single, the big song everybody knows; the gravitational center of an album is the song that contains something of all the others. I don't bring this idea into the sequencing of an album, because this idea is separate from sequence: Sequence is linear. The gravitational center of *The Sunset Tree* is "Pale Green Things"; the gravitational center of *The Coroner's Gambit* is the title track; and the gravitational center of *Transcendental Youth* is "In Memory of Satan," which feels at the heart of the action to me: not before the crisis or after it, but right there in the middle. That there is or was a crisis is an assumption I carry with me into battle, and without which I'd struggle to know where to begin.

29 - CRY FOR JUDAS

Some things you do just to see
how bad they'll make you feel
sometimes you try to freeze time until the slots
are a blur of spinning reels
but I am just a broken machine
and I do things that I don't really mean

Long black night
morning frost
I'm still here
but all is lost

Speed up to the precipice
and then slam on the brakes
Some people crash two or three times
and then learn from their mistakes

But we are the ones
who don't slow down at all
and there's nobody there
to catch us when we fall

Long black night
morning frost
I'm still here
but all is lost

Feel the storm every night, hope it passes by
hallucinate a shady grove where Judas went to die

Unfurl the black velvet altar cloth
draw a white chalk Baphomet
mistreat your altar boys long enough
and this is what you get
sad and angry
can't learn how to behave
still won't know how
in the darkness of the grave

Long black night
morning frost
I'm still here
but all is lost

ΔΔΔ

Famously, in the preface to *Lyrical Ballads*, Wordsworth wrote that poetry "takes its origin from emotion recollected in tranquility." I can't speak to the tranquility part, but I wrote this at the breakfast table, while my toddler son smacked at the puréed fruit on the tray of his high chair. I was at the other end of the table idly plucking a guitar. I remember hitting that pull-off A chord riff, and thinking, Say, there's something, write a little lyric for it, why don't you? The father of a toddler is often pressed for time, so about me the reader now knows that I, faced with a need to juggle several responsibilities at once and lacking time to deliberate about a theme, will simply recollect whatever I might, default to "Some things you do just to see how bad they'll make you feel," and proceed from there.

30 - STEAL SMOKED FISH

Beneath the Burnside Bridge, before
anyone shot their movies there,
we hid from the whipping rain
when we had run out of cocaine.
Dispatch down to Plaid Pantry,
two on point, and two on sentry.
Ah, the joys that the lesser days bring
make you throw back your heads and sing:
God bless all petty thieves,
with tins of oysters up their sleeves!
Feast when you can,
and dream when there's nothing to feast on.

Across a different bridge today,
over the river and down Broadway.
It feels so good to have you here.
Some of you will be dead next year.
I see your destinies above you,
like angels who don't love you:
Let them kiss you and hold you tight,
as long as the money's right.

God bless all my old friends,
and God bless me, too, why pretend?
Feast when you can,
and dream when there's nothing to feast on.

God bless the guys from my old neighborhood,
gone past the point where any blessing can do them any good.

Deploy the C-4 where you must—
disappear in a cloud of dust—
but spare a thought for what it covers up.
Pour a triple, and raise your cup:
We were here once, me and my friends,
but we destroyed all of the evidence
and vanished into the night.
At least we got that part right.
God bless us, all of us, we who learn to shun the light.
God bless all vampires every night.
Feast when you can.
Feast when you can.
Feast when you can.

ΔΔΔ

Set where the upper streams of Simois flow
was the Palladium, high 'mid rock and wood;
and Hector was in Ilium, far below,
and fought, and saw it not—but there it stood!
—MATTHEW ARNOLD, "Palladium" (1867)

. . . like that, but in a meaner place, much further down the timeline from the days when the clouds nearly touched the earth: and yet.

31 - TRANSCENDENTAL YOUTH

Cold through broken baseboards
I despise this town
snow on the sunroof
two stories down
hold hands
wish the snow away
rise in the darkness
of the gathering day
    sing for ourselves alone
    rags on sticks, skin and bone

Cedar smudge our headbands
and take to the skies
soar ever upwards
through air black with flies
shroud ourselves in the cosmos
let the music play
bright star of the morning
shine on its rising way
    sing   in the night   in the moonless dark
    father long gone, but we bear his mark

Learn some secrets, never tell
stay sick, don't get well

Clutch those broken headboards
ride the highest wave
dusky diamonds shining
in the far depths of the cave
try to explain ourselves
babble on and on

by the time you receive this we'll be gone
sing sing high while the fire climbs
sing one for the old times

ΔΔΔ

The superior first refrain, as it occurs on the album—"speak into the microphone" instead of "rags on sticks, skin and bone"—was an ad-lib in the studio, as was "nameless dark" instead of "moonless." One thing music has over poetry is this freedom to improvise, to find something better down in the living breath of the moment. I preserve the earlier draft here so that the reader will see the people in the song, people in a dark room who have not had enough to eat, both because they don't have enough money to eat well and because what money they do have they have chosen to spend on other things.

SEPTEMBER

1 - SOUTHWESTERN TERRITORY

Small screen July evening view
up and down Grand Avenue
where the legends get made
out with the boys' brigade
part of the motorcade

Flew home from Texas last night
slept on the flight
work like a dog all day
born to chase cars away
die on the road someday

I try to remember what life was like long ago
but it's gone, you know

Climb the turnbuckle high
take two falls out of three
blackout for local TV

Stand in these cold empty halls
wait for your name to get called
burn like hillsides on fire
in the squall of the ringside choir
high as wire

Nearly drive Danny's nose back into his brain
all the cheap seats go insane

Keep my eyes open and try to think straight
no one drives on the 60 this late
I feel like the last person alive
Francisquito to Glenshaw Drive

I try to remember to write in the diary,
the diary my son gave me

Climb the turnbuckle high
take two falls out of three
blackout for local TV

ΔΔΔ

This is a song about professional wrestling in Southern California in the 1970s, when it was a low stakes working-class entertainment game; and I don't usually repeat nice things said about me by my betters, but I'll make an exception for the time Chavo Guerrero Sr., my childhood hero, told me over dinner, about this song: "You really got that one right." It was one of the proudest moments of my life, both because it meant I'd given something back to an artist who'd given me so much, and because poetry is largely guesswork. See what you see, make a few assumptions, see if they pan out. They don't always. It's nice when they do.

2 - THE LEGEND OF CHAVO GUERRERO

Born down in El Paso, where the tumbleweeds blow
to the middleweight champ of all Mexico
Dad fought many bloody battles, and he raised four sons
Chavo was the oldest one

Old man Gory could pop like a live grenade
raised his boys in the way of the trade

Hector and Mando, young Eddie G.
but Chavo meant the most to me

look high, it's my last hope
Chavo Guerrero coming off the top rope

He came from Texas seeking fortune and fame
rose pretty quickly to the top of the game
defender of the downtrodden, king of the hill
tag-team champion with Al Madril

Before a black-and-white TV in the middle of the night
I'm lying on the floor, I'm bathed in blue light
the telecast's in Spanish, I can understand some
and I need justice in my life. Here it comes

look high, it's my last hope
Chavo Guerrero coming off the top rope

Red Shoes Dugan holding his arm high, all out of breath
I hated all of Chavo's enemies, I would pray nightly for their death
descending like fire on the people who deserved it most
almost completely unknown outside of Texas and on the West Coast

He was my hero back when I was a kid
you let me down, but Chavo never once did
you called him names to try to get beneath my skin
now your ashes are scattered on the wind

I heard his son got famous and he went nationwide
coast-to-coast with his dad by his side
I don't know if that's true, but I've been told
it's real sweet to grow old

look high, it's my last hope
Chavo Guerrero coming off the top rope

ΔΔΔ

Formally this is an outlaw ballad, a tale of an outsider finding glory in a world that wasn't made for him. I write about a lot of outsiders but the straight glory-to-his-name ballad I don't usually do, because I resist heroes, idols, anybody on a pedestal. Still. It was the lead single from *Beat the Champ*, released on April 7, 2015. Social media was hot at that time, and by the end of that day, Chavo himself, who had a Twitter account, posted that he'd been getting phone calls all day telling him about his song. We reached out and arranged the video shoot; and when the day came, he was so generous with his time and his spirit. He taught me, in the ring, how to grapple, giving of himself so completely over the course of a ten-plus hour shoot that I can point to that day as one in which I learned a lesson about the kind of person I want to be, and about how I hope to be seen by others. We stayed in touch until he died. This book is filled with anecdotes whose conclusions are ambiguous or cryptic, because I see life as a generally ambiguous and cryptic affair, but about Chavo Guerrero Sr., the true champion of the world, I have no ambiguities. My hero then, and now.

3 - FOREIGN OBJECT

Whipped like a dog, down on the cards
square in the spotlight sweating real hard
all soaked in blood like a newborn babe
sharp thing hidden in my hand shaped like an astrolabe

I'm going to stick you in the eye with a foreign object
I'm going to poke you in the eye with a foreign object

March through the red mist, never get my vision clear
learn to love this kind of atmosphere
strike funny poses, keep my weapon hand low
whip my head around a little, get blood on the front row

I'm going to jab you in the eye with a foreign object
I personally will stab you in the eye with a foreign object
foreign object, foreign object, foreign object

Sink my teeth into your scalp, take a nice big bite
save nothing for the camera, play the angles all night
one of these days my legs'll both snap like twigs
if you can't beat 'em, make 'em bleed like pigs

I'm going to jab you in the eye with a foreign object
I'm going to stab you in the eye with a foreign object

ΔΔΔ

That's how the television commentators describe whatever weapon a heel is using to bloody his adversary: "He's got a foreign object." The foreign object is an item of mystical, totemic power. You can't make out its shape, sometimes it doesn't even look like it could do any damage. But the blood is everywhere and the opponent is reeling. Such is the power, the force, the majesty of the unidentifiable foreign object.

4 - ANIMAL MASK

Eighteen-man steel cage free-for-all
through the noise I hear you call

for help;
you can't protect yourself

Frog mask and yellow cape
so desperate to escape
I came to you
hands wrapped in adhesive tape

That was when we were young and green
in the dawning hours of our team

Some things you will remember
some things stay sweet forever

Seen you backstage once or twice
animal gimmick pops real nice
elbow sweep and tiger dance
little extra fighter's chance

"Hold on!" I cried, "I'll be right there!"
Pull your mask down through your hair
they won't see you
not until you want them to

That was when we were green and young
battle cry rising from your tongue

Some things you will remember
some things stay sweet forever

ΔΔΔ

There are several things on *Beat the Champ* that are outside my usual working methods: one of them is allegory, as here. It's not a steel cage, it's the labor-and-delivery room, and every aspect of the match detailed is an account of the birth of my first son, Roman. The elbow sweep is what you see when the fetus, in the third trimester, starts wriggling around so much that you can make out the points of its elbows through the skin on his mother's stomach. One August day the wriggling grew too restive to contain and the battle was joined. We split the purse that day and he is wriggling still.

5 - CHOKED OUT

Diamonds in the firmament
all reserves completely spent
someone set up the oxygen tent
everybody here's real proud to present "Choked Out"

$200 take-all purse
half-nelson to suplex reverse
worried look on the face of the ringside nurse
at one for once with the universe

choked out

I stretch and strain with all my might
drift off into the velvety arms of the night
kick and claw and scratch and bite
fire up the grill, everybody eats tonight

choked out

no brakes down an endless deep incline
most of the boys won't ever cross this line
if they all want to die dead broke that's fine
everybody's got their limits nobody's found mine

crowd screaming like hounds in the heat of the chase
all the colors of the rainbow flood my face
I lift right off into space
I can see the future, it's a real dark place

choked out
choked out
choked out

ΔΔΔ

To my point from the September 4 entry: I don't usually do *a-a-a-a* rhyme schemes—that is Bob Dylan's job. Still, sometimes, in my line of work, you try your hand at Bob Dylan's job, if only to measure the distance from the chokehold to the infinite night sky on the other side of it.

6 - HEEL TURN 1

The ushers and the guys who chuck the popcorn
they feel the rush of stillness in the air
and turn toward the ring from where they're standing
I'm just lying there

But I hoist myself bolt-upright on one hand
and I pull up on my haunches, and I face the crowd
the guy who knocked me down has got his back turned
in comes the great grey pestilent cloud

I'm not going to die in here
I'm not going to die in here

Worked hard to be a hero all my life
always try to turn the other cheek

and save my closed-fist punches for the ones who throw them first
always show some mercy to the wounded and the weak

Always help a bad guy to his feet
always help old ladies cross the street

I see my guardian angel leave the building
I am my only friend
one thing about the good guys that I've noticed—
they always beg for mercy in the end

I'm not going to die in here
I'm not going to die in here

ΔΔΔ

A wrestler "turns heel" when he aligns himself with the forces of evil—when he starts cheating to win, trading scientific holds for eye gouges and embracing a darkness that the babyface, or good guy, seeks to destroy. You can ask anybody who's seen night fall even twice in their life about what luck you might expect to have opposing the darkness.

7 - HEEL TURN 2

Get stomped like a snake
lie down in the dirt
cling to my convictions
even when I get hurt
be an upstanding, well-loved man about town—
in your child's mind, that's how it goes down
but I tried the losing side
I don't want to die in here
I don't want to die in here

Drift down into the new dark light
without any reservations
you found my breaking point:
congratulations!
Spent too much of my life
trying to play fair
throw my better self overboard
shoot at him when he comes up for air
come unhinged
get revenge
I don't want to die in here
I don't want to die in here

Stay good under pressure for years, and years, and years, and
years
president of the fan club up there choking on his tears

Let all the trash rain down
from way up in the rafters
I'm walking out of here in one piece:
don't care what comes after
drive the wedge
torch the bridge
I don't want to die in here
I don't want to die in here

ΔΔΔ

This is a book about lyrics, but the musical coda for this song, Gmaj7 articulations drifting out into space on a grand piano, came to me in a dream during the week when we were tracking the album; the song would otherwise have just ended after the last chorus. This almost never happens to me: a dream of the work during the undertaking of the work, a dream I bring into the work. My dreams don't usually have executable commands in them. The song also didn't have any Gmaj7 in it prior to the dream: It's driven by a straight power G, big and bold and bright. No chord has inherent character, everything's a matter of context, but I can never hear a major seventh without feeling a little of the gravity of life moving in like a fog. This was the news from my dream: Bring in the major seventh and let it do its work.

8 - FIRE EDITORIAL

Two blinded in Detroit!
Something must be done.
Jaws dropping at ringside
in the blood tide
when the fireball hits.

Down Indiana way
make 'em check their guns.
Real tears when it's over
smell the sulfur
when the dark vault splits.

Lord of the hidden pocketknife!
Tawdry dreams all come to life.
Save yourselves.
Save this town, save everything not nailed down.

War in Ontario!
Dead before the bell.
Crushed hopes of the young breed
all the best bleed,
all the proud boys break.

Who'll stand before the flood?
Who will mop up all the blood?
Who, alone?
Skin, bone, steel, stone
swim or drown.
Save this town, save everything not nailed down.

ΔΔΔ

Musically one of the things I'm proudest of having done, an attempt to stretch beyond my working habits into new territory—and succeeding on my own terms; all the heavier cuts on *Goths* are picking up the gauntlet thrown down by "Fire Editorial." Its main character is Ed Farhat, who wrestled under the name "the Sheik" and was known for throwing fire at his opponents. Fire? Yes; it was a magician's trick. Farhat, born the same year as my father to a Lebanese family in Lansing, Michigan, was a promoter in the Michigan territory; as the Sheik, he never broke character once. Wrestling magazines decried his heel tactics in hand-wringing editorials that inspired visions of in-ring death in my young brain, and this song adds another voice to the chorus of voices worried that someday Ed Farhat was going to burn somebody alive.

9 - STABBED TO DEATH OUTSIDE SAN JUAN

The winter's wet, and the summer's hot
take a match in Puerto Rico—why not?

Power and adrenaline flowing like amber
from the recesses of the earth. Put on your waders,
and twitch when the water runs high sometimes
twitch when the tide ebbs low

See the sights, maybe go downtown;
sometimes you get some heat, sometimes it follows you
around

When the blade hits the bone, everybody hears it sing
Shower room full of people, no one hears a God damned thing
Twitch when the current runs wild sometimes
Twitch when the contact howls

All that racket out there in the arena—
I'm on the stretcher. Here come the cleaners

And the sky goes dark, and there I am,
climbing down the Hertzsprung-Russell diagram
I drop from the top of my tall steel cage
drop to the concrete floor

ΔΔΔ

Bruiser Brody, born Frank Donald Goodish in 1946, was forty-two years old on the day José González, who wrested under the name Invader 1, stabbed him in a locker room in San Lorenzo, Puerto Rico. Key witnesses proved unavailable for testimony and González was acquitted: self-defense. He walked free. To die on the road, away from home, at work: This is the stuff of nightmares, and of legends.

10 - WEREWOLF GIMMICK

I was not there for rehearsal, I don't need it any more
when I show up just in time to pop you can clear the God
damned floor
empty out the locker room, let me find my space
let him who thinks he knows no fear look well upon my face

nameless bodies in unremembered rooms
know how a man becomes a beast when the wolfbane blooms

Sail past all the grasping hands, floodlights white and hot
bring my vision into focus, find out what I've got
some sniveling local babyface with an angle he can't sell
full werewolf off the buckle like an angel straight from hell

nameless bodies in unremembered rooms
the pure at heart go putrid when the wolfbane blooms

Half the city sound asleep and safe inside their beds
get lost inside my thoughts and nearly tear his face to shreds

Blood pooling on the canvas as the atmosphere gets hushed
send your heroes to the wolf's den, watch them all get crushed
get told to maybe dial it back backstage later on
anyone left in this building right now: dead before the dawn

nameless bodies in unremembered rooms
run howling through the carnage when the wolfbane blooms

ΔΔΔ

A wrestler's gimmick is his hook, his angle, his persona. People who don't care for wrestling use words like "fake" in talking about it, but when you live a gimmick day in and day out for years, what's really fake? I am what my body does. The promoter who wants me to dial it back does not understand that there is no dial.

11 - LUNA

All gone, all gone
watching it go up out front on the lawn

stay on my feet somehow
I'm strong now
stuck there, no air

Head high, head high
tongues of fire that reach up for the sky
rise through the smoke
the dust of the grave
I will be saved

pause in mid-stride
pause in mid-stride
and ride, and ride, and ride, and ride

Burn hard, burn hard
smoldering pieces landing in the yard
trace names in ash
big names, old friends
and dead ends

Those last few frames
go down so fast
Crawl through the flames and end again in flames at last

Stay free, stay free
invisible armies march by night for me
stay on my guard
burn hard
rage on all gone

pause in mid-stride
pause in mid-stride
and ride and ride and ride and ride

ΔΔΔ

Luna Vachon, whose in-ring persona crackled with a kind of electricity you can neither buy nor approximate by imitation, took her own life in 2010, a little less than a year after seeing her house and everything in it destroyed by fire. Her life story is one of triumph after triumph over adversity after adversity, for forty-eight years. When boxers die they toll a final ten-count at ringside. This song counts ten for a wrestler who came up from the Florida territory in glory and who, in every inch of existing footage, brought her art to life.

12 · SONG FOR SASHA BANKS

We don't get cable in Belle Plaines
but on Thursday nights there's matches on TV
get kicked out of the living room for watching
my brother and me, my brother and me

Keep watching with the lights out back in his room
Chris Jericho starts tearing up the set
I want to do right by my brother
I want to do right by this feeling in my gut

Everybody's got
their own spot
find mine
in 64-point type up on the top line

Head off to camp in Boston
come up through the independents
those who would stand between me and my final destination
get burned up in the fire of my transcendence

California, Minnesota, Massachusetts
they can tell I'm coming up by the expression on my face
I'm gonna make a lot of money
everyone I love is gonna have their own safe place

Everybody's got
their own spot
find mine
in 64-point type up on the top line

ΔΔΔ

Sasha Banks tagged me on social media when *Beat the Champ* came out, asking: "Where's my song, @mountain_goats?" The kayfabe thing to do was write a song for her, and that's what I did. She'd spent time as a child in the same sorts of Iowa facilities where I'd worked when I lived there, I learned. We don't know each other personally but I knew a lot of Iowa kids who dreamed of big futures, and when I learned her story I was glad to have one more wrestling story to tell.

13 - THE BALLAD OF BULL RAMOS

Drive a great big truck
when I'm old, when I'm old
haul the wrecks down to the wreck yard
help the boys unload

Keep my hair nice and long
because I can, because I can
any of my old friends who have a place to turn to
they know to call me any time they come through

Never die, never die
stand with a bullwhip in my hand

and rise, rise
in the desert sand

Work days, work night
finally get laid up
by a piece of broken glass
on the floor of the shop

And the doctor recognizes me
as the operating theater goes dim
"Aren't you that old wrestler with the bullwhip?"
Yes sir, that's me, I'm him

Get around fine on one leg
lose a kidney, then go blind
sit on my porch in Houston
let the good times dance across my mind

Never die, never die
stand with a bullwhip in my hand
and rise, rise
surrounded by friends

ΔΔΔ

Wrestlers, like musicians, keep going until they can't. I'd guess modern wrestlers who hit the big time have 401(k) programs and can conceive of some path to retirement, but the wrestlers I grew up with were lucky if their paychecks didn't bounce. If they managed to leave the game, they went back to civilian life—they might coach high school sports, they might open a gym.

Manuel Ramos began wrestling in 1964 and worked, usually under the name Apache Bull Ramos, for a quarter of a century. He was the inventor of the Texas Rope Match; his heel persona drew heat from crowds in the southwest and around the country, facing Bruno Sammartino at Madison Square Garden and winning championship belts not only in the United States but abroad; Chavo Guerrero told me Ramos was one of the nicest people you could ever hope to meet. After he stepped down he ran a towing service in Houston and lived to be sixty-eight. By the numbers, that's not bad for an entertainer. Whether you're working from a script or not, you're happy when you can beat the odds.

14 - HAIR MATCH

You'll be maybe lunging for the bad guy's hip
no one anticipates the sunset flip
the referee and your opponent will hold you there
and we're going to bring in a folding chair

We'll stipulate that there will be no cameras filming
but of course there will be several in the building
and if by chance somebody hits "record"
and stands real still somewhere back behind the soundboard

Cheap electric razor from the Thrifty down the street
two guys down around your ankles so you'll stay put in your seat
buzzing razor held aloft and just about to strike
I loved you before I even ever knew what love was like

Some people leave before it's over; most of them stay
some hide behind their programs—some turn away
out in the parking lot you look up at the stars
and all the cheap cars

ΔΔΔ

"Breaking the fourth wall," right—getting outside of the action in order to say what the action's really all about, setting up an establishing shot and coming in from overhead like Orson Welles on a crane, letting your thumb into the frame on purpose. Finding out what you're talking about not by talking about it but just by talking. Trying to make sense of something from a long time ago. Getting there.

15 - BLOOD CAPSULES

When the last of the East Coast money ran dry
and the casually dressed bill collectors started casually dropping on by
and the residuals—well, there weren't any more residuals
and me several months behind on the payments to certain individuals

I strolled into the lobby, mouth full: blood capsules
I strolled into the lobby, mouth full: blood capsules

I'm off the juice for seven months—I learn to like living clean
but there just isn't any money on the independent scene
not even if you're cutting corners: staying in nights, eating alone
somebody's got to pay the gas bill, it's not going to go away on its own

I strolled into the lobby, mouth full: blood capsules
I strolled into the lobby, mouth full: blood capsules

I'm the biggest guy in the bank line
everybody else looks tiny
I can almost smell the fear
on the lunch hour car salesman behind me

I know this isn't going to work
I guess I'll see you when I see you

I can't work any other jobs
this was my last best idea

I strolled into the lobby, mouth full: blood capsules
I strolled into the lobby, mouth full: blood capsules

ΔΔΔ

If I, in terrific shape, no longer using steroids because I can no longer afford them but maintaining a meticulous daily fitness program because that is just who I am, walk into a beautiful old bank in downtown Los Angeles and get in line; and if the people in the bank then begin to notice, as I stand there, that blood is streaming from my mouth, quite a lot of blood, and that, maybe, my hands are shaking, or I'm staring menacingly into space; and if the whole scene, as it develops, begins to feel like something outlined and then written down, on paper or on the back of a paperback, something whose dramatic arc, anyhow, needs must culminate in a climax: What is that climax? What am I thinking? What, in my mind's eye, do I see? How do I get money from this? No, really: How do I get money from this?

16 · FOR THE PORTUGUESE GOTH METAL BANDS

Sift the spectrum for the greyscale—that's better
favor bold fonts in black letter
star-crossed lovers and their tragic fates
and that one Celtic Frost record almost everybody hates

Candlelight playing its tricks on the walls of the cave
Hauling these songs to the light from the mouth of the grave

Mark the map out for the treasure, don't say where
find the octave in the shadow, and stay there

sleep 'til sunset, stay up late
bleed bile all night into an SM58

Candlelight playing its tricks on the walls of the cave
hauling these songs to the light from the mouth of the grave

Finally head west, but it's a dead end
come home dead broke but still among friends
keep what's precious, drop what's not
without a second thought

There's not so many of us
there's maybe twenty of us
work like a gravedigger, let the blood spill
headline really big festivals every other summer in Brazil

Candlelight playing its tricks on the walls of the cave
hauling these songs to the light from the mouth of the grave

ΔΔΔ

Our sixteenth studio album was called *Goths* but the working title for the album was *Death Rock Fantasie for Fender Rhodes and Small Band*, because the southern California mini-subgenre death rock, which preceded goth, had an empirically cooler name. "Death rock." Only "speed metal" can really joust with "death rock" in the realm of live-instrument subgenre names. "Goth metal," meanwhile, isn't a proper subgenre but a way of describing metal bands who clearly and obviously have one or more goths in their lineup; European heavy metal, to its lasting credit, showed its goth pedigree early, in the early nineties, when it was terminally unhip to do so. I love the goth metal bands because they are living proof of how small forgotten things grow in the hearts of those who cherish them. They find new life in the work of the people who tended to their memory. We should all be so lucky.

17 - THE GREY KING AND THE SILVER FLAME ATTUNEMENT

In the secret caverns underneath West Covina
half-desperate for peace with the surface dwellers
but coming to no conclusions
and now we emerge, sky grey and misty

The Grey King in his new Pontiac
some of us sworn to the effort, trying get our shapes back
teeth filed down to fine points
framework too tight, strain at the joints

And I'm hardcore, but I'm not that hardcore

Load into the Grand Am, doomed sailors
borne high by the waves, wild with wonder
leather and lace, and good friends
most of them good, most of them friendly

The Grey King at the rail, sparks flying
three of us in the car with him, scared of dying
all eyes on the front seat
assuming his form, reborn in the heat

and I'm hardcore but I'm not that hardcore

ΔΔΔ

In an earlier draft the second line was "Three to two against surface world coexistence"—if you're rhyming "Covina" you either have to get cute ("gardenia," "ballerina," or any number of choices where you pronounce "you" like "yuh" for the rhyme: no thanks) or commit to the hard slant. I ended up going full blank verse with what I'll call "heavy assonance" if I ever get around to writing *John's Glossary of Personal Idiosyncratic Poetic Terms*, and I think this choice is part of what makes this song a favorite—the A verse of each half floats rhythmically over languid major-seventh-intensive café jazz, and then, as the action clarifies and the stakes increase, exact rhymes tighten the corners: the joints and the points, the seat and the heat. The actual scene took place at the on-ramp to the San Bernardino freeway, and I wasn't in the Grey King's car. I was a stranger in the car next to him, and, when I looked at him just before we both turned right, he showed me his fangs. The other people in his car all burst out laughing, and then they were gone. Today as then I salute my King.

18 - UNICORN TOLERANCE

Drawn to the dark
covered by the blood, when possible
called to the corners
to any open crucible

Easy to reach
bearing every mark unmissably
want to leave behind some token
of what I carried with me

Search in the storm drains
sleep in the underpasses
try hard to look hard
in my blackout sunglasses

but I have high unicorn tolerance

Swim with real sharks
those who never speak when spoken to
hard limits fade into memory
once broken through

Scaling the well
every single day, instinctively
feel shame, real shame
for what my friends must think of me

Dig through the graveyard
rub the bones against my face
it gets real nice around the graveyard
once you've acquired the taste

And when the clouds do clear away
get a momentary chance to see
the thing I've been trying to beat to death
the soft creature that I used to be
the better animal I used to be

drawn where I'm drawn
seldom wonder why, just follow You
never blame the rags that swaddled me
for the place the river took me to
long life to the spiders!
safe travels to the crow!
love to the ghosts
who taught me everything I know

but I have high unicorn tolerance

ΔΔΔ

From *Goths*, two titles—this one and "Wear Black" (September 21)—number among the most personal songs I've ever written, and consequently it's always hard to talk about them, because from my vantage point anything that needs to be said is right there in the song. This is me at nineteen: unable to tell anybody "no," incapable of showing my naked face to the world, unhappy in my own skin, resentful of the real me still living under all the layers of hurt and anger—layers that stand in for me to the world, layers that then constitute my knowable self. I am alive today by grace, and because the wounded being at my core—the person I really was and am, the one I could not kill—believed in the magic of fragile things, in the holiness of thin ice, and because he held those beliefs strongly enough to fight back. His victory took years; in the early going, a girlfriend gave me a coffee cup with a gilt image of a unicorn on it, and I remembered how I'd loved unicorns as a child. Hence, in a broad sense: all this.

19 · STENCH OF THE UNBURIED

Incoherent but functional
speeding like a dead comet
purple crushed velvet waistcoat
flecked with Maalox and bits of dried vomit

Say what you will for the effort,
you can't fault the technique
still conscious at sunrise
for the third time this week

But when the blue lights flash
I know we're going to crash
outside it's 92 degrees
and KROQ is playing Siouxsie and the Banshees

Blaupunkt in the dashboard
cracks in the cylinder block
heading up the Golden State freeway
toward Eagle Rock

Ice chest full of Corona
and Pineapple Crush
it'll take twenty years
for the toxins to flush

And when the sirens wail
I know we're going to jail
outside it's 92 degrees
and KROQ is playing Siouxsie and the Banshees

Follow the flame to freedom
the flickering lights of Armageddon
find the foot of the ladder
way down in the pit
keep climbing forever
keep the torch lit

and outside it's 92 degrees
and KROQ is playing Siouxsie and the Banshees

ΔΔΔ

The Fender Rhodes, an electric piano with adjustable tremolo, produces a sound so captivating that lyrics have to compete with it. I play one on every track on *Goths*, whose music—the chords, the changes, the instrumentation—is meant to be pretty: soothing, maybe, narcotizing absolutely. Peter Hughes, in the studio, remarked that the songs were among the funniest I'd written in years, probably the funniest since the early days, and I agree: "Unicorn Tolerance" and "Wear Black" (September 21) are exceptions, but otherwise there's laughs to be had in every song, not at the expense of the goths but with them, which is to say "with us." If you can't laugh at yourself when you're cleaning dried puke from your purple velvet waistcoat and expecting to wake up in jail—well, then, truly I must ask you, friend: What can you laugh at?

20 - RAIN IN SOHO

NO ONE KNOWS WHERE THE LONE WOLF SLEEPS
NO ONE SEES THE HIDDEN TREASURE IN THE CASTLE KEEP
NO ONE LEARNS THE SECRET NAME
NO ONE BURNS IN THE ABSENT FLAME

NO ONE BROKE D. B. COOPER'S FALL
NO ONE HOPES TO HEAR THE BAGMAN CALL
CHILDREN PIPING IN THE MAIN SQUARE
BUT NO ONE'S DANCING, NO ONE'S DANCING DOWN THERE

THE RIVER GOES WHERE THE WATER FLOWS
BUT NO ONE KNOWS WHEN THE BATCAVE CLOSED

NO PROMISE SWEETER THAN A BLOOD PACT
NOTHING HARDER TO GO THROUGH WITH THAN A VANISHING ACT
NO MORNING COLDER THAN THE FIRST FROST
NO FRIENDS CLOSER THAN THE ONES WE'VE LOST

NOTHING SHARPER THAN A SERPENT'S TOOTH
NOTHING HARDER THAN THE GOSPEL TRUTH
THOUGH YOU REPENT, AND DON SACKCLOTH, AND TRY TO MAKE NICE
YOU CAN'T CROSS THE SAME RIVER TWICE

THE RIVER GOES WHERE THE WATER FLOWS
BUT NO ONE KNOWS WHEN THE BATCAVE CLOSED

THERE'S A CLUB WHERE YOU'D LIKE TO GO
YOU COULD MEET SOMEONE WHO'S LOST LIKE YOU

REVEL IN THE DARKNESS LIKE A PAIR OF OPEN
GRAVES
FUMBLE THROUGH THE FOG FOR A SEASON OR TWO

NO TOWN MORE BARREN THAN OUR TOWN
NO HAVEN SAFER THAN THE ONE THEY TORE DOWN
NO GREATER LOVE THAN TO LAY MY LIFE DOWN FOR
A FRIEND
NO SWEETER PLEASURE THAN TO SEE THE CREDITS
CLEAR THROUGH TO THE END
NO ONE KNOWS WHERE THE LONE WOLF'S GONE
NO ONE SEES HIM CAMPED OUT RIGHT THERE ON
THE FRONT LAWN
WE PLAYED FOR YOU BUT YOU WOULD NOT SING
NO ONE'S GOING TO GET AWAY WITH ANYTHING

THE RIVER GOES WHERE THE WATER FLOWS
BUT NO ONE KNOWS WHEN THE BATCAVE CLOSED

ΔΔΔ

All-caps preserved from the draft on my hard drive: It means what it says. When I wrote this, a toddler, who is now a teenager, lived in my house. He was usually by my side as I tracked demos at my office piano, which is why few of those demos have seen release—often, their flow gets interrupted by a father chatting with his charming young son. This song was hard work: good hard work; any song relying on a formula (here, that each line be a negation or denial of something) requires the sort of careful tending you'd give to an English garden. After I'd gotten the demo together I listened to it a fair bit, and then one morning I went for a walk with said toddler son, who couldn't yet pronounce words very clearly, so that, when he began to sing as we walked, it took me a minute to realize that he was singing the line about the Batcave. The Batcave itself was the London club inside which goth was properly born; and here I was, years later, enjoying the privilege of hearing my two-year-old sing some lines I'd written about it as he toddled down the sidewalk one December day many years after its closing, an incalculable distance from the person I'd been when I first heard of it. It's a photographer's studio now. I began a list of writers who could not make this up, but it was just a list of all the writers I could name.

21 - WEAR BLACK

Rain every day, fog all night
wind in the evergreen cypresses
see me, Lord of wind and rain
see me, guardian of the underpasses

Wear black when it's light outside
wear black when there's no light
wear black following the left-hand path
wear black when I get right

Waves at night, hard waves at dawn
all this coast is vanishing
check me out, I can't blend in
check me out, I'm young and ravishing

Wear black on Your forgotten radar
wear black in the present tense
wear black when You come around
wear black in Your absence

Wear black high as a kite
wear black dead sober
wear black when the trouble starts
wear black when it's over

Sun through the trees
head for the sun
can't find the path back to the main road
see me, Lord the Thomas Guide
see me, Keeper of the Source Code

Wear black to the intervention
wear black back to the car
wear black wherever I go
wear black wherever You are

ΔΔΔ

This is the other more-or-less-straight-autobiography song on *Goths*, and it's also a more pure song than lyric—each "wear black" is sung by a four-man chorus in harmony; I did all four parts on the demo, but the album version is sung, beautifully, by Robert Bailey, Michael Mishaw, Everett Drake, and Jason Eskridge, all under Bailey's direction. Typographically, there are ways of trying to capture the effect of voices in conversation—quotation marks, italics, indentations—but none of them can really accomplish what arrangement does simply by setting several human voices on different lines of the stave. The one thing type can do that the song can't do is capitalize that Y. This is a song about feeling lost but declining to feel abandoned. All its constituent parts try to sketch this condition. It was, for me, one of those level-up songs, where I went somewhere, but the place I went was in the past, and I went there to bring some focus from the future.

22 - WE DO IT DIFFERENT ON THE WEST COAST

The papers write about it back in England
it's practically a lifestyle in Berlin
there's probably some pockets in Ohio
almost always something happening in Ohio

I heard some bad reports about Long Island
I don't trust what people say about Long Island
heard some good things from some friends about Chicago
gotta see with my own eyes about Chicago

We do it different on the West Coast

I heard they had a problem with some skinheads
at a show in a machine shop in Pomona
feel like half my friends have moved to San Francisco
I think I'm gonna bleach my hair this weekend

And Dave went to New York, I don't care
you can't shut people up
once they get back from their Christmas out there

skim through such magazines as I can get my hands on
glue circuit boards to plywood on the weekend
trellis modulation for the children
there's a whole new world right up around the corner

We do it different on the West Coast

ΔΔΔ

You got your Florida goths and you got your Minnesota goths and New York heard about it first no doubt and you can't sleep on Chicago, Chicago is really where the movement picks up enough muscle to stay viable, maximum respect to Chicago, but where did we grow it not from cuttings but from seed? Where, I would argue, did the contamination enter the general supply of grain? Once by the Pacific, people, check the photographic record, black eyeshadow was our meat and mascara, mascara our only water. As to Dave, he is a composite of several people who went to New York and about whose doings there we did not, and still don't, care.

23 - RAGE OF TRAVERS

Close the balcony at the Rainbow
because the promoter said so

Aviators and a buckskin hat
how come they dress like that

They break the news to me so gentle
but I start to feel sentimental

This used to be the place to go
still draw pretty good in Ontario

Nobody wants to hear the twelve-bar blues
from a guy in platform shoes

Let's just have a good time when the show's done
ask where the good clubs are, and go find one

Roll up to the curb, spill out of the car
Everyone's dressed up like corpses. I brought my guitar

Set it down by the stage
the singer is locked in a steel cage

Shaking the bars, eyes wild with fear
I don't belong here

Nobody wants to hear the twelve-bar blues
from a guy in platform shoes

ΔΔΔ

I'm telling a story about a guitarist from the rock era showing up at a goth club and trying to sit in, but I'm also doing a formal exercise where each couplet is its own poem that could stand in for the whole song. "Close the balcony" is something clubs do when they haven't sold enough tickets for people to sit there; it looks bad to just have a scant handful of people in a sea of balcony seating. I should say that this story is an exercise in mythmaking about the defeat of the old at the able hands of the new; the new demands a feeling of having claimed a throne, but all that ever really occurs is a displacement. Things don't actually vanish. The album within which the song occurs is only one demonstration of this claim.

24 - PAID IN COCAINE

Crusty boots in the corner of the closet by the tackle box
once-proud shining silver buckles safe behind the normalcy locks
baubles and bangles, a lost age
still all aglow with the radiance of the stage

That's who I was;
this is who I am
work to pay down the interest on the mortgage
used to get paid by the gram

Long Beach, can you hear me?
Can you hear me, Long Beach?

Master tape from the show we did at Fender's back in '85
fresh dark navy paisley from Retail Slut

all four of us fresh and alive
flashes and phosphenes, hard to believe that's me
strapped in, visibly sweating
as happy as I'm ever going to be

And you're by my side,
five years left on your card
you're cashing out, all dressed up
for your date with the emergency ward

Long Beach, can you hear me?
Can you hear me, Long Beach?

ΔΔΔ

Fender's was the club in Long Beach where I saw Christian Death on the *Catastrophe Ballet* tour—and Celtic Frost on *Into the Pandemonium*, and Megadeth on *Peace Sells . . . But Who's Buying?*, and many other shows. Bills at Fender's were usually at least three bands deep, often more; unknown acts competed to snag the local-opener slot supporting some big touring band. Some of these bands went on to bigger things, but most never did. The names of those bands, in small script on Xeroxed flyers, vanish into memory. But did they love their moment on the stage less than the bigger bands whose names we can still call to mind? To the contrary. Theirs was the moment, the heart of it all.

25 - SHELVED

I want to ride the hydraulics
lit up like the North Star
I want to wallow in the spoils before the crowd
I want to play my guitar

Not gonna sit up and beg
not gonna do tricks
not gonna stand here on a soundstage
tethered to a crucifix

The ride's over, I know
but I'm not ready to go

I want to flash my pastel colors by the rail
on a windy day at Pimlico
don't wanna write songs with this clown they set me up with
in a Los Angeles rehearsal studio

Not going to tour with Trent Reznor
third of three, bottom of the bill
you can't pay me to make that kind of music
not gonna swallow that pill

the ride's over, I know
but I'm not ready to go

Maybe Dad is right: I'm still young
and I can write C++ just as good as anyone
I know this guy at LucasArts, he says they're looking for hands
in fifteen years I'll be puttin' back beers with my feet in the sand

ΔΔΔ

There is only one lyrical cowrite in the entire Mountain Goats catalog (there's a couple more in the Extra (G)Len(n)s one) and this is it—Peter Hughes was loving the direction of *Goths* as it took shape, and Peter's engagement with my work inspired and encouraged me many, many times over the years. I wrote this song and tracked the demo with a wordless coda from the song's gothy D minor groove to an imperial D major. The song's about a goth band who've gotten a big contract and who understand that selling out isn't going to work—that momentary gain isn't going to be worth the loss of who and what they are, but that the bargain isn't being offered buffet-style. I wrote four verses and the chorus and asked Peter to write the end of the story; and, gloriously, better than I'd have been able to do it, he did.

26 - ABANDONED FLESH

Robert Smith is secure at his villa in France
any child knows how to do the spiderweb dance
Siouxsie has enough hits to keep the bills paid
every New Year's in Los Angeles, you can still see Richard Blade

but the world forgot about Gene Loves Jezebel
yes the world forgot about Gene Loves Jezebel

They charted once or twice, they were on a major label
when the singer went solo they left money on the table
the two main guys are related, they're at war with each other
now there's two Genes loving Jezebel, one for each brother

But the world
came to agree
what you see is what you get
and what you get is what you see

Whether you're the March Violets, or the Bolshoi—
bands who had to leave the darkness for the sun—
Red Lorry Yellow Lorry were on Cherry Red, I think,
they've been playing clubs since 1981

To be fair to Gene Loves Jezebel, Billy Corgan brought them onstage
it was in 2011, it's on their Wikipedia page
but for the most part, however big that chorused bass may throb
you and me, and all of us, are going to have to find a job

Because the world will never know or understand
the suffocated splendor
of the once and future goth band

ΔΔΔ

Most goth bands renounce goth either earlier or later—"there's so much more to us than that," they'll say. They'll draw distinctions between fashion and style, and say something about judging books by their covers, and they'll be right enough in all that, but still, be all that as it well may be, every goth band is a once and future goth band. Whether they like it or not is only a matter of perspective.

27 - GET HIGH AND LISTEN TO THE CURE

I want to get high
I want to get high
I want to get high, and listen to the Cure all night
I want to get high
I want to get high
I want to get high, and listen to the Cure all night

"One Hundred Years,"
"All Cats Are Grey,"
"A Short Term Effect,"
"Fire in Cairo,"
"In Between Days"

I want to get high
I want to get high
I want to get high, and listen to the Cure all night

"10:15 Saturday Night,"
"The Same Deep Water as You,"
"Always Jumping Someone Else's Train,"
The whole of *Pornography*,
especially side two

I want to get high
I want to get high
I want to get high, and listen to the Cure all night
I want to get high
I want to get high
I want to get high, and listen to the Cure all night

"A Forest," "Secrets,"
"Cold," "The Figurehead,"
"Primary," "Charlotte Sometimes,"
"Let's Go to Bed"

I want to get high
I want to get high
I want to get high

ΔΔΔ

As I see it there are two paths I might take in appending descriptive text to this lyric. One would be to write an essay of no fewer than ten thousand words in which I tell the history of the Cure, a band from West Sussex, and situate their music in its historical and cultural context. The other, which is the one I'm taking, is to claim, fairly I think, that the text really speaks for itself.

28 - SWAMP DUST

You locked yourself
in a studio apartment
somewhere in
the Pacific Northwest
So many things
I never told you
so many small betrayals
I never confessed

You slept in the kitchen
with the window open
cold grey sky
breathing down your neck
Nobody knew
you were rising from this world
'til the bank returned
your rent check

ushering in the changes
breathing swamp dust

next thing I know
it's the Spokane police
asking me questions
all about you
I left my own body
as I watched myself tell them
big things and small things
whatever I knew

I do my civic duty,
look around for you

the few leads that I turn up
don't go anywhere

check in all the places
where you used to spend your time
but it's useless, it's useless
you've become as light as the air

ushering in the changes
breathing swamp dust

ΔΔΔ

This is from the very high stack of unreleased *We Shall All Be Healed* songs, and it's one of the most realized songs of that crew—it has a melody that never left my head, it has a solid refrain, there's an MP3 of it on an unmarked CD-R somewhere in this house and it'll probably never be seen by anyone, including me. I think at one point it was a contender for Extra Glenndom. Here, for the one or two readers who are as rules-bound as I am—that is, for people who are reading one entry each day during a calendar year—it marks a distance traveled. Four months ago, which is to say, fourteen years ago, we were here, in cheap studio apartments from which people vanish without a trace. Yesterday, we just got high and listened to the Cure. Plus ça change.

29 - WIZARD LEVEL

Wake up and recite the lost formulas
scrub my face with cold water at the basin
sketch forgotten trees inside a little notebook
commit their names to memory

trying to get up
trying to get up to wizard level

trying to get up
trying to get up to wizard level

Go walking out behind the house by moonlight
collect dry stems and leaves and small green pine cones
in a muslin bag I got down at the hardware store
blessings on the hardware store

trying to get up, trying to get up to wizard level
trying to get up, trying to get up to wizard level

not everybody gets there
very few can find the path

Go to sleep and dream these holy dreams
scattering to the wind each day at sunrise
always catch the sunrise when I can
held in my heart through trying times

trying to get up, trying to get up to wizard level
trying to get up, trying to get up to wizard level

ΔΔΔ

Unreleased, unrecorded, performed once or twice a cappella, no instruments at all in its history—the Platonic ideal of a song, for me, so tenuous that it can barely be said to exist; momentary; self-contained.

30 - HAND OF DEATH

Rehearsing for the tournament of champions
somebody's going to have to cleanse the temple
train by moonlight
all night

Practice with a blindfold on
try not to think too hard about the neighbors
up on my balcony that overlooks the harbor
preparing to deploy the hand of death

Preparing to deploy the hand of death

Rest among the ruins of old empires
rise from my heavy sleep at sundown
byways on my pathways,
beckoning

Stay focused on the target
feel close enough to taste its beating heart
hungry as a captive of the King
preparing to deploy the hand of death

Sure and steady,
almost ready

Remind myself to breathe. Heed thou my counsel,
skin and bones and blood and tender flesh—
there will be no return to these beginnings.
Preparing to deploy the hand of death

Preparing to deploy the hand of death.

ΔΔΔ

My initial plan for *In League with Dragons*, which had a whole host of other titles before I was accepted into the ranks and joined up with the league, was for each song to be in a different time signature. This one was in 2/4: march time. I still dream fondly of how awkward the interview cycle would have been, me trying to count 9/8 to interviewers over the phone. By the time we got to the studio, this was more of a bossa nova, and it was good, but didn't feel important to the rest of the record. It's one of my favorite lyrics, because it's just a metaphorical description of me in my employee-housing room back in Norwalk, teaching myself guitar and setting off on the path that would lead me to . . . well, to this book, three decades later.

OCTOBER

1 - GOING INVISIBLE 2

Look in the cellar where the cinders blaze
sift through the shadows for days
look in the corners but you can't see me
you can't see me, I'm free

I'm going to burn it all down today,
down today, OK
I'm going to burn it all down today
and sweep all the ashes away

Count up the keepsakes in the cabinets
the keyboards and the chemistry sets
look in the attic where the blinds are drawn
you won't find me, I'm gone

I'm going to burn it all down today,
down today, OK
I'm going to burn it all down today
and sweep all the ashes away

Etch an outline on your heart
I'm going to blow the whole circus apart

Reckon the remnants when they land at last
the shattered aftermath of the blast
look for me everywhere the burn marks form
trying to find a place to keep warm

I'm going to burn it all down today,
down today, OK
I'm going to burn it all down today
and sweep all the ashes away
I'm going to burn it all down today,
down today, OK
I'm going to burn it all down today
and sweep all the ashes away

ΔΔΔ

That "OK" doesn't sit with me right, on the page—my whole notion of some songs not really having an existence outside of the air in which they resound finds support there: but not elsewhere in the song, where rhymes like "cabinets" and "chemistry sets" practically cry out to Heaven for somebody to notice them. Accordingly, we printed the lyrics in the liner notes in an almost completely illegible font.

2 - NO, I CAN'T

You bought me some candy
and you bought me some flowers
and you brought me a sofa
and you brought me a radio:

Thank you for the candy
thank you for the flowers
thank you for the sofa
thank you for the radio

Now I have everything I need
Now I have everything I need

You brought me a puppy
and you brought me a lamp
and you brought me some books
and you brought me a filing cabinet

Thank you for the puppy
thank you for the lamp
thank you for the books
thanks for the filing cabinet,
I don't know what I ever did without it

Now I have everything I need
Now I have everything I need

You came by, and you came in
and you let the wind in
it must be cold outside
we looked out through the sliding glass door
but I'd forgotten what we were looking for

Thank you for coming by
it's nice to see you, once in a while
thank you for the coat I forgot to mention
I've been freezing in here. I've been freezing in here

Now I have everything I need
Now I have everything I need
Now I have everything I need
Now I have everything I need

ΔΔΔ

From 1993, a song as much about its chord progression as its lyrics, which were half improvised live onto cassette while I learned, in real time, how you can make three chords out of an E minor shape by fretting the B string first at the third fret, then at the second, and then leaving it open for the straight minor. Precisely because songs were being born during the process of recording back then, they also preserve a moment of me in real time, a younger me than the one who'll hear them years later, and maybe build on them—which is to say, cf. October 8.

3 - DONE BLEEDING

Recite the songs that kept me whole
on the day I hand over command control
try to let them all flow into this one
list alphabetically
the toxins the doctors found in me
during my time in prison

Count my fingers, every last one
when I get done

Clean the floors well, sweep and swab
do a thorough job
leave the old place nicer than I found it
wish well as the neighbors cheer and shout
finally taking their earplugs out
things were even worse here than they sounded

Grim-faced pilots back from the bombing run
when I get done

Take a picture or two
just to remember the view

leave a mark on the door
as an empty warning sign from one who went before
but isn't here any more
let the crust form on my skin in the sun
when I get done

Sweep the front porch, make it new
put the broom away when I get through
no passers-by need know of my lonely tenure
all this riot of light, the shock of leaves
wind rippling in my sleeves
swirling against my skin as in a blender

Red thread drying behind me, hand-spun
when I get done

ΔΔΔ

This is a song about leaving a room forever. Sometimes when you leave a room, the you that you were during your time in there stays behind. Who knows why he does this, but he does. What you see in the world outside the room is something about which he can only know rumors and secondhand reports. Still, you should send him those reports from time to time. It is only because of the jolts he withstood that you are able to report on anything that happened later. The phrase "as in a blender" is from, and for, that good man Alastair Galbraith, down all the years.

4 - AN ANTIDOTE FOR STRYCHNINE

Dig around in the garbage
save up some halibut bones in a jar
scrape a winter's worth of salt deposits

from the rusty frame of my car
ask the experts, maybe they'll know

Call up my teacher in Cambridge
see what he remembers
throw white phosphorous in the fireplace
look for clues in the embers
call the hotline, give them a phony last name

Trying to find an antidote for strychnine

Time's running short
always seems to run shorter
have some supplies sent
from up just past the northern border
keep a line out to the people who take the long view

Only share my research
with sick lab rats like me
trapped behind the beakers and the Erlenmeyer flasks
cut off from the world, I may not ever get free
but I may, one day

Trying to find an antidote for strychnine

So many suffering from the same affliction
coming up on the breakthrough
the clock's ticking

Dig down amongst my calculations
check my math
up there on the surface
everybody's getting ready for the bloodbath

stem the tide
they're calling down for reinforcements

Trying to find an antidote for strychnine

ΔΔΔ

Haunting the halls of secondhand bookstores, twelve years old, I gravitated toward titles by Michael Moorcock, with their iconic Michael Whelan cover paintings and their author's peerless knack for a title. *Stormbringer. The Dancers at the End of Time. A Cure for Cancer.* That I was not, then, quite mature enough to read his books with full comprehension only made them more alluring. This song grew from its title: Who wants this cure and why? It is a science fiction story of its own in the style of a for-hire Tod Browning, under contract to Universal but unable to stop being Tod Browning.

5 - IN LEAGUE WITH DRAGONS

It's so hard to get revenge
the human element drags you down
lead a solitary life, if you can
try not to show your face in town
let the rumors find such bridges as they may
reckon up the variables
find a way
make it real
make a deal
until my protector comes

It's so hard to be yourself
when you've already seen the inside
try to navigate the turns as best you can
headed on down the slide

strong friends are where you find them
people talk all kinds of trash, never you mind them
make it real
make a deal
until my protector comes

Huge wings blotting out the sun
remembering everyone

Be so hard to look away
gotta be strong in the face of suffering
cut a good figure just in case somebody's watching
even if it ends up meaning nothing
let the breezes spread such scandal as they may
maybe Boris Vallejo paints the back of your head someday
make it real
make a deal
until my protector comes

ΔΔΔ

The hardest song for me to write about, not for lack of trying; because this is as good as I get, to my ear. As a reader, I hear in my line here what I hope to achieve. But it's not like the others: There's mainly resignation instead of hope, and such hope as remains looks toward a devastating event. A dragon who "remember[s] everyone" is no benign force. If all my songs were like this, there'd be only a couple dozen of them at most, and few people would ever have heard them. But in the future, that will be true anyhow, in a sense, and this song is perhaps a visitor from that distant future, depending on how one measures distance. Or, as Paul Celan would and in fact did say, in a translation by Pierre Joris:

Standing for-no-one-and-nothing.
Unrecognized,

for you
alone.

6 - WAYLON JENNINGS LIVE!

Drunk at the Meskwaki casino
right where God intended me to be
looking up at the one man in this room
who's handled more cocaine than me
think back on the good times, just an hour or so ago,
before I got myself this drunk
when the valet parked my rented Mitsubishi
with the beat-up old brown suitcase in the trunk

Full of firearms and flash drives
full of passports, and international money orders
for just in case I make it 'cross the border

Get a postcard from the gift shop
let my family know I'm doing fine
looking up at a map up on the ceiling
to find the place where we all meet up, further on down the line
head back to my table
get another scotch and soda for the road
the band onstage is really working up a head of steam
close my eyes and lean my head back, dream a little dream

Full of firearms and flash drives
full of passports, and international money orders
for just in case I make it 'cross the border

ΔΔΔ

A story: I was at a stoplight in Chapel Hill. I was going to a bookstore where I was either giving a reading or moderating a discussion, I forget which. *Honky Tonk Heroes*, the Waylon Jennings album that kickstarted the outlaw country movement of the seventies, was playing on the car stereo. During an instrumental passage I ad-libbed the opening line of this song. My ad-lib made me deliriously happy; I recalled seeing a Merle Haggard date listed at a casino in Iowa long ago, and wanting to go then, but not being able to justify the expense. And I remembered a note on Merle Haggard's website at that time advising the prospective concertgoer that all dates were potentially tentative. "Always make the call before you make the drive," it said. All this happened in my brain while I was waiting for the light to change. I opened up a voice recording app on my phone and sang this song's opening line in my best Waylon Jennings impression, and then I went on with my evening, but the sprout from the stoplight grew into the story you hear in the song.

7 - DOC GOODEN

Wheels down in Seattle
three years ago in this town
they sent their best and brightest to me
I sent them all back down

Deluxe coach to the ballpark
there's champagne on the snack trays
summon up the spirit of a brighter time
looked bad last week against the Blue Jays

when my name was everywhere—
none of you were there,
when my name was everywhere

Potholes in the parking lot
you feel the jolts a little harder every year
the batboy hands out yellow slickers
it never stops raining out here

when my name was everywhere—
none of you were there,
when my name was everywhere

when the speedball would squeal
with the highlight reel
when the headline hype
was on the front page in extra-large type
it was me,
for all the world to see

Don't call it a comeback
I've been here for years
maximum respect to all the warriors
who choose to fall down on their spears

when my name was everywhere—
none of you were there,
when my name was everywhere

ΔΔΔ

I will confide in the gentle reader that when a man makes his living jumping up and down onstage while singing songs, and spends about a third of the year sleeping badly in a bunk on a tour bus, he is a very funny man indeed if he writes a song with the line "you feel the jolts a little harder every year," performs that song on a stage while jumping up and down, and then returns to the bus that will carry him across many bumpy parking lots before it takes him back home.

8 - YOUNGER

Crank that siren high
drain the wellspring dry
map out your coordinates
send out scouts by day
dole out mercenary pay
for restless young subordinates

It never hurts to give thanks to the local gods
you never know who might be hungry
it never hurts to scan the windows on the upper
floor
I saw a face there once before
when I was younger

Set the torch aflame
call the night by name
stake out your dark position
lie in wait
by the gleaming city gate
try not to lose sight of the mission

It never hurts to give thanks to the broken bones
you had to use to build your ladder
moment close at hand
half of you will never understand
and it doesn't really matter

Big smile on my face
capsule just in case
underneath my tongue there
voices on the breeze

I heard voices once like these
when I was younger

Blood rushing to my face
I know that sweet warm taste
and the bitter trace

Storm right down that hill
if I don't, no one will
follow me right through the chaos
this whole house is doomed
even the bit parts get consumed
prepare a grave for Menelaus
it never hurts to give thanks to the navigator
even when He's spitting out random numbers
I knew what those figures meant
and what they hoped to represent
when I was younger

ΔΔΔ

I don't write a lot of songs in dressing rooms. I don't trust myself to balance thought and feeling right if I'm going through the vicissitudes of touring, the peaks and valleys. But this one came through like a transmission from another realm while I was at a dressing room mirror in Chicago, at the Vic on Sheffield. It's written around the riff from "No, I Can't," a song that preceded it by fifteen or twenty years, in which the narrator says, repeatedly, that he has everything he needs. What do you look like when you actually do get everything you need? A little different from whatever your guess might have been when you were younger.

9 · POSSUM BY NIGHT

When the house lights all go dark
shuffle on down to the park
spent stars in the winter sky
days of refuge in short supply
all you parasites climb aboard!
all you vagabonds, praise the Lord!

When the compost pile grows high—
climb to the top, if I try
long-haul truckers still wide awake
guard their pathways for Jesus' sake
all you garbage trucks to the curb!
true sons of the Living Word!

Try not to get stuck in the intake vent
grow fat and grow old and go blind and be content

All you pack dogs, have your say
let me just find my own way
moon in the trees my guide
walk with my jaw hinged wide

Once more unto the breech!
safe in the spots that the light can't reach

ΔΔΔ

There were three possible titles for *In League with Dragons*. I knew I wanted the album to take its title from one of the songs: "Younger" was the leading candidate for some time. "Possum by Night" succeeded "Younger" for a good while—I think during most of the recording session it held its place. But the noble possum does not seek the spotlight, and it's not right to put him here. Let those who understand his central position seek him out but give him the space he needs. Before we leave our possum to his business I'll mention also that "Possum by Night," as a title, is me conceding that a different title I'd had in my notebook since at least 2007—"Possum Bit the Watering Can"—simply wasn't ever going to happen, no matter how long I waited for its moment to come.

10 - CLEMENCY FOR THE WIZARD KING

We who train in the way of the blade
we who sleep in the accursed glade
we come before you now
we come before you now

We who in his favor would stand
who lovingly await his most fearsome
command
we come before you now
we come before you now

Cut loose the handcuffs
let him go free

We who travel by starlight
we who slipped past your guards in the night
we come before you now
we come before you now

We who boldly lay claim to our own
we who've seen the chamber of the true throne

We who've seen the kindness of the cracks of his
face
we who will die if we must in this place

we come before you, outnumbered and unafraid
well trained in the way of the blade
cut loose the handcuffs
let him go free

ΔΔΔ

A little inside baseball here. This song's a personal favorite—when I find a formula and really commit to it, that's me at my most content; were I an essayist I'd have a long one about how "formulaic" should almost always be taken as a compliment whether it's meant that way or not. For me, the climactic long adjectival clause of this song—"outnumbered and unafraid / well trained in the way of the blade"—is a high point not just of the album but of my entire creative life; Matt Douglas and I sang the vocal take in harmony live on either side of an omnidirectional microphone as the musicians, all in isolation booths of their own, played on. It was glorious. So when, for this book, I opened the document from the lyrics folder I used for the *In League with Dragons* recording session, I was very surprised to see that the song originally concluded:

we come before you now
and as one from the waist we all bow

Well! That's fine, I guess, I can see it's trying to add a little more movement to the scene, give some more visible character to the Wizard King's acolytes. But you know what's better than action, for my money? A foreboding, nay threatening eleven-word adjectival phrase followed by the refrain.

11 - SICILIAN CREST

In these times of wanting prophecy
and false witnesses up to all manner of deviltry

drench a kitchen rag in heretics' blood
wash the windows and prepare for the flood

Look to the west
look to the man bearing the Sicilian crest

Portents in the sky say that the time is near
dial into the signal coming in loud and clear
sacrificial victims out of the cage
smiling as they're taking the stage

Look to the west
look to the man bearing the Sicilian crest

Out of the blue, everything's new
all the talk we heard was true
the legends we all heard once
the whispers from the storefronts

Hope for the best, prepare for the worst
we wait like stockpiled landmines, ready to burst
wait all your life to see what you see
open up your eyes and be free

Look to the west
look to the man bearing the Sicilian crest

ΔΔΔ

We live in a time of intensely diaristic impulses, we insist on the obsessive documentation of the moment; I consider these impulses unhealthy, and I resist them. Incessant documentation of the present moment inevitably blurs all moments into a continuous now. Within this rushing current no ripple can be retained in memory. It just keeps happening. But against this I wish to mark that I'm writing this on November 4, 2024, the day before the United States will decide whether to pursue the course of open fascism a little further down the road or not. "Sicilian Crest" was written on or about June 15, 2018, and sought to examine the mindset of people who'd cast their vote for a fascist. One avoids saying "I told you so" in any context; it's gauche. And yet.

12 - MARSH WITCH VISION

Break into shining storefronts up and down the avenue
do six months for burglary, get a fresh tattoo
dad buys a PA system, I invite some friends around
just some guys I know from town

All the normal things to do around here just bore me
What is this I see before me?

Take a job up at the slaughterhouse, hammer in hand
happy on the weekends, singing with my band
and then one day we're bound for Denmark, one change of
clothes in tow
so let's go

when the spirit moves within you, how can you resist the call?
I love you all!

ΔΔΔ

There are so many alternate-universe versions of the Mountain Goats in my mind, so many imagined pasts instead of the one herein chronicled. Given that "Marsh Witch Vision" wasn't written until 2014 or released until 2017, it would be impossible for a person to say, of the Mountain Goats: "Oh, yeah—weird band. They just write songs about Ozzy. Strictly and exclusively Ozzy unless maybe the guy writes a song about Bill Ward, or about Tony Iommi's missing fingertip or something. One song is about how Ozzy's dad bought him a PA to keep him from getting into more trouble and then it just goes on from there for thirty years, single theme. Just Ozzy." Still, together, for the next eight days, let's imagine exactly that, and let's lean all the way into it. I will see you back in the real world on October 20.

13 · SHIRTLESS IN HAMBURG

sleep two to a bed
four to a room
prophets from the countryside
glad tidings of doom

too broke to play around
like the soldiers do
all up and down
the glittering avenue

anything's better than the future
I can see that from here

stack the amplifiers high
turn up the bass
spring wild from the wings
with glitter on my young face

it's miserable outside
but in here it's warm
it always feels so stable
at the center of the storm

snake on my chest for protection
why the hell not

ΔΔΔ

The first single by the Mountain Goats, "Shirtless in Hamburg," was released on October 13, 1992, a Tuesday; albums were released on Tuesdays for more than twenty-five years, until digital distribution so completely overtook brick-and-mortar that it no longer mattered whether hard copies might run into snags in shipping, requiring a weekend's worth of padding time just in case. It was the year of Leonard Cohen's *The Future* and 10,000 Maniacs' *Our Time in Eden*; maybe the labels felt lucky, or maybe they were still on drugs, but they gave us the full-court press. We weren't a proper band at this point: The song is just me and my acoustic guitar, singing about the early years of Black Sabbath slogging it out on the continent. The front cover of the 7″ was a black-and-white image of a very young Ozzy Osbourne in Europe, having painted a serpent onto his chest before going onstage. The Osbournes sued, and the terms of the settlement are still sealed, but the lawsuit made all the papers, so the single, now sleeved in black text on a white background with a BANNED WORLDWIDE sticker affixed directly to heavy cardstock, went directly into the charts, and stayed there for twenty-seven weeks.

14 · SONG FOR BLACK SABBATH'S SECOND NORTH AMERICAN TOUR

Hang my hammer on a nail
never see it again
set sail for the cosmos
high above the world with its beaten-down men

Not long for this world
have to be reminded

to stay away from windows
not to leave important things behind

All gone
All gone
With the dawn

And then I'm in an airplane heading west
over the ocean
unsteady on my feet again
a body in motion

So far from the slaughterhouse
new creatures with new hearts
landing at LaGuardia
tearing up the charts

All gone
All gone
With the dawn

ΔΔΔ

The lawsuit gave us juice, the kind of juice you can't buy. I'd been signed to record an acoustic singer-songwriter album, and the album was in the cans, ready to go, but now the label thought we could go bigger if we rerecorded everything with a full band and a bigger producer. They gave it the full-court press: I ate on their dime at the best restaurants in LA for months. Cha Cha Chá, Posto, Pinot—they'd drive me all over the Valley trying to talk me into it. I was young. "It's just a song on an acoustic guitar," I said. "The last one did great," I said. "Allen Reynolds will not get what I'm doing," I said. I stuck to my guns. It could have all gone sideways but it didn't. Instead of suing again, Ozzy covered the song live; he'd played what was supposed to be his farewell show in

Costa Mesa, on November 15, 1992, but the rise of the Mountain Goats had changed up all the math inside the Osbourne camp. Needless to say it had upended my life, too. I was still in college. Weird times.

15 - CALIFORNIA JAM

helicopter in from Los Angeles
land at Ontario, there's guys with cameras
        hey you—
        can I get a quick interview

beat-up stretch limousine to the speedway
in the baking sun, stay high all day
        take to the stage
        lords of the age

drums rolling like buffalo down the plain
and I am an oncoming train
me and the ghosts of Birmingham
me and the ghosts of Birmingham

light rigging overhead, rainbow behind
and the cloudless sky, and the infinite distances in my mind
        arms in the air
        sun in my hair

rise like dancers, stick the landing
feel kind of beautiful, everybody here is beautiful
        and that's just how I feel
        and it's real

drums rolling like buffalo down the plain
and I am an oncoming train

me and the ghosts of Birmingham
me and the ghosts of Birmingham

ΔΔΔ

I was working from the memory of a news story I'd seen as a kid when I wrote this—Black Sabbath landing on a private jet, getting into a limo to go play the California Jam, a big concert at a speedway, and then some footage of the show itself. When our single about the memory of that footage hit number one in England, the label sent a car for me and brought me to their big offices on Sunset. They put me in a soft chair and dimmed the lights, and screened the actual film itself, not video but film. I tried to mark the moment for myself—I, in my own life, was living through such times as the ones I'd written about in the margins of my class notes just a year ago, distractedly jotting down couplets while my fellow students asked questions about material they hadn't read but that I'd already been over twice. I remember MTV News asking Chris Cornell if he liked "the guy doing all the songs about Black Sabbath"; he smiled, then said: "I can relate, you know, because we love Black Sabbath, too." Being in the conversation: It feels nice, at first, and then you start looking for other words, because "nice" only lasts for so long.

16 - PASSAIC 1975

Write something down in illegible script
as we're approaching the landing strip
new Gibson SGs, inlaid with pearl
tonight Passaic, tomorrow the world

In a Holiday Inn by a nameless river
renew the assault on my lungs and my liver
and while I'm waiting for the company man
slip on my kimono that I bought in Japan

tell the crowd, tell the world
I want everyone to get high
tell the press, tell the cameras
I want everyone to get high

And the tech crew in Memphis has a present for me
a screen that scrolls lyrics
like the ones they have on TV
the deluxe model, one of only four thousand made
black out that night
in front of ten thousand paid

And in the back lounge, in between stops
contingency plans in case the new one flops
sometimes I wake up coughing up blood
tonight Indianapolis, tomorrow the flood

Tell the person next to you:
"I want everyone to get high"
tell the crowd, tell your mother
I want everyone to get high

ΔΔΔ

You can't imagine the resources big labels had in those days. If you were hot they'd get you anything. Dope, girls. I didn't want dope or girls, but I did want to know if they were sitting on a giant cache of old live tapes, stuff they might release in the future. They were. Black Sabbath didn't actually play Passaic on the *Sabotage* tour, they played Asbury Park, but for reasons I'd hope are obvious, I wasn't going to call the song "Asbury Park 1975."

17 - MID MORNING FLORIDA

parked by a mansion with an airstrip
sun rising up so crisp and bright
old dudes holed up in their bunkers
chasing down the light

faster than a speeding bullet
smart as a whip
dead in a parking lot in Leesburg
this is it

going back to California

burned-up jewelry at the inquest
cold now to the touch
last time I ever saw him
he told me how I drink too much

feel like I'm going to crumble
what will become of us
take two weeks to think about it
get right back on the bus

feel so bad
so afraid
of the road
up ahead

going back to California

ΔΔΔ

They didn't want to let me release this; they had, get this, a small focus group listen to the songs, and they all said this one was "sad." This was my first sign that things weren't going to last, no matter how heady the days seemed at the time. Of course it's sad! It's about Randy Rhoads dying at the age of twenty-five in the middle of a tour, and his band just forging ahead, not knowing what else to do! It's bleak! "Nobody wants bleak," they told me. "We'll see about that," I said. And so we did.

18 - NO MORE TEARS

insane in a studio in Los Angeles
rudderless and hungry and high
ideas of no earthly consequence
float across my consciousness
and then go dark as bullseyes

go down the devil's way
go down a twenty-devil way

twenty years on they'll be asking what I remember
go where the dry dust crawlers tread
the fire in the vocal booth
the doctor who filed down my teeth
dreams from the ether overhead

go down the devil's way
go down a twenty-devil way

lit candles pressed into the walls down there
three cans of Aqua Net in my greying hair

arsenic drifting down through the hourglass
track-lit hallways that go on for days
floating like a Portuguese man-o'-war

pretty hardcore
fire offerings, burnt offerings, thanks and praise

go down the devil's way
go down a twenty-devil way

ΔΔΔ

This was the last single from the album, and it didn't do what the others had done; it charted, but only in North America and the UK, and only in the top 20. "Take a year off," I was told. "Maybe think about something to write about besides Ozzy." I was young and very successful. I took six months. I felt bulletproof.

19 - THE VIDEO WITH LITA FORD

I'm just going through my things
trying to get the place clean
when I find this thing on VHS
damnedest thing I've ever seen
I'm in some kind of magician's robe
desperate grimace on my face
somewhere on a soundstage
lost in space

and I stare at the TV
and I cry out to the Lord
trying to remember
the video with Lita Ford

and that's where my family finds me
when they get home from the mall
run faster than the wind at midday if you like
when the darkness comes you'll crawl

and they help me put myself together
map out the lost time in the deep
I make like I'm whole again
wait 'til everyone's asleep

and then I stare up at the screen
and I cry out to the Lord
trying to remember
the video with Lita Ford

I see us both, I have no idea where we are
I'm singing pretty good
there's too much chorus on that guitar

I keep on sifting through the wreckage
to see what I can see
all these guys in suits and frosted hair
that look more or less like me

and then I stare up at the screen
and I cry out to the Lord
trying to remember
the video with Lita Ford

ΔΔΔ

You haven't heard this song, because the label declined to exercise their option when they heard it. I was furious; both musically and lyrically it seemed to take my Ozzy project to new heights. To them, it was, quoting here from the severance letter they sent, "another song about Ozzy Osborne, a subject we don't think the public is anxious to keep revisiting." "Keep revisiting." Fuck you. I did stop writing Ozzy songs, though; the sudden rift soured me on the prospect. I stand by the legacy of these tunes, the mark they left on music, briefly, before the onward rush of culture erased the whole affair. I used the money I'd made to pay off my student loans.

I moved on.

20 - ALMOST EVERY DOOR

Cower in the corner,
try hard to disappear
the moment's never going to come
when anyone can say that the coast is clear
maybe turn around, find a wall to break your fist on
almost every door's an exit
just not this one

Dream about the outside
sprinting down the open plain
barefoot and outclassed
bloody up the broken grain
every cartoon keg, TNT and nitroglycerine
almost every door's an exit
just not this one

Pause before each door like a sinner lost in prayer
always one more hallway at the bottom of the stair

I get knocked down,
but I get up again, like a dunce
cave's all sealed up
nowhere to hide out in the winter months
aiming for the blackout, spare a prayer for souls in prison
almost every door's an exit, just not this one

ΔΔΔ

From a two-song session at Electrical Audio, the late Steve Albini's labor of love in Chicago. Working at Electrical, for a guy who bought Big Black records as they came off the presses in the eighties, is always a little fantastic: Wait a minute—I get to do this? Matt Espy from Dead Rider did percussion. I think it's no accident that the lyric itself stands a little apart from the kind of stuff that ends up on the albums—it's denser, it takes a little longer to work through. For me, the stuff that takes a little longer to work through is the stuff most worth doing.

21 · SONG FOR TED SALLIS

Into the source of the squall
        I inevitably fall
Toward the wellspring of all agony
        shuffling endlessly
Whether or not it was always going to be this way
        Only mattered yesterday

No skin like the skin you woke up in

Up from the earth and the clay
        melting away
Never lose enough to find my form
        trudge through the storm
wait in hope
        for some as-yet-undiscovered isotope

No skin like the skin you woke up in

When, at last
        the die gets cast
read the numbers out loud
        with your head bowed

Try to find a face to focus on
    but the memory's gone
Wherever my former self went,
    it was an accident
try to picture him in my mind's eye
say goodbye

No skin like the skin you woke up in

ΔΔΔ

The other song from the Electrical session with two Matts, Douglas and Espy. Astute readers will clock that the format on the page is different here—it was already this way in my notebook, for the record. More of that old "what if I were a poet?" stuff—if I were, my books would have pages that look like this one, that play with internal long-line nonce rhyme schemes to see where they lead. Ted Sallis is the Man-Thing, a shambling heap of organic matter. "Whatever knows fear burns at the Man-Thing's touch": He can't tolerate fear in others; it causes him physical pain, which he seeks to end by touching the source of it. I repeat: He seeks to end his pain by touching its source. He had a name before he got this way. You'd never recognize him now.

22 - TUCSON FOG

The fog rolled in,
and it's never going to lift, I guess.
Breathe against the window facing the street.
Scribble with my finger on the glass.

Trying to read the horoscopes
of animals long extinct.
Trying to read the omens in the kitchen sink.

The fog took shape
like a golem with a vengeful eye:
limbs like rippling swans' necks
at least a hundred stories high.

Trying to read the horoscopes
of animals long extinct.
Trying to read the omens in the kitchen sink.

Trying to force an ending
where everything turns out well.
Don't really mind the ritual,
just the smell.

Get word sometimes
from distant outposts much like mine—
places where the fog rolled in one day.
Try to tell them it'll work out fine.

Trying to read the horoscopes
of animals long extinct
trying to read the omens in the kitchen sink.

ΔΔΔ

Sort of the definition of a B-side here—a title nobody will quite clock ("fog" obvious enough from the lyrics; "Tucson" because musically it's a Meat Puppets pastiche), a chorus only maniacs would sing along with, a bridge that lands on the phrase "just the smell." There is almost certainly at least one person who'd assert that a forgotten B-side like this is the best song in the catalog, and that person is in every instance almost certainly correct.

23 - WHAT HAVE YOU DONE TO THE MAGICIAN?

I taste the air in here
I know the stench of fear
scope out the exits, get a picture inside my head
warning signs all flashing red

What have you done to the magician?
what have you done to the magician?
here where the half-burnt light bulb shines so dim
what have you done? what have you done to him?

You're gone, but you can't be far
back in the parking lot, I've blocked your car
you'll need a tow truck with a flatbed and some long, strong
chains
I'm here on my hands and knees trying to scrub out the stains

What have you done to the magician?
what have you done to the magician?
here where we roll the dice, and the odds seem grim
what have you done? what have you done to him?

Scratch in the concrete like a mark on the moon
think as I look at the evidence: It's got to be my turn soon

Save my description for the cops, but the cops won't come
promise myself I won't let myself go numb
you can bear out the metaphor if you like, but you won't like
what you see
maybe better to let all the deeper tide pools be

What have you done to the magician?
what have you done to the magician?

here where the payoff is nothing, and the margins real slim
what have you done? what have you done to him?

ΔΔΔ

A fully realized song—the demo has a rhythm track and overdubs, the whole nine yards—preemptively relegated to B-side-or-below status right before the COVID pandemic. These days if I release a song like this and too many normal people hear it, they will be confused and ask for clarifications, a situation greatly to be avoided, so you have to be careful with the weird songs. Over time, you can mark how the weirder stuff ends up in the back seat; but the *best* stuff, the stuff you're going to remember on your deathbed, is what you did in the back seat.

24 - GETTING INTO KNIVES

I hit the cul-de-sac on the spiritual path
retraced my steps back home
but the house burned down before I got there
and I found myself alone

I tried to keep things in perspective
as I hunted down the perpetrator
loaded my toolkit up with every hateful instrument
now here we are thirty years later

I'm getting into knives
I'm getting into knives
I've been up and down the buffet several different times
I'm adjusting my focus, I'm getting into knives

I sought wisdom from the ancients
consulted with master tacticians

met up with some guys who wouldn't tell me their last
names
they specialized in nonconventional munitions

stayed on the scent like a bloodhound
followed the clues where they led
taste of hot ashes on my tongue all day
I took my rifle with me to bed

but I'm getting into knives
I'm getting into knives
it's a gift to be simple, it's a gift to be free
I'm adjusting my focus, I'm getting into knives

held to my vision all these days
while stray signals kept flooding the switchboard
came all this way for hunger
may I be worthy of my reward

I stood at the door, and I listened
rustled through my rucksack quiet as I could
you can't give me back what you've taken
but you can give me something that's almost as good

I'm getting into knives
I'm getting into knives
behold, I stand at the door, and I knock, and then I knock twice
I've adjusted my focus, I'm getting into knives

ΔΔΔ

I have so many notebooks, and in them, when I can get to one in time instead of just reaching for a stray junk mail envelope, are many song titles. Some notebook pages—specifically, those in one of several 2⅞ ×

4¾ notebooks that say "Rodeo Queen" on them—are just lists of titles, begun one day when I thought up a good one and added to it over the months and years. "Getting into Knives" was one of half a dozen titles on one such page for a very long time—years, though how many of them I'll never know, I don't date my pages unless they're to-do lists. I would see it occasionally, and say, "'Getting into knives,' I like this idea, what does it mean?" And in this way the title percolated, maybe incubated, for a very long time. Naturally it ended up being a song about murder, which benefits from a long incubation time.

25 - AS MANY CANDLES AS POSSIBLE

When stray dogs finally catch you in the alley
you don't consider their point of view
but when the wounds are healed, and the scars are shiny,
sometimes then you do

The terms are vicious
time is tight
no one gets
too much light

When you see the risen beast in your nightmares,
you treat him like a long-lost brother
but when you pass him on the streets of the city by day,
you pretend you don't recognize each other

The lake is boiling
the fish won't bite
no one gets
too much light

Seek out a cave by the ocean while you wait out the rain
dial down the weak bits and crank up the gain
listen for the prophecy somewhere in the static
once you've saddled up your pony, burn down the paddock

When pigs gather in the sty to greet the sunrise
they all begin to squeal for joy
it doesn't sound like joy to the untrained ear
and there's plenty of distortion, and it's not real clear

You've got a friend downstairs
he howls all night
no one gets
too much light

ΔΔΔ

The line about the pigs—this is an important point to me, there's something in it. I was staying at Farm Sanctuary in upstate New York, a place I've supported for decades; they give farm animals, animals who would otherwise have been slaughtered, a place to live out the term of their natural lives. The animals come to Farm Sanctuary from all over by different routes, and then they live in safety and comfort. The pigs get real big; when you see pigs being taken to slaughter, they're still quite young. The pigs are fed in the morning, and I heard them, at dawn. A sound like something from a horror movie, or an industrial noise band. This immense polychoral squeal. It is the sound of the pure pleasure of eating, that pleasure unchained and unrestrained, expressed with full throat and whole heart. They don't get a chance to eat like this in the slaughterhouse. Neither, if you follow me, do we.

26 - GET FAMOUS

You were born for these flashing lights
you were born for these endless nights
you always knew, sooner or later,
you were destined for something greater
you took notes on what you had to do
to get the piece of the pie that belonged to you
you've been waiting for this ever since you were young
be careful not to choke on your tongue

Get famous
you should be famous
go on and get famous
I want you to be famous

Cold, grey world—all these obedient sheep
they act like they know, but they're all sound asleep
waiting for something to wake up to
some nice juicy bone to chew

You arrive on the scene, like a message from God
listen to the people applaud
this is what you were born to do
Wesley Willis taught me how to write about you

Get famous
You should be famous
You go on and get famous
I want you to be famous

Light up the sky like a comet
make yourself want to vomit
shine like a cursed star

show everybody
exactly who you are

Get famous
you should be famous
go on and get famous
I want you to be famous

ΔΔΔ

I'd like to dedicate this song to Emily Dickinson, who knew the deal. (By "dedicate" I do not mean "address," because I know my place—at the feet of the master, head bowed, gaze averted.)

27 · PICTURE OF MY DRESS

Here at a truck stop in New Mexico
just before dawn
somebody's grandma behind the wheel of a big rig
pulling in with her headlights on
we smoke a cigarette as the sunrise runs riot
someone's got to break the quiet

And she says "What are you doing here, anyway?"
and I smile and say "You'd never guess"
she holds it up for me by its skinny white shoulder straps
while I take a picture of my dress

I'm in the bathroom
of a Dallas, Texas, Burger King
And Mr. Steven Tyler's on the overhead speaker
he doesn't want to miss a thing
out there at the counter

blending in with the lunchtime crowd
try not to laugh out loud

I eat half my Crispy Chicken Club
I have extra mayonnaise, it's a mess
take the other half back to the parking lot with me
pop the trunk,
and take a picture of my dress

it still looks good
I only wore it once
four years ago
four years, and seven months

it may be a long while
before the highway decides to finally set me free
I'm going to have to chase down the remnants
of something special that you stole from me
it may be hiding in the sunset
or in distant corners of the dawn
or maybe it's gone

but I say some prayers above the engine
bless everything there is to bless
run out of gas in the middle of nowhere anyway
stand by the roadside, smiling
and take a picture of my dress

ΔΔΔ

I've told this story before: Maggie Smith, who wrote "Good Bones," posted a thought about taking her wedding dress, postdivorce, on a road trip. I answered with the title "Picture of My Dress." It was a Sunday morning. I wasn't busy that day, and I wrote it.

28 · BELL SWAMP CONNECTION

Toward the tail end of the age that's almost finished,
where the highway starts to crack and nobody fixes it,
I was wandering through an undeveloped tract
out near the ocean.
"100 acres, we will build to suit!"
See what there is to see before it's gone:
Somebody's always just about
to put some kind of awful plan in motion.

Eastern red cedars, and the pines,
and suddenly an elevated stone slab
in what must have been a clearing once.
Try to recognize the signals and the signposts,
but my curiosity
will likely always get the best of me—

It's like that one thing
my dad kept trying to tell me
as the twilight
inched its way on up his body:
Get out! get out! get out! get out!

Well, of course I climbed atop the slab and lay down on it;
I am a child.
I had my face toward the sky
lying there in the sun with both my eyes closed.
Woke up after sundown. What the hell is wrong with me?
Volunteer pines in their hundreds in the dusk like military
tentpoles.

Let my eyes adjust,
try to read the markings on the slab:

weird alphabets I felt sure I hadn't seen just before I passed
out.
Stars growing brighter,
and me looking up
like a lobster in a cage, down in the depths,
beneath the bottom of a glass boat—

And I heard a voice
from somewhere out beyond the free fall
like a captive soldier
trying to warn his brothers:
Get out! get out! get out! get out!

ΔΔΔ

From this lyric, a personal favorite, it's the lobster who gave me the most trouble. He was a crab at first. A "wayward crab," specifically. I knew even as I was writing "wayward crab" that probably this was a placeholder for whatever phrase I landed on to convey the image of some trapped animal out in the North Carolina Outer Banks, waiting to be hauled up from the depths forever. This is the thing about the depths: Sometimes it's better to remain in the depths! I think a lot of people have missed this very important point, but I'm not a life coach, they'll have to figure it out themselves.

29 · WOLF COUNT

Live among the starveling wolves
get lost inside the pack
pull at a carcass 'til my tooth breaks
your grown-up teeth—
they don't grow back,
they don't grow back.

Find a clearing in the forest
wait for word from the battlefront
sing to the moon until your throat's raw
the Lord of the manor—
he won't be coming back from the hunt,
he won't be coming back from the hunt.

Soon, it'll be my time to go,
I know.

Breach the perimeter with my brethren
know who your friends are when you need them
sleep soundly with the enemy
and remember me—
too dumb to trade his cloak for freedom,
too dumb to trade his cloak for freedom.

Run, run ahead, all of you—
I'll catch up when I'm able to.

Seek the manor grounds anew
too dark to find the path
sleep on the road and dream the only dream worth dreaming—
the thronging plain,
the bloodbath.

Soon, it'll be my time to go,
I know.

ΔΔΔ

"Wolf Count" is of personal importance to me because it seeks to honor the late Robert Mezey, under whose tutelage I learned to write verse. Without Bob, this book would not exist; he was an exacting teacher, and his stringency was nothing but pure love of the craft. He would recognize, in this song, its origin, a Borges poem I first heard in the Mezey-Barnes translation; and then he, without any hesitation, would say, through his inimitably nuanced smile, "Borges did it better," and he'd be right; but Bob's students knew—and know—that a line like this from Bob was like hysterical, unadulterated praise from anybody else. May I somehow pass along guidance as good as Bob's here and there before I go, "grey and furtive in the final twilight."

30 - THE LAST PLACE I SAW YOU ALIVE

I'm not thinking of you
when I swing left onto Gordon Avenue—
it's just the way the traffic veers.
Haven't driven down these streets in years,

But then I pass the last place I saw you alive.

I walk the narrow path these days.
Can't see going back to my old ways.
Call to mind sometimes that bloody, stinking mess—
us worms turn into butterflies, I guess,

But then I pass the last place I saw you alive.

It's changed since you were here, or else it hasn't—
it was special, it was deadly;
it was ours, and then it wasn't.

It's only now and then you come to mind.
There's a trillion things you left behind.
It's just the way the math works out—
nothing really to get worked up about,

But then I pass the last place I saw you alive.

ΔΔΔ

As you grow, there are more and more places that are the last place you ever saw someone while they yet lived. These places may or may not have retained any other connection to the people we remember—they may have been way stations, accidental points of contact, third-to-last known addresses. They can be hotels, or the sidewalks in front of hotels. Maybe at some point somebody knocks down the building where the meeting took place: Probably this happens, to be honest. It doesn't matter. You don't need the building. You just need the coordinates.

31 - SKELETON'S TOOTH

I see the shadows of the prophets in the parapets
truly they have their reward
trade you a map of the castle grounds
for some proof that you got past the guards

There's dried blood on the wrought-iron gates
spies in the tower
I crawled up from the dungeon last night
under my own power

Spit blood at the sidewalk
try to stay out of the headlines
scan the guts of fresh roadkill
looking for bad signs

Stay safe in the shadows
I know the real truth
better a mouth full of bloody gums
than a skeleton's tooth

I hear the howling of the helpless in the surface noise
scratch out their names in the dirt
trade you some tales from a vanished kingdom
for some earplugs that fit

Recall the proverb of the prodigal son
not sure who it applies to
threats of my enemies run loops in my head
the way that lullabies do

Take the road where it leads me
I should probably know better
just up ahead see the shining sign
of the debt collector

Sleep and peace attend thee
all through the night
skeleton's tooth gleaming down in the darkness
all fine and bright

Once I walked in splendor
back in the bloom of my youth
better to bury all the better days
than a skeleton's tooth

ΔΔΔ

People ask how becoming a parent changes your craft, and the real answer is "I have less time in which to practice it," but children are also sources of ideas. I sat down at the piano and found a chord sequence and asked my son, then very small, to give it a name, and he said "Skeleton's Tooth." I reflected on how a skeleton's tooth is really just a person's tooth once he can no longer use it, and I wrote this.

NOVEMBER

1 - THE PLAGUE

There will be blue skies
above the green and verdant plain
churns will swell with fresh butter
there will be an abundance of sweet grain
and we will rise from our sleep
we won't have time to choose what things we'll keep

And rivers will all turn to blood
frogs will fall from the sky
And the plague
will rage
through the countryside
la la la la

There will be cotton clouds
above the fields as white as cream
there will be loud singing in the churches
as we all come out to take one for the team
and all our great schemes and plans
will slip like fishes from our hands

And rivers will all turn to blood
frogs will fall from the sky
And the plague
will cover the country
with its anger
la la la la

ΔΔΔ

Again with the representative challenge of the "la la"—it's an essential part of the song here, possibly *the* essential part, but the page can neither contain it nor fairly represent it: It's something that has to happen, in real time. Even if it's rehearsed it retains that sense of occasion, and this page is only a record of the occasion, not the occasion itself.

"The Plague" is older than most of its November brethren by a couple of decades, but it belongs here, because its November brethren were born in two recording studios in the first two weeks of March 2020, and, well—you remember how it was.

2 · PEZ DORADO

Echoes from a nursery rhyme
hide in plain sight all this time
here you come splashing in your summer clothes
you and your pale pink toes

Just there where the shadow falls
there we follow one and all
can't resist the creeping dark
ready to make our mark

Little red fish beneath the surface of the water
testing the break point in case we get lucky

Ancient blood is patient blood
we were here before the flood
waiting for our time to shine
sparks in a silver mine

Shorebirds deal death all day long
we are weak but they are strong

lose some friends along the way
then in you come one day

Little red fish beneath the surface of the water
scales in the sun, stars in a shot glass
testing the break point in case we get lucky

Take your time, we've got all day
days beyond that, come what may
if you get home tell all your friends
the spawning tide never ends

Say what you felt when you found us here
here where the waters are crystal clear
one summer day in your summer clothes
the day you saw several ghosts

Little red fish beneath the surface of the water
hungry for years, senses sharpened by the hunger
testing the break point in case we get lucky

ΔΔΔ

I had some Japanese incense with koi on the wrapper, and the name of the incense printed in several languages: *pez dorado*, "goldfish." But it got me thinking of El Dorado, the lost city of gold, about which I know absolutely nothing more than the words I've just said, and that got me to thinking about lost cities underwater like you might find in Lovecraft, but fish don't have cities. They live a different sort of life. They see things differently from us. Different to us, as people overseas sometimes put it, a prepositional substitution that feels worth chewing on a little in the context of this tune.

3 - TIDAL WAVE

It's not the barnacles that do all the damage
figure this out too late
it's not the destination that makes the difference
it's the freight

Everything becomes a blur from six feet away
get used to this
every card ever turned over remains in place
get used to this

not every wave is a tidal wave
not every wave is a tidal wave

It's not the mutiny that gets written down in the diary
it's the manifest
forgotten cargo in obsolete measurements
anybody's guess

Even the proud, even the very proud
probably die on their knees
twin masts out on the open seas
mistaken for trees

Not every wave is a tidal wave
not every wave is a tidal wave

ΔΔΔ

"Everything becomes a blur from six feet away"—that's true! It's not really anything to be sad about, but if you notice it one day and you get a little time at the piano later, well, then, maybe get sad about it a little and see what shakes out.

4 - RAT QUEEN

Meek subjects by torchlight come to pay their respects
as foretold by the ancient texts
line snaking down the sewer
reverent hush upon the crowd
one by one we approach
the figure in the shroud
        new dreams
        new dreams for the rat queen

Great warm throbbing hum of the undercity
at one with the purpose
I am a faceless, nameless acolyte
here tonight at your service
take my visions, make them real
impose them on the world above
all the dead sleepwalkers
who never learned how to love
        new dreams
        new dreams for the rat queen

Brand new dreams, great visions
something heady and threatening
on the boil in the kitchen

Arise from the storm drains, take to the street
we who've never once tasted the stench of defeat
victory sweet as the dregs of the fast-food dumpster
look how they jump when we show up
like they've just seen a monster
        new dreams
        new dreams for the rat queen

ΔΔΔ

Written on the occasion of the coronation of the Rat Queen: Long may she reign!

5 - YOU'VE GOT TO HAVE A MOUSE IN YOUR LIFE

Oh, you'll want to have something to eat
perhaps a plate of sweets for the sweet
you'll want to keep your business simple,
and keep your cheeks dimpled;
remember not to chew on your feet—

And you've got to have a mouse in your life.
You've got to have a mouse in your life!
You've got to have a mouse, you've got to have a mouse,
you've got to have a mouse in your life.

Well, you'll want to always try to behave;
when your face is getting scratchy, you shave.
You'll want to keep your blades sharp, and learn to play the harp;
saddle up your glow sticks and rave.

And you've got to have a mouse in your life.
You've got to have a mouse in your life!
You've got to have a mouse, you've got to have a mouse,
you've got to have a mouse in your life.

What will you do without a mouse around the place—
Amble to and fro with your mouse-deficient face?

Well, you'll want to wipe your nose when it runs
gobble candies by the hundreds of tons

yes, but swallow down your pride, and set a few aside,
'cause someone's going to need 'em,
they'll be angry if you eat 'em,

And you've got to have a mouse in your life.
You've got to have a mouse in your life!
You've got to have a mouse, you've got to have a mouse,
you've got to have a mouse in your life.

ΔΔΔ

This is a long story.

In the autumn of 2011 I was in Halberstadt, Germany, on assignment from *Harper's Magazine* to write about the changing of the chord in John Cage's *As Slow as Possible. As Slow as Possible* is a piece for organ with no time signature and the tempo indication given only in its title; what could it mean? So it's a thought experiment, but at Halberstadt, where the first twelve-tone Gothic organ was built, they did some very fun math and set a playing length of 639 years. Every so often, pipes are added or subtracted to an organ in a deconsecrated medieval church, and the chord changes.

I spent a week in Halberstadt, getting a sense of the place and the people behind the John Cage Organ Project, wonderful people; and on a weekend morning I wandered into the town center where, on a stage, for the kids, some performers were singing a song that seemed to be about a mouse, specifically about the mouse in whose costume one of the performers was dressed. It was bizarre, and charming, and I shot some film of it, and then went back to my business.

A week later I played in Cologne for the first time in many years, and the head of the label that released *All Eternals Deck* (whose German pressing is one of the best-sounding vinyl pressings I've ever had the honor of hearing) was driving me to dinner or somewhere when I saw a statue of the same mouse I'd seen dancing in Halberstadt the week before. "That's *hatte manne* mouse!" I cried, quoting the lyric to the tune I'd heard as best I could. "Stop the car! It's *hatte manne* mouse!"

"Yes, that's the mouse," said my label rep; he explained that it's a popular children's program, or more accurately, a children's program that had been very popular for a previous generation. I dashed into the store to buy some mouse gear for my then infant son, including a plushie of the mouse himself, whose name is Die Maus, and the tour continued.

Back home in the States, I gave the plushie to the baby, who enjoyed it, and one night he was making a fuss at about two in the morning and I went up to see what the matter was, and he'd pushed the mouse plushie through the slats of his crib; and, speaking in the way fathers do to their fussing babies, I said, "Well, here's the problem, your mouse is missing, you've got to have a mouse in your life."

As we would learn over the years to follow, *Die Sendung mit der Maus*—"the program with the mouse"—is a children's program so gentle, so loving, and so fun as to make you yearn for what children's entertainment can and might be when creative adults set their minds to it. Die Maus is a problem solver; with his friends Elefant and die Ente (a duck) he goes through life in the form of three-minute vignettes. If he's riding in a three-wheel motorcycle and can't fix a flat tire, he asks Elefant to sit to the left and rides on two. If he can't lift a barbell, he paints the ends to look like soccer balls, and now they're lighter.

Die Sendung mit der Maus came to mean a great deal to our little house, and this song was part of that moment. It is unreleased, but it's a sort of pre-bop jazz lilt, and its lyrics, as you can see, speak to a universal truth.

6 - THE GREAT GOLD SHEEP

I'm going to do what I like
I'm going to live how I want

I'm going to build myself a great estate
with lots of statues out front
    choirs from the Curtis Institute
    singing me to sleep
    wake up and worship the great gold sheep

I'm going to walk the pathways of the ancients
I'm going to let my name be known
I'm going to seek the wild haunts of this world
and carve a place out all my own
    heat up the iron until it glows
    burn the brand so deep
    wake up and worship the great gold sheep

There's only one, splendid and fine
the ages attest its wondrous design
you and me stand somehow above the fray
and name every one who's throwing their chance away

I'm going to write my name on everything
I'm going to leave a lasting legacy
and when my body's thrown with great force from a window
the dogs will fight for whatever's left of me
    shallow grave among the weeds
    where the pale worms creep
    wake up and worship the great gold sheep

ΔΔΔ

Originally "The Nebuchadnezzar League" and based on a mishearing of my toddler son singing the Hebrew alphabet—he was probably trying for *qof resh shin*, though I'm not sure, I took a year of Hebrew in college (in order to be able to at least do a little of the Old Testament in the original) but I don't have any exposure to the alphabet songs. Once I'd clocked what "the great gold sheep" was rooted in, anyway, it was a cinch I'd write something about the golden calf.

7 · WHEN A POWERFUL ANIMAL COMES

We move by night
cover our tracks well, and we pack light
follow the shoreline when we've run clean out of land
speak in gestures only we can understand
we've made mistakes
everyone spots their own mess when the dawn breaks

We get so exhausted
lost kids, just wasted
sleep in short shifts and then rise up to our feet
life is short, and life is hard, and life is sweet
the tree line shakes
we roll hard along some long odds when the dawn breaks

See soft peaks off in the distance
those people in the mountains—
they will never know what hit them

We shed dead weight
it gets pretty hard to concentrate
practice our prayers until some small hope crystallizes
follow the shoreline 'til some better hope arises
behold, the beast awakes
stand trapped in that great shadow when the dawn breaks

ΔΔΔ

Between *Getting into Knives* and *Dark in Here*—two albums written during one of my most concentrated bursts of creativity since the mid-nineties: I had a lot of ideas—there are even more songs about animals than usual, but this animal has no specific identity. The vague is a better threat than the specific, as all we who seek to conjure threat and menace know, though the specific threat does have its moment now and then. A few days after we tracked this one, the NBA canceled their season because of the incipient pandemic. We were stationed in Alabama, making an album. Wasn't that, as the Weavers would remark in the imperative voice instead of the indicative, a time.

8 - CORSICAN MASTIFF STRIDE

We sail we sleep we scry dry land
we dig a pit beneath the sand
a place to keep the sun at bay
at dark we rise and find our way

with our faithful companion by our side
put it all on the table and let it ride
close to the drop-off on our long slide

the land we left becomes a dream
the ghosts we knew, they rise like steam
they leave some trails against the sky
all but invisible to the eye

with our faithful companion by our side
put it all on the table and let it ride
close to the drop-off on our long slide

call off the search party,
let mourners wail by the shore
point to the spot where our ship disappeared
we're not coming home any more

should you succeed and breach the coast
you tell your friends you've seen a ghost
you tell them all there's nothing here
worth dying for   you leave it there

with your faithful companion by our side
put it all on the table and let it ride
close to the drop-off on our long slide

ΔΔΔ

A distance: Had I, in 1992, heard the words "Corsican mastiff" in sequence, I'd have picked up a guitar then and there and the song would have almost certainly have had the words "Corsican mastiff" in the chorus. That chorus might have gone a number of ways: "Hunkered down in the bunker with your Corsican mastiff," maybe (honestly: probably), or "With the Corsican mastiff you brought home from the war." I could not, in 1992, have been satisfied with just mentioning the Corsican mastiff in the title and not affording myself the supreme pleasure of saying the phrase aloud at least once. I still take great pleasure in the sounds of words, in the way syllables click and clack against one another, I think that's clear. But over the years my interest in the story has overtaken my lust for sheer sonics, my incantatory fascination with the sounds of the words themselves. However the song shaped up, in 1992 the final chorus would probably have run: "Corsican mastiff / Corsican mastiff / Corsican mastiff / Yeah." Now I let the Corsican mastiff run on a much longer leash.

9 - PARISIAN ENCLAVE

Signal drawn upon the bricks of a clinic for the dispossessed
collect the brine from the rain gutters let the devil take the rest
rats returning home to our nest

Beneath the streets of the city with my brethren in the
never-ending shadow
Beneath the streets of the city with my brethren in the
never-ending shadow,
there I go

Secret hymnal with the words in a version of the mother tongue
Walls envelop all of us like a mother who protects her young
Spores at play deep down in our lungs

Beneath the streets of the city with my brethren in the
never-ending shadow
Beneath the streets of the city with my brethren in the
never-ending shadow,
there I go

ΔΛΛ

The phrases are dictated by the rhythm of the melodic line, which is the opposite of how I usually write: Usually, one or two important phrases—the chorus and the opening line, maybe—are formed by melody and rhythm, but after that the song has to shape itself around the words. This one went the other way, which is a lot trickier, which may account for its brevity, but it packs a fair bit of story into six lines and a chorus. Sometimes I make good on threats like "the whole album should be like this!"—*Goths*—and other times I force the entire weight of the concept onto a single song that's under two minutes long. I like the results either way.

10 - MOBILE

Jonah went down to the docks
to flee from the wrath of the Lord
but the mark on his forehead was visible

to everybody on board
they threw him down into the water
but he did not drown
I'm on a balcony in Mobile, Alabama,
waiting for the wind to throw me down

Now the Lord told the great fish:
"Be free of your burden"
and Jonah emerged from his darkness
like a dancer crashing through the curtain
and the plant grew, but it withered,
and shriveled up and turned brown
I'm on a balcony in Mobile, Alabama,
waiting for the wind to throw me down

Lord if you won't keep me safe and warm
then send down the storm, send down the storm

Jonah was sure he heard voices
maybe just one voice, but real clear
and where he went the voice followed
sometimes hardly loud enough to hear:
"Shall I not spare the wise with the wicked?
Hold back my wrath from this town?"
I'm on a balcony in Mobile, Alabama,
waiting for the wind to throw me down

May I address the foreman of the jury?
Why do You hold back your fury? Don't hold back Your fury.

ΔΔΔ

There was another song from the *Getting into Knives / Dark in Here* group called "Shores of Tarshish," Tarshish being the city to which

Jonah flees to escape from the Lord. I've said, here, "to flee from the wrath of the Lord," but I'd like to linger a moment on that—the book of Jonah begins: "And there is a word of Jehovah unto Jonah son of Amittai, saying: 'Rise, go unto Nineveh, the great city, and proclaim against it that their wickedness hath come up against me.' And Jonah riseth to flee to Tarshish from the face of Jehovah, and goeth down to Joppa, and findeth a ship going to Tarshish, and he giveth its fare, and goeth down into it, to go with them to Tarshish from the face of Jehovah" (Jonah I:1–3, Young's Literal Translation). Is the Lord wrathful when Jonah flees? I would say "no," on the face of it, but I would also argue "no, but also yes," and so this song is a meditation on the nature of God's wrath, which may or may not be wrath, depending on who you ask.

11 - THE DESTRUCTION OF THE SUPERDEEP KOLA BOREHOLE TOWER

Stick bright reflective tape to the collar of your shirt
mind your business and you won't get hurt
be true to the things you said you'd be true to
always keep your objective in view

Keep two working contacts among your effects
see the tall poppies with their tender fragile necks
Solomon in all his glory not arrayed like these
bending in the wind like pilgrims on their knees

those who came to learn these lessons
left no trace of their presence

Always have a flashlight, just in case
show the world your true face
burn such fuel as you need to burn
learn to wait your turn

Count the heads in the bunks before you turn in for the
night
lace your boots up tight
secure the rope to the pole
keep a sense of wonder when you finally reach your goal

those who came to learn these lessons
left no trace of their presence

Leave nothing behind
keep a positive thought in your mind
if you can't find anything nice to say
drift away

Retain a sense of grace when it's time to cut the cord
crack through the crust fall to your knees and praise the
Lord
listen for the voices calling out from down below
steady as you go

What will they say back home about you—
who always kept your objective in view
whose effects included contacts that finally got found
inside the Arctic Circle, scattered on the ground

those who came to learn these lessons
left no trace of their presence

ΔΔΔ

One of two songs in this book that has its origins in a story that ran in the *Weekly World News*, "Going to Lubbock" (July 27) being the other. Word along the evangelical wire was that the Soviets had drilled so deep they pierced the vault of Hell, deep beneath the earth.

There was a recording of what they'd heard—the screams of the damned. Then funding disappeared, the well was capped, and the site abandoned, and over time the tower collapsed, which means that the site where the screams of the damned were or weren't recorded by Soviet oilmen is now a windswept relic of another time. Yes: The "truth" about the recording has been widely disseminated online, you can look it up. It is there to delude the gullible, who regurgitate it where and when they can. But we know the truth.

12 - THE NEW HYDRA COLLECTION

Down in the lab
with the hopeful few
hell-bent on doing
the work that you cowards won't do
weaving the future
from bright new threads
prices on their heads

Someday the abomination
is going to finally make land
we stay silent as a snowdrift
focused on the task at hand
dream of the day
when the calm waters break
and something rises from the lake

Someday, all of you people will know
the safe path isn't the only way to go

Movement in the grid
as fish leap in the air
it's only a test run,

and still the tension's too delicious to bear
all around the monitor station
big smiles, high fives
according to my projections
everybody's going to run for their lives

Still we wait until our time has come
down here where the engines hum
exiled priests of Rome
bringing our troubles back home

Someday, all of you people will know
the safe way isn't the only way to go

ΔΔΔ

Some things about yourself you know and remember but don't have any reason to share—probably most things about yourself are like this. When I got to college I couldn't wait to write a thesis; I hoped one day to write a dissertation. Every semester for three years I'd contemplate the specter of the senior thesis not with dread but with the blissful anticipatory hope of the lover. In my notebooks I would scrawl ideas for it. One that stuck around until it vanished was the general theme of monstrousness in literature—the image of the monster, the idea of the monster, the whole general monster concept. When push came to shove I ended up writing instead about what I called "tragic vision," but one way of thinking about what I've done since is to pursue the monster thesis idea at a very leisurely pace.

13 - LIZARD SUIT

Take the trouble to pronounce the street names right
people like it when you show respect

look out the window at the softening asphalt
dreamy shimmer of the haze effect

Wear my lizard suit to the party
it's so hard to get noticed in this town

Almost invisible aboard the train
so many people who you just can't read
dawdle when I reach the final station
don't make a move until the crowds recede

Wear my lizard suit to the party
it's so hard to get noticed in this town

Wait for my cue
search for one clue
I have to trust that my compass stays true

Let my phobias control my habits
let my habits form the shapes of days
all alone up on the rooftop sometimes
among the beacons where the lightning plays

Wear my lizard suit to the party
it's so hard to get noticed in this town

ΔΔΔ

Interviewers like this question: "Tell me about your creative process." I try always to be a good sport about it, but as a question it's both too vague and too big to elicit many useful answers. Everything's part of my creative process; creative work is the tangible record of a process that exists before and outside of language and shape and chronological time; nothing is not the creative process, and this isn't just true for me but is the birthright and legacy of everyone who lives—and, if this were generally known, a just world would be right there within our grasp. One part of my process is that when I write I do not have a theme, I just have stories, from which my theme eventually makes itself known: So it's not accurate to say I don't have a theme, but it is accurate to say I'm ignorant of it until later on. This song, quite transparently a song about alienation, was, when I was writing it, a song about a guy who wears a lizard suit to a party. The phrases in the song surrounding that image were written to fit the rhythm of the lines, as in "Parisian Enclave," and their meaning was secondary to their function of leading up to the image. It is impossible for me to answer the question "tell me about your creative process," but this is part of it.

14 - DARK IN HERE

Steal away at sundown, pick a place to hide
check for signs of ambush, hunker down inside
tired of running, tired of never standing still
hear them riding up the hill

Men whose ribs are showing through their skin
bringing up the rear
it's high noon somewhere, it's dark in here

Stack my ammunition, be ready when you come
you who thirst for action, I will give you some
when the smoke dies down, you can rest assured
we will know who kept his word

You who stood so proud once
I can taste your fear
you blazed like torches, it's dark in here

It's dark as a coal mine filling up with gas
I stand ready for the blast

Will you be ready when your moment comes?
Will your hands be steady when you reach down for your
guns?
Did you leave your house in order when you came for me?
Is this really where you meant to be?

Just beyond your limits
find the new frontier
I live in the darkness
it's dark in here

ΔΔΔ

This song resists the page—it wants the breath-pause between phrases, possibly slashes between phrases instead of commas or line breaks, possibly italics on the chorus, possibly typographical play: intentionally misspelled words, inexplicable initial capitalizations mid-line, simple line drawings in the margins. Readers are hereby encouraged to do this work themselves, on this actual page, and to document their work with a photograph, not for me but as a way of getting down inside the song while revisiting this photograph occasionally over time, not on any particular schedule but as the occasion calls for it, if it ever does call for it, you never know.

15 · TO THE HEADLESS HORSEMAN

Set out early, every seasoned rider knows
keep an even pace, steady as she goes
headed back to town after several nights away
I rode past you on the road again today

Gentle shadows in the mist among the trees
Who awakes prepared to face such sights as these?
God keep the bounty hunter who shows mercy to his prey
I rode past you on the road again today

and as you approached, I could sense the threat
but a stranger's just a friend who hasn't shared their
secrets yet

Make camp by sundown, watch fire burning bright
Songs bloom in the dark and throb down in the night
I seek the gate of wisdom, the secret state of play
I rode past you on the road again today

Rise up restless, get ready for the waterworks
Shun the hollow places where my marksman lurks
One of us will tire, and one will rise and ride away
I rode past you on the road again today

ΔΔΔ

The original draft of this is more hopeful. That is why we revise.

16 - BEFORE I GOT THERE

The acrid smell of burning branches
the relics all in ruin
broken blades behind the altar—
cheap substitutions

And the tapestry above,
torn down, trampled, then rehung
now illegible forever
an oracle with no tongue

All of this, all of this, all of this before I got there.

And in a pit behind the altar
the bodies of the fallen
heavy tracks up to the lip
just to prove that they were crawling

Faces turned toward the sky
that they would never see again
victims of the fallout
I have failed you, sweet young men

All of this, all of this, all of this before I got there.

ΔΔΔ

One way of reading dreams is to regard every character in the dream as yourself: I find this strategy persuasive and useful. As to this song: Who has failed whom here? All these absent agents of destruction: How far away are they now, really? That illegible tapestry—I'll bet somebody still in the room with us could tell us what it said, no matter how burnt it looks now. I would stake my life on it.

17 - UNMASKED!

Rain beats down, down on the outer walls
down on the skylight, where the streetlights
shine like unquenchable coals.

I'm up high, trying to say goodbye
the only way I know how—
crude and graceless,
peeking through the eyeholes:
seeing the real you.

And just after midnight,
when it feels like it's getting late,
I will reveal you.

Crowd's half gone, just a few hangers-on
come to see me finally tear through the stitching at last.
And you don't care; you look almost relieved down
there—
like you're free, like you can breathe now.
Like they've sawn off your cast.
One more sleeper to see through.

And by way of honoring
the things we once both held dear,
I will reveal you.

Cast of thousands.
We were the real two.

And when I'm alone
before a mirror late at night
I will reveal you.

ΔΔΔ

This is a wrestling song, a partner to "Hair Match" (September 14)—I think of old wrestling movies, the ones from Mexico where the masked wrestler appears in dramatic non-wrestling scenes, talking to people who don't regard the mask as anything unusual, people for whom the mask is no longer part of an imposed context. You can take the wrestler out of the ring, but you can't take the ring out of the wrestler. He gets to stay there no matter how much distance you put between him and the actual noise of the crowd.

18 - LET ME BATHE IN DEMONIC LIGHT

Down at the end of a bombed-out street
the shell of a house where my friends and me used to meet
someday the old flesh will give way to the new
find a functioning mirror inside and slip right through

And there, there I'll be
and who? who's coming with me?
to show me my one true face
when I arrive in my preordained place

Chain of command maybe ten years long
I emerge in Manhattan, still young and strong
someday the hellhound will pick up the scent on the trail
zero in on my penthouse and pierce the veil

And there, there I'll be
and who? who's coming with me?
to show me my one true face
when I arrive in my preordained place

Hopeless but free
lit up like a marquee
over the freeway
where will my long trail end?
here, here with my new friend

Fruits of the spirit
heavy on the vine
undying hunger
deep in the bloodline
dodge the hook like a steelhead
swim through the night

break the surface and rise like a geyser
when my time is right

And there, there I'll be
and who? who among you? who's coming with me?
to show me my one true face
when I arrive in my preordained place

ΔΔΔ

We talked a lot in college about identity as social construct—about the malleability of the self, you know. When I say we I mean I, but I'm not sure I still buy what we were selling back then. This is kind of a heavy song about predestination and the solid core one suspects is lurking down there at the center where one used to suspect there wasn't any fixed quantity at all. Time and age have a way of wearing away at attractive ideas like the malleability of the self. You have to give a song like this a nice lilting rhythm to buffer the message a little. It's the only way.

19 - YOUNG CAESAR 2000

When I was twelve years old, they put me on the throne
When I was twelve years old, they made me king
From the ocean south of here to the northern hemisphere,
they gave me everything

Now I'm thirteen, and no one takes me seriously
Now I'm thirteen, and they're trying to take away control
I don't know how stupid you all think I am
But as sure as flowers grow along the western wall,
some heads are going to roll

ΔΔΔ

I used to write about antiquity a lot: I was in college, studying antiquity. Among the many angles you can look at the past from, two stand out as questions one needs to answer before moving forward—were the people of the past a lot like us, or were they really not like us? If it's the latter, you still end up at "we're like them," and that's sort of, you'll forgive me, the hermeneutic approach of my stuff set in Rome, or, as here, in a Rome that never actually existed except for the purposes of this song.

20 - THUCYDIDES II:58

Red face at noon
strip naked but can't get free
and doubling over in the street,
dozens just like me

Spreading like a rumor
spreading like a rumor

And the doctors come traveling house to house,
and they visit the sick each day
sit with them there until they're gone
die quicker that way

Save who they can save
on their way down to the grave

Spreading like a rumor
spreading like a rumor

Run to the altars, beg for shade
take to the high sea thousands strong
hang on to your goodness while you can

sweat it out all night long
and listen for the old melody
as it comes to me
on a high wind down from Ethiopia

On a high wind down from Ethiopia.

ΔΔΔ

This is the one that got away, or one of the ones that got away, but there are only so many hours in a day; it was written for a project involving Anonymous 4, a vocal quartet who specialize in medieval chant and polyphony. I'd loved their music for years. That project became a live presentation using songs from *Transcendental Youth*, and the concurrent idea I'd had working—writing songs based on ancient texts, to be arranged for the Mountain Goats and Anonymous 4—retreated to the place where the projects for which neither world enough nor time could be found must go. The onward march of life, and the blessing of increasing success, consigns many such half-begun projects to the back of the file cabinet, whose eventual end is obscurity. I'm glad to give "Thucydides II:58," a song about a plague, this tiny bit of light that its brethren from the same notebook won't get.

21 - AULON RAID

Come riding with your soldiers
see how they fare
keep yourself out of the action
arrows flying through the air
your reputation precedes you
something must be done
here in the heat of the onslaught
I am the one

Me and my crew
we will deal with you
we will deal with you,
me and my pagan crew

Come to lay down the edict
come for the spoils
come for the temple attendants
anointed in oils
come flanked by your big guns
ride with the pack
come screaming for tribute
go out on your back

Me and my crew
we will deal with you
we will deal with you
me and my pagan crew

ΔΔΔ

We were in Muscle Shoals recording *Dark in Here*, quartered after-hours at an Airbnb on the river. I was reading a book called *A Chronicle of the Last Pagans* by Pierre Chuvin; that just happened to be the book I'd brought with me. By the end of our recording session the COVID-19 pandemic had upended the entire world; Matt Douglas and I rented a van to drive home in rather than risk getting on an airplane. A day or two after I got home, everything shut down. It seemed clear that all the plans we'd made for the upcoming year would be, even in a best-possible-case scenario, delayed. I did what I do when I am indoors without a lot of prospects in the outside world: I started writing songs inspired by the book I was reading. The book was about how to understand the disappointment over time of a people who had once held sway and influence throughout much of the world. Its question, like all questions of history, was: "What happened?" I was trying to get out ahead of the question.

22 - UNTIL OLYMPIUS RETURNS

Go through the motions every day out in the square
listen for the hidden rhythms on the air
nod in agreement when the tyrant holds forth
look for a beacon from the north
protect yourself, vouch for every member of the team
this is just a momentary ripple in the stream

Join in the rebuilding, sing loudly at your labor
make friends with the new guys, be nice to your neighbor
profess keen interest in the welfare of the state
taste everything they feed you, say it tastes real great
spit it down your sleeve every time you get the chance
this is just a brief improvisation in the dance

Raise up the columns, take the statues down
praise the columns, spread the word around town

Behold the temple where the old one stood!
is it not a thing of beauty? don't it make you feel good?
is it not a big improvement on the way things used to be?
is it not a stately beacon for the whole world to see?
we will be right here on the day it finally burns
everybody hold a spot until Olympius returns

ΔΔΔ

Local workers conscripted by conquering forces to build monuments to their glory on the sites of their own places of worship: This is a familiar story in history. Olympius was a local agitator who went missing in

North Africa and whose return was imagined by the vanquished in victorious terms. He was probably killed, but we are still waiting.

23 - LAST GASP AT CALAMA

Out in the street, free and young
songs of the great god wild on my tongue
here come
the new guys again
humorless men

Let he who's without sin throw the first one,
like you said
let anyone else throw the second
as long as it connects with your head

One summer, then all of this is gone
one more summer, then no more swan

Hand me a torch, why not?
Let's get some kicks in while the flame's still hot
they'll do
what they were going to do anyway
but Carthage may rise again one day

With the measure that you use,
so shall it be measured to you—
so you say, and it's true

One summer, then all of this is gone
one more summer, then no more swan

ΔΔΔ

History records the resistance of the locals—"pagans," from one perspective; "the people who already lived there," from another—to the arrival of the interloper. Rome was the interloper par excellence, and was met by robust and usually futile resistance, but what, really, is futility? This is a gigantic book by a singer-songwriter of whom most people presently living will never hear. We don't traffic in notions of "futility" here.

24 - FOR THE SNAKES

All your brambles, all your creeping vines
all the trash that people leave behind
all your fine, fine columns
poking up through the pond scum
we will have uses for these things when we come

Cracks in the marble you hauled in from the quarry
these will be seen by all in all their glory
long hidden shadows of the places they came from
we will bring memories of these things when we come

All your abandoned things
once fine vestments, statues with wings
they have their uses, every one
let me slither across them in the sun

Pale imitations that you brought back from afar
we will show them to you as they are
wind through the ruins, high and lonesome
we will have uses for these things when we come

ΔΔΔ

It is good practice to understand that everything eventually comes to ruin, and that ruin is in the eye of the beholder, and that the eventual beholders will be creatures whose uses for our big dreams made real upon the earth will be entirely practical. It is for these creatures that we sing, whether we know it or not.

25 · THE WOODED HILLS ALONG THE BLACK SEA

Cause no trouble
keep to our own kind
known to exist
hard to find
neck-deep in our passions
serve who we serve
enshrouded in moonlight
bucking the curve

Under the radar
just out of reach
among the thick woods
a mile from the beach

The burden of exile
gets easy to bear
sometimes forget
there's cities down there
woodsmen with axes
they come and they go
snitch to the prefect
about what they don't know
smell the ocean breeze
we will never run out of trees

Under the radar
just out of reach
among the thick woods
a mile from the beach

ΔΔΔ

A story: I bought a Casio SA-7 at some point in the late eighties or early nineties, and it's the one heard on a number of early Mountain Goats releases. (Its use was quite divisive at the time, though the numbers to be divided were still quite small.) I didn't bring the Casio with me when I moved from California to the Midwest, and that was the end of the Casio on Mountain Goats records. But at some point I got it back, and by then I was a father, and my toddler son took a liking to it, playing again and again the pre-installed demo song that highlighted the many possibilities of the instrument. I hadn't heard this song in many years; it was a jaunty, swinging tune, although it's hard to swing without two or more human players involved. The song, we learned, years and years after I'd first heard it in the employee housing apartment in Norwalk, was "American Patrol," a march from 1885 best known in a version by Glenn Miller and his orchestra.

When I started recording *Songs for Pierre Chuvin* into my boom box, recording the songs direct to tape as soon as they were written, in the old style, I thought that I'd need one Casio song to keep things in the spirit of the old tapes. But the toddler had wrecked the SA-7 pretty definitively several years earlier. So I got a new one from eBay and I wrote a song about pagans in exile, which is one way of describing SA-7 composers waiting for their moment to return.

26 - JANUARY 31, 438

When the hunger turns in on itself
it begins to devour its host

who do you turn to for help?
who do you love the most?

I dance with the ones that brought me
I dance with the ones that brought me here

When the word comes down the wire that they're looking
to make an example of you
skin and bones around a campfire beneath the stars
no good end in view

I dance with the ones that brought me
I dance with the ones that brought me here

I dance in the dark, all alone
I dance for the god on the throne
if they come catch me and arrest me, mid-step
let me go down dancing, let me be the last one left

Crushed like a seashell by a seaside warrior's foot
trying to turn the tide
when the hunger's all that holds you together
who do you want by your side?

I dance with the ones that brought me
I dance with the ones that brought me here

ΔΔΔ

Sky Masterson, addressing luck personified in "Luck Be a Lady," sings: "Stick with me, baby, I'm the fella you came in with." If you read many nineteenth-century novels where people dance at the ball, you'll eventually run across a scene where somebody causes a scandal by dancing with someone other than their escort. But what if your dance partner is doomed? Or the orchestra? Or the hall in which they dance and play, oblivious to the ruin that's—well, any minute now, really, it's only a matter of time.

27 · HOPEFUL ASSASSINS OF ZENO

Get tired of coming in from the mountains every year
find some place to set up shop around here
spread out a little, circulate
a log that floats down river will surely take on
  weight

Meet some people, make some friends
How long 'til we get sent back to the mountains?
It all depends

On the hopeful, and the cunning, and the faithful
the well-positioned
filthy but graceful

Get familiar with affairs of state
foretell the future, get a pretty good success rate
notch some wins, take some losses
be nice to the guys who wear necklaces with crosses

They will stab you in the back
you gotta turn the other cheek
you gotta learn to love Jesus,
so to speak

Like the hopeful, and the cunning, and the faithful
the well-positioned
filthy but graceful

Real filthy, think about getting clean
even hear the soldiers talk about it, down at the canteen

Little kings keep coming, one another's head
which is exactly how the portents read
Watch with wonder, fail to discern
These people never learn

How long until the snake devours its tail?
Longer than we think
Still it's gotta happen sometime
Until then, raise a drink

To the hopeful, and the cunning, and the faithful
the well-positioned
filthy but graceful

ΔΔΔ

Songs for Pierre Chuvin benefits from the self-imposed criterion of writing one song a day for ten days—under such restrictions, either you're going to relax into your habits or you're going to reach for less familiar registers. "Conversational" is the tone I'm always reaching for—in my personal poetics, the best poems are those that can be imagined as spontaneously delivered monologues—but the mark's easy to miss. Here the rhyme lines keep pulling the vocabulary back down to ground level—"around here," "so to speak," "it all depends." Given more time I might have revised the spit and vinegar out of this song, but it wants more spit, and more vinegar, and because it only had an hour to get born, it gets both.

28 · THEIR GODS DO NOT HAVE SURGEONS

They came like beasts who'd tasted blood
first a few and then the flood
coursing over hill and dale
wet paw prints on their bloody trail

Return the peace you took from me
give me back my community
show us the goodwill you were shown
but leave us alone

And restore the temple of Isis at Memphis
restore the temple of Isis at Memphis

Their hunger like a worm inside them
no sacred place could be denied them
they who talk all day of beauty
call all the plain things dirty

Melted holes in celluloid
give me back what you've destroyed
you who come demanding proof
let your God rebuild this roof

And restore the temple of Isis at Memphis
restore the temple of Isis at Memphis

Make it whole again, if you can
stand in the smoke and say some prayers
wave your hand

And restore the temple of Isis at Memphis
restore the temple of Isis at Memphis

ΔΔΔ

A song about the displacement and destruction of local communities by colonizing Roman forces, but I remember singing "give me back my community" in the condenser mic on the corner of the boom box. It was early in the pandemic. Nobody was seeing anybody. The streets were empty outside. I did not register what I was feeling as anger: I had a family to take care of, songs to write, work to do. There was nobody to be angry at, unless you were an idiot. These things happen. But I hear anger in this. Losing something forever is hard. Sometimes a song will tell its author something he still has to wait a while to learn. In the temple at Memphis there was of course no celluloid. I was thinking of an album I have of music drawn from film found in a wrecked Iranian movie theater. I am still thinking of that.

29 - GOING TO LEBANON 2

We came down to the shore
always some desperate people there
anywhere people congregate for pleasure
they'll go hunting for treasure

come one, come all, fortune-seeking brothers
pick up the faint scent of the faith of our fathers
their names were known once to me
I hear them sometimes on the song of the sea

Take note of what will be gone
in the blink of an eye
the blue, blue water, the bone-white sky

You can set your watch by these guys
we will be high on the highway

before they've even opened their eyes
picture them scouring the sanctuary
looking for gold
it never gets old

But there is no gold and there is no silver
"the South takes what the North delivers"
reverse the circuit sometimes, every couple seasons
remember our grandfathers
whenever we need a reason

Take note of what will be gone
in the blink of an eye
the blue, blue water
the bone-white sky, yeah

ΔΔΔ

The original "Going to Lebanon," on *Zopilote Machine* but absent here, was a leveling-up song for me—it did an interesting up-the-neck chord pattern and its chorus was simple, wistful, and kind of pretty. As my ten-day early pandemic project neared its projected conclusion, "wistful" was the soft way of describing my feeling for the past and the future.

30 · EXEGETIC CHAINS

Look closely at the shadows on the ground beneath the trees:
the labors of Hercules
wild grasses on the hills, rippling in the wind:
Cybele unchained

The songs you sing at Christmastime,
the stories that you tell—

I knew them well
Yes, I knew them well

Say your prayers to whomever you call out to in the night
keep the chains tight
make it through this year
if it kills you outright

The coins they toss at dancers whirling in the city square—
music on the air
the places where we met to share our secrets now and then:
We will see them again

Change will come
stay warm inside the ripple of the Panasonic hum
it grinds and it roars
headed somewhere better
If I have to crawl there on all fours

Say your prayers to whomever you call out to in the night
keep the chains tight
make it through this year
if it kills you outright

ΔΔΔ

My whole life I have resisted the image of the writer who speaks directly from the present moment of his life to the imagined listener. There's more to it than that, I say. But this song was simply me addressing the people whose faces I would not see for over a year, the people who gather in rooms to hear me and my band sing and play: the people for whom we sing and play. It was hard, painful, to be separated from the audience. From you. A performer exists only in the context of the audience. Someday, I will perform no more, and that's all right, too: Everybody eventually needs rest. But 2020 was not rest. It was a separation. This song spoke into that separation in hope, naming images from antiquity to suggest continuity within the broader phenomenon of music over time. It's a song apart from the rest of the album, and from most else in this book, despite its allusive connection to, you know, that other song.

DECEMBER

1 - GRAVE DIGGER

The pumpkins grew in neat rows
we waltzed toward the center of the field
steady as she goes

And blue heavens made wishing wells
brightening the patch
fattening the pumpkins in their perfect orange shells

We turned right by the smooth orange big one,
the wrong way

We tapped on the pumpkins with our thumbs,
and you know how you wait a year or so for something,
        but nothing comes?
It was like that

Empty bottles washed clean by rain
nothing to lose here,
no reason to complain

We turned right by the smooth orange fat one,
the wrong way

Tell me a secret
what does it matter?
override the red clouds hanging on the otherwise clear sky

And then little raindrops like tiny knives,
and I turned to you,
and the field came alive

We took a smooth turn around the fattest pumpkin they had,
the wrong way

ΔΔΔ

As I said back on July 27, the Extra Glenns got a lot of my better earlier songs—the ones that took a few more chances with structure, the ones that aimed a little higher. The rhymes here are nothing special, but the story is my favorite kind of mystery: one where you can't say exactly where the mystery is, but you sense its presence. Yes, I'm Catholic, why do you ask?

2 - TUG ON THE LINE

Sun shone down on a cloudless sea
and we were out on the water, my father and me
with several friends of the family along for the ride
and out on the calm water, we killed the motor
and spread our nets wide

Keep your face to the wind and you'll be fine
and wait for the faint tug on the line

Everyone getting restless when we pulled up the net
we dropped it down on the deck and everyone's feet got wet
and the fish that looked like monsters from way down where the
water gets cold
slid down the deck like shuffleboard coasters
and made for the hold

Everyone's eyes like saucers
nobody saying a word

Keep your face to the wind and you'll be fine
and wait for the tug on the line

Sailed home in silence across the cold sea
several friends of the family, my father and me
and something down below deck that we would try to forget
shapeless and probably nameless
as of yet

Keep your face to the wind and you'll be fine
and wait for the faint tug on the line

ΔΔΔ

"He has a real thing about fish," remarks the alien librarian tasked with summarizing this book for the database.

"The people who lived on this planet made too many books for us to spend time critiquing them," his assistant replies. "Look around. We'll be lucky if we don't die down here."

The librarian sighs, looking up from the volume you yourself are holding right now. "You're right," he says. "You're right. Still, he has a real thing about fish."

3 · PROGRAMMED CELL DEATH

Up and down the shining aisles
of the all-night grocery store on Melrose
dozens of us exiles from the mothership
the whole wide Western world is at our fingertips

But while the moon hangs high above the city
and while the night begins to flex its jaws
we meet up like a loose-knit congregation
or like spies who need to pass on information

How much longer are we supposed to stay alive,
gathering by the Portuguese sardines in aisle five?

Mounds of California avocados
like offerings to an unresponsive god
I wore my suit from Hong Kong to the store tonight
'cause it fits me just right

And suddenly the lights out in the parking lot
begin to burst like sodas under pressure
one by one they throw themselves against the night sky
and almost unremarked upon the moment passes by

Though one or two of us point our fingers outside
eyes glazed, mouths wide

Listening to that still small voice within us
doesn't seem to do us any good
try to take that in stride
try to let the moment slide

And we fiddle with our cell phones
until our thumbs are sore
and the music on the speakers overhead
is fainter than the voices of the dead

How much longer are we supposed to stay alive,
gathering by the Portuguese sardines in aisle five?

ΔΔΔ

This is a riff on a Douglas Coupland scene, I think—maybe something from *Shampoo Planet*—and Liza Minelli is never going to sing it, so I will never hear Liza Minnelli singing about the Portuguese sardines over on aisle five. It's just never going to happen, let's be realistic. I will die angry about this, and bitter.

4 - THE MUMMY'S HAND

If you prick us, don't it sting?
if you kick us, won't it hurt?
I am wrapped in scraps of linen
and pieces of people's old shirts
but way, way underneath
all these sticky bands
I hold all my dreams
right here in my hands

I will rise
from the tomb
like an infant
emerging from the womb

I spent several thousand years
down here all alone
no way to stem
the lonely old ache in my bones
say the spell three times
crank up the special effects
I'm gonna cast off all my bandages
and see what happens next

I will rise
fully formed
like an infant
freshly born

I've been trapped too long
underneath the ground
in the hollow darkness
but ain't no grave gonna hold my body down

I will push
my hand up through the earth
and I will rise like the cry
of an infant at its birth

ΔΔΔ

Reasons why as a child I was more drawn to the Mummy than to Dracula, the Wolfman, or Frankenstein (partial list):

1. Obscurity of the Mummy's motives for mischief as vs. Frankenstein's (revenge), Dracula's (sustenance), or the Wolfman's (primal rage)
2. Obscurity of the Mummy's generally unspecified powers as vs. Frankenstein's (strength of large body, motivated anger), Dracula's (hypnotic sway plus fangs, shape-shifting), and the Wolfman's (feral strength)
3. The Mummy is free from the burden of speech in a way none of the other big three can accurately claim.
4. Frankenstein movies are about Frankenstein. Dracula movies are about Dracula. Wolfman movies are about the Wolfman. Only the first Mummy movie is about the Mummy; he is otherwise seldom the center of the story that bears his name. Someone must speak up for the Mummy and give him a story

of his own. It took me a while, and he still didn't get to be on an official release, but this one is for the Mummy.

5 - TRAINING MONTAGE

Water dripping from the pipes down in the basement
bare feet on a concrete floor
notches on the wall of my solitary cell
sweat dripping out of every pore
it feels like it takes forever
it's maybe five minutes on-screen
but the horns will swell and the strings will sound
when that flipped quarter hits the ground

I'm doing this for revenge
I'm doing this to try and stay true
I'm doing this for the ones they had to leave behind
I'm doing this for you

Keep cool down in the quiet of the morning
sweat blood when the sun comes through
thick mist on the pond before the temple
headed down for the final rendezvous
everybody ready for justice
just another mile to go
but the strings will keen and the horns will cry
when it's just me against the sky

I'm doing this for revenge
I'm doing this to try and stay true
I'm doing this for the ones they left to twist in the wind
I'm doing this for you

ΔΔΔ

Here's what happened: By December 2020 we had been off the road for almost an entire year; it was the longest I'd been continuously at home in at least a quarter century. I was one of those people who was lucky to find upsides in being locked in at home: I love to play music, but touring takes me away from my family for months out of the year; I hate being away from the children, and I hate leaving my wife to do the work of two. Sleeping in my own bed every night, luxuriating in the reliability of routine—a rare and precious gift if it's something to which the other circumstances of your life deny you access—led to the best physical health I've ever been able to claim; my running distance increased from 5k to 10k to twenty miles, nearly to the marathon before my aging body began to register serious objections, which it still holds today, four years later.

People kept talking on social media about binge-watching TV shows, but I didn't care about any of these TV shows; I gave one or two of them a shot but could not connect. For movies I like either art house or junk (the same is true for literature), and if it's junk, I don't want big-budget junk that made a mint at the box office. I want movies most people forgot, like *American Rickshaw*, or, for that matter, anything from the later work of Donald Pleasence. And so I resolved to try to watch a movie or two—action movies were what I landed on, and while I was watching, I started taking notes on the action itself. Which was more or less how I used to write back in the *Hot Garden Stomp* days: watch TV with a guitar in my lap, mute it when I get an idea.

I think it took me about a month to write *Bleed Out*. I watched movies and wrote songs. I do not do writing seminars, but if I did, there would be a TV in the classroom, and we would feast on second-string genre titles.

6 - MARK ON YOU

When this is over
when we leave this all behind us
deep in the moonless night
when the rescue team finds us
it's going to get so dark for you
I'm going to leave a mark on you

Can't trust anybody
even the tough ones crack
train up a swordsman
to stab you in the back
I Know This Much Is True
I'm going to leave a mark on you

No man knows
the hour, or the day
but the mark is going to be visible
from several blocks away

Maybe you'll make it
to the far side of the hill
maybe you will see me coming
but I don't think you will

Make peace with your family
walk softly on this earth
I'm going to leave a mark on you

ΔΔΔ

The line in the second verse is, of course, a direct quotation from Spandau Ballet's biggest single, "True." If I get going on Spandau

Ballet, I will go long, and at this late stage of the game I'm not sure going long is really the right look for any of us assembled here at the end of the year, waiting for the turn of the calendar—still, let us share, if only for a moment, this vision. Tony Hadley, ageless in Versace, a skinny-stem microphone of unknown vintage in his hand—is it a Turner, maybe? It's got an external housing like a Turner. Stationed around him on the spacious stage, the remaining members of Spandau Ballet: Gary Kemp at the synth; his brother, Martin, on bass; Steve Norman with his Yamaha Custom EX in hand, brass instead of the bright copper of the Buffet Prestige he used to play; and John Keeble behind the drums. They're all here, and they are playing "Mark on You," by the Mountain Goats, but the drums are languid, and the bass liquid, and the synths breezy. They play before an enormous billowing curtain lit in washes of purple and yellow. I am in the audience. When Hadley reaches the line "Make peace with your family / walk softly on this earth" and really sells the crescendo, a camera pans from the stage to the audience. That guy you see who looks like he's about to leave his body for sheer joy? That is me. I have been waiting for this concert for a very long time.

7 - WAGE WARS GET RICH DIE HANDSOME

Floor the pedal at the green light
watch the traffic all drift right
barrel forward unimpeded
switch lanes as needed

Be flexible, be unreplaceable
in a world of heavy footprints, be untraceable

Wage wars, get rich, die handsome
Wage wars, get rich, die handsome

Live once, you get to pay twice
keep your nose clean
keep your wheels nice
open highway on the horizon
queen of queens, anima rising

Stay independent
make adjustments as needed
it's losers all the way down
you stay undefeated

Wage wars, get rich, die handsome
Wage wars, get rich, die handsome
Wage wars, get rich, die handsome
Die handsome

ΔΔΔ

I don't imagine I have to tell anybody that the "anima rising" bit is a Joni Mitchell quotation. I am not fit to carry Joni Mitchell's shoes, but it is a matter of scientific record that in an alternate universe, referred to by mathematicians as ZL-405 (the "ZL" stands for złoty; one of the mathematicians was Polish and considered the project a waste of his time, remarking more than once "this whole plane is not worth a złoty"), she and I were both character actors who mainly featured in action flicks. We were only on set together once, in the 1986 Charles Bronson vehicle *Assassination*. It's a crowd scene, you won't see us. We both get killed.

8 · EXTRACTION POINT

You never learn to tell the difference between
the probable projections and the best parts of the dream

the fragments that stick with you, the ones you really feel—
those parts aren't real

But high in the cold Midwestern air
they shimmer before us there
almost out of reach but not quite
stay up thinking about it all night
waited so long for days like these
I'm tired of living on my knees

Pull your hair back tight, head right for the extraction point
and if you don't hear from me, let them all go free

I'm on the Kennedy Expressway at dawn
don't know where we got this car from
I'm driving with the fog lights on
the angles you don't plan for, the things you might have missed—
those things exist

But under the waxing winter sun,
I feel like we're almost gone
just pick a lane and drive right through
headed off to freedom with you
dreams of the future up in the front of my mind
leave a couple dozen bodies behind

Pull your hair back tight, head right for the extraction point
and if you don't hear from me, let them all go free

ΔΔΔ

As I have said, I don't do advice, I consider the whole notion of advice a little arrogant, but the bit about the angles you don't plan for existing whether you see them or not—it's worth considering.

9 - BONES DON'T RUST

Never any call for a lone wolf
you have to learn to go with the flow
but they can find a use for a scarecrow
depending on your stomach for crows
always going to need a little muscle
if you prove yourself worthy of trust
your bones don't rust

Haven't checked a mirror in years
don't need to know the bad news
there's not going to be a gold watch
after thirty years of paying your dues
show up five minutes early as usual
work on just a couple hours' rest
your bones don't rust

They stay hard as diamonds
they cut through steel
they still sing when they're hungry
they ache when they're angry

Listen for the voice of the spirit
maybe something wrong with your ears
always on the edge of collapse now
absolutely nobody cares
but everybody loves a professional
not a single track in the dust
your bones don't rust

ΔΔΔ

The appeal of the assassin who wants to retire but can't is that now he feels bad about all the murdering he still has to do, which liberates us to enjoy his work; but this is also pretty audibly (to me now, not to me when I was writing it) about how touring bands keep getting better at their craft even as their bodies grow rebellious about the way they've chosen to live. "I don't want to go on tour," I say on Monday, and I really mean it, and then on Wednesday play one of the best shows of my life. It would be the same if the finger that slipped the silencer onto the barrel were arthritic. Somebody'd still have to die.

10 - FIRST BLOOD

Mail-order body armor
map to the Blue Bucket Mine
guy who had a place down by the lakeside
changing water to wine
devastating schematics
rough drafts of the twenty-third psalm
Paul Kersey never left his apartment
John Rambo never went to Vietnam

Armor-piercing Black Talons
from the first production run
nobody's seen them in the wild
since 1991
out in the cul-de-sacs at midnight
where the candy for the cannons comes from
I heard Buford Pusser was dirty
John Rambo never went to Vietnam

Shall we rise to the occasion
or go to sleep for good in the trenches?
dug in beneath a brilliant blue sky
helmets hanging high in the branches
empty vessels by the dozen

diamonds in the sun
we worship nothing in the foxholes
John Rambo never went to Vietnam

ΔΔΔ

One of the best song titles of all time is the Minutemen's "Political Song for Michael Jackson to Sing." The song itself is a fairly dense text that lands here: "Coming together, for just a second, a peek / a guess at the wholeness that's way too big"—remarkable—but not before stopping here: "If we heard mortar shells / we'd cuss more in our songs." We do hear mortar shells, but only through the speakers of our home theaters, for which we paid good money. This song's secret other title is "Good Money" as of about thirty seconds ago, and now you know why.

11 - MAKE YOU SUFFER

I'm going to rise up early every day
overcome every obstacle in my way
keep a secret chamber in my heart clean
polish every surface to a brilliant sheen
remain positive and stay on the grind
and banish every other thought from my mind

I'm going to make you suffer
I'm going to make you suffer
let your yes be yes, and let your no come from deep in your belly
I'm going to make you suffer

There was a captain many years at sea
living the life of the sailor, rugged and free
nothing but the sky to sing him to sleep at night

safe in the arms of the ocean   no land in sight
out on the waves, you try to keep warm
nobody here to sound the alarm

I'm going to make you suffer
I'm going to make you suffer
the first in line will receive the full brunt of the blow
I'm going to make you suffer

Woke up from a dream whimpering like an infant
over time people tell me their dreams grow distant
and they learn to love the lives they lead
no more hungry ghosts in the chimney to feed
you often hear stories like these
someday I will see you on your knees

I'm going to make you suffer
I'm going to make you suffer
say what you like—there won't be anybody listening
I'm going to make you suffer

ΔΔΔ

A big part of the appeal of genre fiction is that people have reasons for the choices they make and the things they do with those choices. Real life is only occasionally like that, and literary fiction, whatever "literary" means, also seeks out the less tidy explanations of what happened and how. My favorite thing about this song is the jump that registers on the faces of half the crowd or better when we get to the chorus, because it's not only the writers of genre fiction who would like, just once, to have a simple solution to something that's been bugging them for a long, long time.

12 · GUYS ON EVERY CORNER

From the front door to the drugstore
from the drugstore to the bakery
from the loading dock to the chimes of the city clock,
they're about to make their play for me

But I will rise, I will rise
'cause I got guys
guys on every corner

With your tabloid stars, and your unmarked cars
with your special forces, and your inside sources
with your radar fields, and your riot shields,
and heavy horses

I'm coming to swat you down like flies
'cause I got guys
guys on every corner

They don't look so special—
T-shirts and tennis shoes,
blank expressions
a couple of Chicago guys
a robust East Bay delegation

From the far ends of the earth,
they have loosely gathered
to stand in doorways
making small talk about the weather

They look like nothing, they look like your neighbors
you won't remember their faces later
run like rats, look to the skies

I got guys
guys on every corner

ΔΔΔ

This song is an open admission that I have been cultivating a global surveillance network for more than thirty years, and that none of you are safe from my all-seeing eye—in your most private moments, my guys are there, cameras clicking, voice-triggered handheld microcassette recorders from the eighties in their vest pockets; and the beauty of the whole thing, the cherry on top of it, is that I can tell you directly about it in a book marketed and sold to the general public, and you won't blink an eye. Ah, good old John Darnielle, you'll say. He tells so many stories. He's so convincing. JD and his little stories.

13 - HOSTAGES

There may come a day someday
when we all look back and laugh
but there's lots of noise in the break room
nasty points on the graph

And they're breaking into the broadcast now
special update from Action News!
some of what you'll hear in the footage that follows
may not reflect our station's views

We may run out of bullets
we're never going to run out of hostages

There's disagreements on procedure
vocal, bitter divisions

as is often the case in situations like this one
I'll be the one who makes the final decision
some of you have been here before
most of you have not
some will dwell on the details in the future
or work to keep it out of your thoughts

We may run out of bullets
we're never going to run out of hostages

There's a team up on the rooftop—
good luck to the team!
when you know you'll never make it out alive,
you kind of get to live out your dream
helicopters in the distance
music of the spheres on the wind
it's going to be a rough ride from here down to the exit
some might look back and laugh at the end

We may run out of bullets
we're never going to run out of hostages

ΔΔΔ

I have this reputation for being hopeful, for supplying comfort where needed—because of "This Year," because of "Up the Wolves," because I favor the jaunty melody in a major key at mid-tempo or better. This one's in a major key, too, and the people in it do have all kinds of hopes—hopes in which they're possibly more invested than they've ever been in their lives or will ever be again, I'll give you that. Otherwise, well, yes, guilty as charged, I tend to see the glass as half full, but I'm keenly aware that the metaphor never specifies what's in the glass, or what will happen to you if you drink it.

14 - NEED MORE BANDAGES

Stockpiles of ammunition in wooden crates
stenciled with exotic ports of call
white rags stuffing up glass jugs
clean-burning overproof alcohol
    I did not seek out the mission, but the mission found me
    twenty-one years old
    I mean to learn what it's like to be free

We're going to need more bandages
we're going to need more bandages

Cheap overseas tobacco
hidden treasures within
you can even smoke it if you're desperate
we do get desperate now and again
    I am not the first to follow the plan,
    just a cog in the machine
    I'm just here to run interference
    dancing like a fly on the screen

We're going to need more bandages
we're going to need more bandages

More bandages—more shovels!
when the shovels break,
we've still got our fingernails!

Why wait until tomorrow?
victory awaits with the dawn!
if we all get blown to pieces,
we can leave a nasty mark when we're gone

I did not hunt down the moment,
it found me in a dream
struck down as a warning to the others
nothing without my brothers

ΔΔΔ

Can I talk nuts and bolts here? This song started with the chords and some wordless syllables—me in my room working through a progression without a clear concept of what I'm going to say, although it was during the whirlwind month of *Bleed Out*, so I knew I'd have some kind of action/intrigue framework. So the first draft of the first line would only have been some syllables in the air following the riff on the guitar—*ba-BAA-ba-da-da-da-da*, a place marker for where my composing brain figured the lyric would fit. Then, as the shape of the song began to gel, I needed actual words. I work like this some of the time—but not all of the time. *Ba-BAA-ba-da-da-da-da* might have gone elsewhere in somebody else's hands: "These lonely winter mornings," "White whales and baffled sailors," "You need a good shellacking." We could fill this whole book, and many more besides, with the possibilities. So it tells you something about me, maybe a big something, if you understand that my brain, in need of words to fill that space but without an extant plot framework to dictate their import, chose "Cheap overseas tobacco," and that I then filled in a little melodic phrase with "in wooden crates." It's the same terrain as "Sax Rohmer #1" (July 30) which is to say, the same world as the one in which the early stuff lived—images first, their meaning later.

15 - (UNTITLED)

Louder than your Windsor V8, dusty tennis shoes
ten years since I'd seen you on the day I heard the news
no one riding shotgun for seven years at least
short of breath and bitter on the 60 headed east

stack em up
like unanswered letters
stack em up
you got sick and you never got better

Six foot two and flawless, still some baby fat
two guys one year older, here we are, imagine that
Dan went to prison, he shot someone, you said
your beautiful blond ringlets bouncing up against your head
stack em up
try to understand it
stack em up
too pretty for this planet

Some you lose track of
some you have to bury
some dash back toward the darkness they emerged from
some you have to carry

Crawl toward the sweet sap on a prehistoric tree
feel your feet get stuck, try to jerk them free
never see the moment coming 'til the second it arrives
I knew you before the amber got you, when you were alive
stack em up
keep a candle burning bright
stack em up
to sleep in your shadow every night

ΔΔΔ

If I can confess an unflattering tendency: One reason I keep songs like this one unreleased is that they're personal, but they resonate, so people end up singing along if I play them. What kind of grinch is it who doesn't want people to sing his song? It's too complicated a question to address from the stage, so I just let the songs recede back into their caves. But I am grateful for the last time I saw Brad, who spotted me on a Portland street corner when I'd flown up there on impulse a year after leaving. "I thought you went to California," he said, appearing by my side in sunglasses at a crosswalk. I can hear his voice. It is a sweet thing in my life, to hear his voice in my mind. I don't think any photographs of Brad exist. "I thought you went to California." Yes, I did.

16 - INCANDESCENT RUINS

Here inside the final diorama
charting weather patterns for kicks
there are several fairly weighty problems
I'm pretty sure the simulation won't fix

Never any better at bottom
than the signals I'm set up to receive
choking on the blood of the androids
wiping off my mouth on my sleeve

Shining on the inside, maybe
shining on the inside, maybe

Somewhere in the monument garden
suggestions of a tunnel to freedom
every hour the crack of the rifle
never any guns when you need them

I have to test my chin on the concrete
it's the only way to be sure
only the desperate ever make it to the exit
only the brave and the pure

Shining on the inside, maybe
shining on the inside, maybe

Shining like a deep-sea creature
only temporarily bearing the pressure

Sniffing at the walls of the maze
all the ancient rumors were true
you only see the jump cuts and the close-ups
you never get the aerial view

content to maybe serve as an example
set up a sign or two on the trail
there's a lot of things that can happen
all for the want of a nail

shining on the inside, maybe
shining on the inside, maybe

ΔΔΔ

Not sure I'd call this a "rule," maybe a guideline, but when you see a superficially scattershot collection of images and phrases in a Mountain Goats song, the likelihood that I'm tucking any confessional urges I have into those images and phrases is high. "Never any better at bottom / than the signals I'm set up to receive," "I have to test my chin on the concrete / it's the only way to be sure," "only the desperate ever make it to the exit": I was working fast when I wrote these songs and never stopped to ask what I was writing about, what the next layer down might have been. Stick to the story and let the meaning take care of itself—that's a guideline for me. But this one feels personal.

17 - BLEED OUT

Every time they knock me down
I rise to my feet
every time I take a bullet, they send a medic
to patch me up real neat
you only have to run the numbers to know
sooner or later everybody's got to go
bleed out
I'm gonna bleed out

I'm gonna bleed out
I'm gonna bleed out
there won't be anybody waiting to rush me to safety
I'm gonna let the long night take me
bleed out
I'm gonna bleed out

Every bender needs a blackout
every gauge deserves a top line
every story needs a child who believes
the brave hero's gonna be just fine
you only have to check the papers to see
some of these children end up just like me
bleed out
I'm gonna bleed out

I'm gonna bleed out
I'm gonna bleed out
I'm gonna make a gigantic mess
but it meant something important, I guess
bleed out
I'm gonna bleed out

Somewhere beyond imagination
somewhere beneath the final delta
washed up on the banks of a river at the height of the storm
everybody seeking shelter
I'm gonna dive right in
I can't swim
bleed out
I'm gonna bleed out

I'm gonna bleed out
I'm gonna bleed out
there's gonna be a big spot where I once lay
and there won't even be a spot one day
bleed out
I'm gonna bleed out

There was a chance we'd make it through this
it's safe to say now that we missed it
and I will never lose hope, and I haven't lost hope
I'm just realistic
I will go down punching, but I will go down
and my cornerman won't bring me back around
bleed out
I'm gonna bleed out

The blood is pooling underneath me
flowing freely from my mouth
you want to call a medevac now,
knock yourself out
you can tell them when they get here
you tried
but the smallest hole was several inches wide

bleed out
I'm gonna bleed out

I'm gonna head into the darkness
I'm gonna head into the light
I will surrender to the slow, lurching tide
and drift off into the night
there won't be any words of wisdom from me
just a lake of blood for all the world to see
bleed out
I'm gonna bleed out

I'm gonna bleed out
I'm gonna bleed out
I'm gonna tell my friends to all go to Hell
and wish my enemies well
bleed out
I'm gonna bleed out

I'm gonna bleed out
I'm gonna bleed out
if it's blood you want, I've got plenty of it—
you're gonna love it!
bleed out
I'm gonna bleed out

ΔΔΔ

This is my "Hallelujah" insofar as the morning I wrote it I thought: I just want to do this, I want to spend years doing this, my whole life, I want "Bleed Out" to become my legacy, I want it to have a thousand verses but I only use six of them; I want to grow to resent "Bleed Out" and hear it sung by people who would no sooner bleed out on the concrete than swallow thumbtacks for their breakfast, I want to wash up on the shores of "Bleed Out" where my bleached body will serve as a warning to others, viz., that to linger is to languish, indulgence is its own reward and also its only reward, I'm going to call the band right now, I thought, Hey fellas, throw all those other songs away, *this is it*, no further songs are needed, I found the One. And I think this happens to everybody in their normal lives, like when you make toast and it's perfect and you think: Just this toast forever, let this moment freeze in time and I'll be fine—that was me writing this, bleeding out in my own imagination, having lived an entirely different life from the one I have actually led, palpably lying on the concrete in an alley: toast.

18 - JENNY III

Jenny was a warrior, Jenny was a thief
Jenny hit the corner clinic begging for relief
never thought we'd see the day when she wiggled free
but she did
long before we did

Nights in crackling emerald
signal hot and live
fastest in production
as of 1985
didn't guess we'd ever come to dread that engine's roar
but she did
long before we did

Nobody will ever know for certain
the names of all the secrets
she held back behind the curtain

Jenny came to get me
she'd been gone for several years
aging motorcycles purr like cats when they grow near
I was crying, I could barely make the frame out through my tears
she did
long before we did
Jenny, you did
long before I did

ΔΔΔ

What happened was this: I was at the piano with a chord progression I liked and no fixed idea of what to write about, and I sang aloud, to the melody suggested by the chords: "Jenny was a warrior, Jenny was a thief," which is a version of a rhyme I knew from illustrated Mother Goose books in my childhood: "Taffy was a Welshman, Taffy was a thief / Taffy came to my house and stole a piece of beef." Jenny is if not from Texas then at least partially defined by having become Texan, but her restlessness, her refusal to stay pinned to a map, is her most notable trait. "Taffy was a Welshman" seems pretty clearly to me a bit of regional spite from a time when such fare was common and acceptable, so I'm glad to lift a few phrases from it and leave that bit in the fog of the past, and to reclaim the good name of the thief for Jenny, who steals only what she dearly needs.

19 - GROUND LEVEL

You can make out all the exits
from a static position
one quick walk-around will give you
all the relevant information
never going to break my neck
falling downstairs

tan and mustard yellow I-beam
visible from the air

Tall space heater
down the main hallway
blue pilot light
hissing all night

We sleep light in the shadow of the cloverleaf

You can light a cigarette
against the cooktop if you need to
feel the heat against your forehead
let it bleed through
you're never going to get by
on three hours' sleep a night
unless you absolutely have to
and then you get by all right

Move in silence
if you can't stay still
nobody sees your face
through the security grille

We sleep light in the shadow of the cloverleaf

ΔΔΔ

Jenny from Thebes is what I've called a "fake musical"—it's the songs for a stage musical that doesn't exist. I'm not the first to do something like this—*The Lamb Lies Down on Broadway* is basically the same notion, ditto *Bat Out of Hell*, and I'd argue that Shadow Morton's entire career is a version of this approach to songwriting. But when you're doing this without the benefit of actual sets in real space you need to paint a picture, and that's what this is: the southwestern ranch-style house in which Jenny lived for a while. The place "I" arrived at when I'd reached the end of my rope. The place where others did the same for a while: maybe a long while, and maybe not.

20 - ONLY ONE WAY

You're gonna get a wrinkle on your forehead
you're gonna get a click in your knee
you're gonna tell the doctor that you can't sleep
and you're up every night until three

You're gonna make a bargain with the bad guys
you're gonna make some choices you regret
there's no place to hide from the prophecy
since nobody told you it falls to me

There's only one way out
there's only one way out
there's only one way through
no matter what you do

You're gonna have to watch for the signs
you're gonna have to learn how to read
nobody's gonna hand you a flashlight
you're gonna have to steal what you need

You're gonna have some trouble at the border
they're never gonna let you forget
I'm just passing on the information
beaming down to me from a distant station

There's only one way out
there's only one way out
I've been told there's only one way through
no matter what you do
but if all that's true,
what about you? What about you?

ΔΔΔ

Warnings are preferable to advice. Advice is presumptuous but warnings carry weight, almost a cosmic sort of weight: Warnings are the terrain of the oracle. There should be more oracular pop music. I am trying to do my part.

21- FRESH TATTOO

Tattoo of the seventh shield
still wet on my skin
you're all crumpled up at the curb there
I think I'm going to take you in
always had to follow my instincts
usually I'm out on my own
you there by the road, wet and helpless
what happens if I take you home?

Well, you may forget the whys and wheres
of an old tattoo on your forearm there
but usually you recall the day you got one
and usually it fades in the sun

Headed for a season in exile
as the oracle predicted
according to reliable sources
in thirty days I'm getting evicted

trying not to scratch where it itches
it takes a certain level of discipline
not even half a second by the light switch
let the future flood right in

Well, you may forget the whys and wheres
of an old tattoo on your forearm there
but usually you recall the day you got one
and usually it fades in the sun

Usually the lines grow faint
like old house paint
just a way to mark the years gone by
you lay on the couch three weeks
until the color came back into your cheeks
I'd seen ones like you before
plenty came through before

Legend on the shield in Greek
"What's that say?" you said
I gave you an answer that I thought you'd buy
all of this will disappear in the twinkling of an eye

Well, you may forget the whys and wheres
of an old tattoo on your forearm there
but usually you recall the day you got one
and usually it fades in the sun
but not this one

ΔΔΔ

"Give Jenny a tattoo," I thought to myself while contemplating a whole album of songs about her. The chorus is a simple statement of fact for myself: I remember the days of each tattoo I've gotten as events in time. I am prouder of the song that emerged from the title "Fresh Tattoo" than of almost anything else in the catalog—"Extraction Point" can compete, "The Legend of Chavo Guerrero" is up there, "Running Away with What Freud Said" but that's personal. In "Fresh Tattoo," according to my own criteria—which, as this book surely makes clear, are a little esoteric—I succeed in letting a character be herself. If I relate to her it's because she has succeeded in the difficult task of coming alive, not because she is actually me, as turns out to be the case with too many of my narrators for comfort. Here she breaks free. I'm the other guy, who she's helping, because he needs her help.

22 - CLEANING CREW

You were passed out on the sofa
cigarette burns and coffee stains
loose change in your pocket
naltrexone in your veins

They got a scanner at the airport now
and a dropout in a Kevlar vest
I can hear the timer
ticking in my chest

What are you gonna do?
what are you gonna do?
what are you gonna do when the cleaning crew comes through?

When you get out on your own again
if you ever do shake free
if you find yourself in Portland,
ask about me

Dig up the first revision
the one who's got less to lose
look on every lamppost
from here to Baton Rouge

Ask yourself one question,
then ask yourself again:

What are you gonna do?
what are you gonna do?
what are you gonna do when the cleaning crew comes through?

I saw the future in an oil slick
it told me what I need to know
leave a little stain behind you
everywhere you go

ΔΔΔ

"True love leaves no traces," says Leonard Cohen, and he's Leonard Cohen, I'm sure he's right, but if you even work in the shop next door to Cohen's sometimes you want to start a little argument (here, the coda) just to see where it gets you. I was only administered Narcan once—naltrexone is the generic—and spent the next week of my life in the sort of fugue state that tends to follow an overdose. Here, Jenny addresses the stray in her care, certainly a stand-in for the version of myself who pursued his interests further than I, in this timeline, could bear, asking him what will happen on the day when only he is left to take care of himself. She hints that she understands his condition better than her modest accommodations might suggest. One mark of progress as a writer is reading something and knowing that you couldn't have written it earlier than you did. I wrote this in 2021, right on time.

23 - FROM THE NEBRASKA PLANT

I recall the curb
waiting for the bus
flaky yellow paint
what's become of us

searching in the snow
for something in the distance
when the vision comes
I have no resistance

it's one of several iterations
it gets hard to keep track
on your custom Kawasaki
with the stinger on the back

walk across the bridge
used to get so scared
signed out AMA
no one really cared

it wasn't in your nature
taking in the strays
but you handed me your helmet
I clung to you for days

but I am strong now, I am strong now
that was all years back
on your custom Kawasaki
chrome yellow and black

it's somewhere in a wreck yard now
never see it again on this earth

let the scavengers proclaim
how much it was worth

out here on the median
not sure what to do
figure something's going to happen sometime
wait all day for you

flak jacket full of holes
Kevlar coated and dusty black
on your custom Kawasaki
with the stinger on the back

ΔΔΔ

The Kawasaki GPz750 Turbo, manufactured from 1983 to 1985, was assembled in Nebraska to bypass import tariffs. In "Jenny," I name a bike with a 900cc engine: that's the Ninja, which superseded the GPz Turbo. I did so out of metrical necessity; the bike I once wanted to ride and on which I would surely have died had I been able to afford one was the 750. Few songs in this book better illustrate how I like to fold autobiographical detail into fiction, and how those details achieve clarity when forced into the confines of a plotline. Me: I'm the guy who signed out against medical advice while being assessed for overdose in Portland in March 1985. Me: waiting for a bus back to my apartment on the other side of town the same day, cold, wet, directionless. Me: dreaming of a motorcycle in that time, imagining the freedom. And me, proud husband and father of two beautiful boys, remembering those days and those dreams years later, seeing the vanished young man who lived and dreamt them; and assigning him a Jenny to take him in, to see how he fares with someone more able than himself to bandage his wounds.

24 - SAME AS CASH

You were still attached to your Civic sedan
although the brakes always needed repair
you were headed out to buy some supplies
you could smell the threat of rain in the air
I can only see the scene secondhand
I can only try to understand
how a small amount of pressure in the right place
breaks the strongest link in the chain
in your car with your head in your hands at the far end of the
Walmart
parking lot
trying not to buckle under the strain

Every single night after prime time
loud enough to hear in your sleep
the salesman from the lot half a mile from here
yelling down the hood of his jeep
I'll take anything that the others won't
I can see the value where others don't
just a small amount of pressure in the right place
two fingers to the temporal vein
in your car with your head in your hands at the far end of the
Walmart
parking lot
trying not to buckle under the strain

Striking a bargain with the imp in your brain
prepared to take another knock for the short gain
but you can ask any veteran running back:
eventually your joints complain

You were headed home at eighty miles an hour
with your fingers sweating under your gloves
everyone deserves a little light in their hair
everybody needs to love and be loved
that's what all the people say, anyway
I can save my thoughts for another day
maybe a small amount of pressure in the right place
anything to help with the pain
in your car with your head in your hands at the far end of the
  Walmart
parking lot
trying not to buckle under the strain

ΔΔΔ

This is the origin story of Jenny buying the Kawasaki, obviously, and I hope the story speaks for itself—for me, the thing I mark most about it is its composition. I'd been on the set of a TV show (*Poker Face*) for a month or so, and the episode had finally wrapped, and I was spending my last night in the Hudson Valley at a hotel across the street from a Walmart. I didn't have an instrument with me, but I did get an idea about the parking lot, and I recorded it a cappella into my phone's camera. When you're forced to write without an instrument you often think big, and that's reflected in the sweep of the lyric here, a single moment in a person's life that comes to define who she will be in the future.

25 - MURDER AT THE 18TH STREET GARAGE

I'm in the repair bay casting spells
mystic in the glow of the shop light
ringing out the funeral bells
tending the fires, gathering power
may I present the man of the hour

Placing his faith in the strength of the safety visor
placing his faith in the strength of the safety visor
leaving only slightly diminished
older but wiser

I'm down on the concrete with a bucket and rag
when you've got a big job to do
you notice how the moments drag
live in the present, savor the grind
relish the time before you have to leave it behind

Placing your faith in the strength of the safety visor
placing your faith in the strength of the safety visor
leaving only slightly diminished
older but wiser

Smarter but scared, now,
wearing an exile's mark
one that's going to glow in the dark

I'm out on the sidewalk, scrubbed clean
take all your worry and care
feed it to the big machine
once you commit to the turn, you're going to have to follow
  through
it's the only thing you can do

Placing your faith in the strength of the safety visor
placing your faith in the strength of the safety visor
leaving only slightly diminished
older but wiser

ΔΔΔ

Here and on "Fresh Tattoo," vocal harmonies are sung by Matt Nathanson, without whom there is absolutely no way this book, nor the career that has preceded and will follow it, could exist. He ran the open mic night at Pitzer where I first showed up almost too late to play, just as he was asking if anybody else had a song. I had just gotten off work in Norwalk and driven into Claremont, remembering that I'd seen a flyer about the Sunday night Grove House open mic. My thought was that if the stuff I'd been tinkering with wasn't good, that'd be clear once I played it for strangers: I didn't really know anybody on campus. I played some songs about which I would surely be dismissive today, but delivered them with all the conviction of a young fellow who feels the music in his body, and Matt pressed me to come back the following week. I did. I am still coming back the following week. My debt to Matt can't be overstated. He probably thinks all this would have happened whether I'd run into him or not. I'm considerably less sure of that.

26 · WATER TOWER

Moving lights on an overhead map
have to be headed somewhere
there's probably going to be a building burning in
 town
when you smell smoke in the air
small hopes are seen to still be small ones
when the hour grows late
and a body floating in a water tower
is bound to take on weight

Somebody comes bearing the standard
just when you need to see it held high
you never miss your water
until you're parched, riding home from the slaughter

oracles are seen emerging
from the northern mists
and a body floating in a water tower
is bound at the ankles and wrists

Bound at the ankles and wrists
marks in the skin
from where the ropes have been digging right in

Men of legend built the cities of the prairie
to rise from the horizon at night
feel something bigger than me
when I see them trapped in the headlight
head east, head north by northeast
get my bearings and know
that a body floating in a water tower
only has one way to go

Float downstream
let me float downstream
floating downstream

ΔΔΔ

Trina Shoemaker, whose production on *Jenny from Thebes* brings the album to life, took issue with the intrusion of the first person in the coda: Whose body is it? It can't be the narrator's, since she's the one who put the body there, right? In this question you can sort of locate an explanation not just for this song but for the rest of them, without exception.

27 - CLEAN SLATE

One from East St. Louis
with a scar beneath his eye

left the kitchen spotless
on the day he said goodbye
breakaway republic dude
supremely filthy mouth
Copiah, Mississippi,
points much further south

It's never light outside yet
when they climb into the van
remember at your peril
forget the ones you can

Leave home feeling empty
change planes in Taipei
stay awake the whole time
end up several worlds away
the house was almost full that day
they made a space for you
this world is sad and broken
gotta fix a crack or two

Rest until you're rested
climb back onto the caravan
remember at your peril
forget the ones you can

And then just when you think
you've learned how to forget
you learn it's just
the ones who haven't risen to the surface yet

absence after absence
keep the place secure

this will be the last time that I do this
I'm pretty sure
no one lasts for long in this profession
so they say
maybe see you again someday

every end point fixed forever
on the day its arc began
remember at your peril
forget the ones you can
forget the ones you can

ΔΔΔ

In the early days, repetition was a greatly valued weapon, the most reliable arrow in the quiver—I would talk to you about it at length if you asked me. At some point I retreated from repetition, and got curious about songs without choruses, songs that travel from one point to another instead of returning to a center. In several recording sessions there's been if not pressure then mild encouragement, always resisted, to attach a repeat of the chorus to the end of the song: That is how songs that are trying to be heard tend to do things. In "Clean Slate" I repeat the chorus's final line one extra time at the end, and in this moment I remember why I loved repetition so much in the early times. It's because sometimes only when you say something twice can it become real, and other times only when you say something twice can you understand that it's never going to be real no matter how many times you say it.

28 - SEVERAL OTHER THINGS

There came a day when all the treasures I'd
  gathered
began to weigh me down like chains

I got a blowtorch from a friend down at the body shop
it's always good to have good friends

Picture me at the curb before sunrise
fresh flame noisy and blue
getting rid of the dead weight,
and the evidence,
and several other things I'm never ever going to confess to

There came a day when all the promises gathered
out there at the vanishing point
and the glitter and the shine of this world
began to chip away like old house paint

See me stationed on the brink of departure
waiting on the word from you
getting rid of the dead weight,
and the evidence,
and several other things I'm never ever going to confess to

Never in this world, nor in the next one
never at the point of the blade
never in the living memory of anybody now present
never when the memories fade

Long ago by a fire in the canyon
the prophets sang about the troubles to come
traitors and vandals, cracks in the city walls
gas leaks in the critical zone

Picture me among the desperate, forever
doing what I have to do
getting rid of the dead weight,

and the evidence,
and several other things I'm never ever going to confess to

ΔΔΔ

I do what I call "overwriting" for most albums—I keep going after I know I have more songs than we'll need, more songs than we'll be able to complete given the constraints and costs of studio time. Jenny's disappearance from the scene is central to her story: Did I want to have a cinematic sort of lead-up to the vanishing? That song ends up being "Going to Dallas," which is also a dramatic monologue, but more introspective, as befits second-act monologues from characters to whom you've grown attached but whose nearly invisible final traces will very shortly be eaten alive by the horizon point. In this world but not of it. Free among the contradictions.

29 · GOING TO DALLAS

Nobody's ever gonna pour
plaster in my tracks
my exit will be clean
when I vanish from the scene
you won't find any thumbprints
to dust your powder into
just mute donkeys still as statues
in each saloon I've been through

Going to Dallas,
as far as anybody knows
maybe Montana
depending on the way the wind blows

No blinking red light on the line tonight
or any night out in the future

kiss the people you hold dear
forget that I was ever here
if word should reach you from the field
be cool
try not to talk out of school
make them beat it out of you if they want it
live like a pack mule

Going to Dallas
as far as anyone's concerned
maybe Montana
depending on the way the roads turn

And if they steer me wrong,
I'm just going to play along
remember this when the time comes
try to let it soften the blow

let me go to no haven anyone would yearn for
burn a hole in something for me
turn around and let me go free

Going to Dallas
in the morning when the wind is fair
maybe Montana
if I've got enough gas to get there

ΔΔΔ

The song moves fast enough to hide its most important line, a crucial ethos for me, but "burn a hole in something for me" defines Jenny's view of the world beyond the house she's fashioned into a sheltering place, and her intentions for the world once she has to leave that house behind. There is a lot of leaving in my songs. It's rehearsal, right? Everything is rehearsal.

30 · GREAT PIRATES

On the morning when I stop looking back
I'll be up to see the sunrise in deep bruised
  black
and bright blood red, and pale desert rose
and several other colors like those

great pirates testing the waves
great pirates testing the waves

Everybody gone from here
may you all emerge free and clear
and may you do some good where you go
high in the hands of the crosswinds,
  or in the arms of the undertow

great pirates testing the waves
great pirates testing the waves

and calling the roll—let's see:
just me
and checking the rigging, before
heading off to war

Peach rose black sky up early
carry what I need to carry
bury what I have to bury
dancing, whistling, singing past the cemetery

great pirates testing the waves
great pirates testing the waves

ΔΔΔ

"Pirates" because of Brecht's "Pirate Jenny," the original inspiration for the character's name, but also because of Rickie Lee Jones: "I'm just tryin' to have some fun / until the Pirates come / and take me." The first line of this song is "On the morning when I stop looking back," which is something of an irony, because I resist looking back when I can, but a book collecting a few decades' worth of work can't help but to be looking back the whole time, and because there is only one day left in the year.

31 - AMBIVALENT LANDSCAPE Z

Out where the water tower climbs
higher than God
crop dust in billowing clouds and the outlaw corn
glinting goldenrod

Cold gaze of the universal harvester
glittering on the horizon line
every creature on earth needs a fallout shelter
this one's mine

I'll never see you again,
so until then—

Down by the Morton building
where I first met you
nothing but energy fields and their bright pink edges
doing what they do all day

You threw your car keys away
left a bunch of dummy footprints on the clay
I try to follow directions as they're printed on the tin
but I need a shelter to fall out in

I'll never see you again
so until then—

ΔΔΔ

And I will, of course—see you, I mean—because a poem is never finished, only abandoned, this per Paul Valéry, who would know, and the main thing I'm doing is trying to write a poem, one in which I'll certainly locate pieces of myself even if it's being put together from noir images that of necessity conceal more than they reveal, but still, you know, after a whole year of this and more years to come until they don't: until then.

—SAVANNAH, GEORGIA, 4 DECEMBER 2024

ACKNOWLEDGMENTS

Everything I do, I do because I've been encouraged, supported, challenged, and lifted up by people who believed in me. This book exists because of those people. This is necessarily a partial list. My teachers: Sister Mary Claude, Mrs. Wyatt, Debbie Vancil, Terry Kneisler, Betty DiCarlo, Rosemary Adam; Robert Mezey; Barry Sanders; Ellen Finkelpearl; David Claus; Kitty Wilkinson. Anthropology Records roster and staff: Joel Huschle. Mark Givens. The Shrimper scene, including but not limited to Dennis Callaci, Allen Callaci, Franklin Bruno, Bob Durkee, and everybody else who came to or played at Munchie's in those indelible early summers. People at labels who made a way for me: Tim Adams. Craig Stewart. Cory Brown. Russell Hill. Jod at Oska whose last name I never knew. Gregor Kessler. Jamie Tugwell. Chris Sharp. Ed Horrox. Mac McCaughan and Laura Ballance; everybody at Merge. My former booking agent, Adam Voith: of inestimable importance to this story. My management at Ten Atoms, singling out in particular Ryan Matteson, who has brought us to new heights. My bandmates, past and present: Rachel Ware Zooi, Sarah Arslanian, Amy Piatt, Rosanne Lindley, Peter Hughes, Jon Wurster, and Matt Douglas. In the book world, my agent, Chris Parris-Lamb, and my editor, Sean McDonald; my production editor, Carrie Hsieh; Amber Manning, who compiled every lyric for which I hadn't written an entry: without her attendance to this task I might never have finished the book; and everybody at MCD / Farrar, Straus and Giroux who makes my books possible. My parents, Max Darnielle and Mary James Noonan, who delighted in my early efforts when I was very young. My family, Lalitree Darnielle and our sons Roman and Moses, who make each day a new delight. My friend Donna, whose guidance has made me a better writer. Everyone who has listened to our music, and everyone who has engaged with my writing: I dreamed, as a child, of having readers, and in the most real sense possible, it is you who have made my dreams real. Thank you. Finally, John Hodgman. Why John? Because I like John. What's happening, John? How have you been? You are the last guy in the acknowledgments list. Please turn out the light when you leave. We are not trying to light the entire neighborhood.

INDEX OF SONGS

A Note About the Author

John Darnielle is a writer, a composer, and the guitarist and vocalist of the band the Mountain Goats. He is the author of the novels *Devil House*, *Universal Harvester*, and *Wolf in White Van*, which was nominated for the National Book Award. *Rolling Stone* has declared Darnielle the "Best Storyteller in Rock." He lives in Durham, North Carolina, with his wife and sons.

The OLYMPIC
RI. 9-5171